Galaxy Tab
The Missing Manual®

Galaxy Tab: The Missing Manual

BY PRESTON GRALLA

Published by O'Reilly Media, Inc., 1005 Gravenstein Highway North, Sebastopol, CA 95472.

O'Reilly books may be purchased for educational, business, or sales promotional use. Online editions are also available for most titles (http://my.*safaribooksonline.com*). For more information, contact our corporate/institutional sales department: 800.998.9938 or *corporate@oreilly.com*.

Editor: Nan Barber

Production Editor: Holly Bauer

Proofreader: Rachel Leach

Indexer: Potomac Indexing, LLC

Compositor: Dessin Designs

Cover Designer: Karen Montgomery

Interior Designer: Ron Bilodeau

Print History:

September 2011:   First Edition.

ISBN: 978-1-449-39685-5

[LSI]

Contents

Part 1: The Basics and Getting Online

Part 2: Getting Social and Finding Your Way

Part 3: Books, Media, and Games

Part 4: Getting Productive

Chapter 13
Calendar 313

Chapter 14
Getting Work Done with Your Galaxy Tab 337

Part 5: Advanced Topics

Chapter 15
Controlling Your Galaxy Tab with Your Voice 349

Chapter 16

Part 6: Appendixes

Appendix A

Appendix B

The Missing Credits

About the Author

 Preston Gralla (author) is the author of 40 books that have been translated into 20 languages, including *Droid X: The Missing Manual, Droid 2: The Missing Manual, Big Book of Windows Hacks, Windows Vista in a Nutshell, How the Internet Works,* and *How Wireless Works.* He is a contributing editor to Computerworld, a founder and editor-in-chief of Case Study Forum, and was a founding editor and then editorial director of *PC/Computing,* executive editor for *CNet/ZDNet,* and the founding managing editor of *PC Week.*

He has written about technology for many national newspapers and magazines, including *USA Today, Los Angeles Times, Dallas Morning News* (for whom he wrote a technology column), *PC World,* and numerous others. As a widely recognized technology expert, he has made many television and radio appearances, including on the CBS *Early Show*, MSNBC, ABC *World News Now*, and National Public Radio. Under his editorship, *PC/Computing* was a finalist for General Excellence in the National Magazine Awards. He has also won the "Best Feature in a Computing Publication" award from the Computer Press Association.

Gralla is also the recipient of a 2010–2011 Fiction Fellowship from the Massachusetts Cultural Council. He lives in Cambridge, Massachusetts, with his wife (his two children have flown the coop). He welcomes feedback about his books by email at *preston@gralla.com.*

About the Creative Team

Nan Barber (editor) has worked with the Missing Manual series since its inception—long enough to remember booting up her computer from a floppy disk. Email: *nanbarber@oreilly.com*.

Holly Bauer (production editor) lives in Ye Olde Cambridge, MA. She's a production editor by day and an avid home book, DIYer, and mid-century modern furniture enthusiast by evening/weekend. Email: *holly@oreilly.com*.

Nancy A. Guenther (indexer) indexed this book on behalf of Potomac Indexing, LLC, an international indexing partnership at *www.potomacindexing.com*. She has been a full-time freelance indexer since 1983, specializing in computer software, American studies, and business. Her website is *guenther.bizland.com*.

Rachel Leach (proofreader) is a librarian and freelancer specializing in fiction, history, and IT. She offers editorial, project management, and research services through her website, *www.squidinkediting.com*.

Acknowledgements

Many thanks go to my editor, Nan Barber, who not only patiently shepherded this book through the lengthy writing and publishing process, but provided valuable feedback and sharpened my prose. Thanks also go to Brian Sawyer, for making the introduction that ultimately led to this book.

I'd also like to thank all the other folks at O'Reilly who worked on this book, especially Holly Bauer for bringing the beautiful finished product to fruition, Rachel Leach for excising errors, and Nancy Guenther for writing the index.

—*Preston Gralla*

The Missing Manual Series

Missing Manuals are witty, superbly written guides to computer products that don't come with printed manuals (which is just about all of them). Each book features a handcrafted index and cross-references to specific pages (not just chapters).

Recent and upcoming titles include:

Access 2007: The Missing Manual by Matthew MacDonald

Access 2010: The Missing Manual by Matthew MacDonald

Buying a Home: The Missing Manual by Nancy Conner

CSS: The Missing Manual, Second Edition, by David Sawyer McFarland

Creating a Web Site: The Missing Manual, Second Edition, by Matthew MacDonald

David Pogue's Digital Photography: The Missing Manual by David Pogue

Dreamweaver CS5: The Missing Manual by David Sawyer McFarland

Dreamweaver CS5.5: The Missing Manual by David Sawyer McFarland

Droid X2: The Missing Manual by Preston Gralla

Droid 2: The Missing Manual by Preston Gralla

Excel 2007: The Missing Manual by Matthew MacDonald

Excel 2010: The Missing Manual by Matthew MacDonald

Facebook: The Missing Manual, Second Edition, by E.A. Vander Veer

FileMaker Pro 10: The Missing Manual by Susan Prosser and Geoff Coffey

FileMaker Pro 11: The Missing Manual by Susan Prosser and Stuart Gripman

Flash CS5: The Missing Manual by Chris Grover with E.A. Vander Veer

Flash CS5.5: The Missing Manual by Chris Grover

Google Apps: The Missing Manual by Nancy Conner

The Internet: The Missing Manual by David Pogue and J.D. Biersdorfer

iMovie '11 & iDVD: The Missing Manual by David Pogue and Aaron Miller

iPad 2: The Missing Manual by J.D. Biersdorfer

iPhone: The Missing Manual, Fourth Edition, by David Pogue

iPhone App Development: The Missing Manual by Craig Hockenberry

iPhoto '11: The Missing Manual by David Pogue and Lesa Snider

iPod: The Missing Manual, Ninth Edition, by J.D. Biersdorfer and David Pogue

JavaScript: The Missing Manual by David Sawyer McFarland

Living Green: The Missing Manual by Nancy Conner

Mac OS X Snow Leopard: The Missing Manual by David Pogue

Mac OS X Lion: The Missing Manual by David Pogue

Microsoft Project 2007: The Missing Manual by Bonnie Biafore

Microsoft Project 2010: The Missing Manual by Bonnie Biafore

Motorola Xoom: The Missing Manual by Preston Gralla

Netbooks: The Missing Manual by J.D. Biersdorfer

Office 2007: The Missing Manual by Chris Grover, Matthew MacDonald, and E.A. Vander Veer

Office 2010: The Missing Manual by Nancy Connor, Chris Grover, and Matthew MacDonald

Office 2008 for Macintosh: The Missing Manual by Jim Elferdink

Office 2011 for Macintosh: The Missing Manual by Chris Grover

Palm Pre: The Missing Manual by Ed Baig

PCs: The Missing Manual by Andy Rathbone

Personal Investing: The Missing Manual by Bonnie Biafore

Photoshop CS4: The Missing Manual by Lesa Snider

Photoshop CS5: The Missing Manual by Lesa Snider

Photoshop Elements 7: The Missing Manual by Barbara Brundage

Photoshop Elements 8 for Mac: The Missing Manual by Barbara Brundage

Photoshop Elements 8 for Windows: The Missing Manual by Barbara Brundage

Photoshop Elements 9: The Missing Manual by Barbara Brundage

PowerPoint 2007: The Missing Manual by E.A. Vander Veer

Premiere Elements 8: The Missing Manual by Chris Grover

QuickBase: The Missing Manual by Nancy Conner

QuickBooks 2011: The Missing Manual by Bonnie Biafore

QuickBooks 2012: The Missing Manual by Bonnie Biafore

Switching to the Mac: The Missing Manual, Snow Leopard Edition, by David Pogue

Switching to the Mac: The Missing Manual, Lion Edition, by David Pogue

Wikipedia: The Missing Manual by John Broughton

Windows XP Home Edition: The Missing Manual, Second Edition, by David Pogue

Windows XP Pro: The Missing Manual, Second Edition, by David Pogue, Craig Zacker, and Linda Zacker

Windows Vista: The Missing Manual by David Pogue

Windows 7: The Missing Manual by David Pogue

Word 2007: The Missing Manual by Chris Grover

Your Body: The Missing Manual by Matthew MacDonald

Your Brain: The Missing Manual by Matthew MacDonald

Your Money: The Missing Manual by J.D. Roth

Introduction

What's a spectacular entertainment device, runs thousands of apps, connects you to the Internet, lets you take high-resolution photos and videos, handles any email you can throw at it, is a wizard at Facebook and other social networking services, lets you video chat with people across the world, opens the world of electronic books and newspapers to you…and that's just what it can do before breakfast?

It's the Galaxy Tab—the tablet that puts the world at your fingertips and has enough tech specs to make anyone's heart skip a beat. The Galaxy Tab brings together superb hardware from Samsung with Google's powerful Android operating system. Many people consider the Galaxy Tab to be the best tablet on the planet. If you're holding this book in your hand, you're probably among them—or soon will be.

This book will help you get the most out of your Galaxy Tab, and there's a lot you can get out of it, as you'll see. Whether you're looking just to get started, or want to dig deep into the tablet's capabilities, this book's got you covered.

About the Galaxy Tab

The Galaxy Tab is a tablet computer with a gorgeous 10.1-inch screen. (A smaller, 8.9-inch version was being prepared as this book went to press. Since that tablet uses the same Honeycomb operating system as the 10.1-inch tablet, you'll find most of this book relevant to the smaller tablet; for more details, see the box on page 16.) As a tablet, it can perform all kinds of magic that a big, expensive computer can't, like record video or take

5-megapixel photos. It's also got a whole range of built-in sensors such as a magnetometer, 3-axis accelerometer, GPS, and more.

The Galaxy Tab lets you browse the Web just as you do on a larger computer, and get fully formatted email with fonts, colors, and pictures. It has a GPS locator and even gives you turn-by-turn directions. It's got a calendar and contact app that syncs with your Google account. It's a calculator, alarm clock, stopwatch, traffic reporter, text-message maven, and that's just a start. Using apps you can download via the Android Market and elsewhere, you can make it do just about anything, including pointing it at a landmark and having it identify it for you.

About This Book

The only printed guide you get to your Galaxy Tab is a small leaflet. After that, you're on your own. There's an entire world to explore in the Galaxy Tab, and a leaflet doesn't begin to give you all the help, advice, and guidance you need. This book is the manual that should have accompanied the Galaxy Tab.

The brain running the Galaxy Tab is a piece of software from Google called Android. The Galaxy Tab runs Android version 3.1, called Honeycomb, and it's been tweaked a bit by Samsung.

 There's a chance that since this book was written, there have been changes to the Galaxy Tab. To help keep up to date about them, head to this book's Errata page at *http://tinyurl.com/galaxytab-mm*.

About the Outline

Galaxy Tab: The Missing Manual is divided into six parts, each of which has several chapters:

- **Part 1, The Basics and Getting Online,** covers everything you need to know about using the Galaxy Tab. You'll get a guided tour of the Galaxy Tab, and learn some fancy tablet tricks. This part tells you everything you need to know about the Tab's remarkable online talents. You'll find out how to get online, master email, browse the Web, and download and use countless apps from the Android Market. And as a bonus, you'll find out about 10 amazing apps for your Tab that you absolutely, positively, must have.

- **Part 2, Getting Social and Finding Your Way**, is your guide to using your Tab for social networking using Facebook and Twitter, using chatting and video chat, keeping track of all your contacts, and using maps, GPS, and turn-by-turn navigation.

- **Part 3, Books, Media, and Games,** gives you the rundown on using your Galaxy Tab as an entertainment and information device. So you'll learn all you need to know about taking pictures, recording videos, viewing pictures, playing videos, and playing and managing your music. It also covers getting and reading books, reading newspapers and magazines, and getting news delivered to you straight from the source.

- **Part 4, Getting Productive,** shows you how to get to work on your Galaxy Tab. Here you'll learn how to master Gmail and email, get the most out of your calendar, and get real work done with your tablet using office documents. You'll also find out how to set up the Galaxy Tab with your company email account, and hop on to your company's network via a Virtual Private Network (VPN).

- **Part 5, Advanced Topics,** gives you the most comprehensive listing you'll find anywhere about all of the Galaxy Tab's settings. It also shows you how to control the Galaxy Tab by talking to it.

- **Part 6, Appendixes,** has two reference chapters. Appendix A shows you how to set up your Galaxy Tab, and what kind of accessories you can get for it, such as cases, chargers, and screen protectors. Appendix B offers plenty of help troubleshooting issues with the Galaxy Tab's operation. It also covers how to encrypt your Galaxy Tab.

About→These→Arrows

In this book and the entire Missing Manual series, you'll find instructions like this one: Tap Settings→Wireless & Networks→Wi-Fi settings. That's a shorthand way of giving longer instructions like this: "Tap the Settings button. From the screen that opens, tap Wireless & Networks. And from the screen that opens after that, tap Wi-Fi settings."

It's also used to make it easier to understand instructions you'll need to follow on your PC or Mac, such as File→Print.

About the Online Resources

As the owner of a Missing Manual, you've got more than just a book to read. Online, you'll find example files so you can get some hands-on experience, as well as tips, articles, and maybe even a video or two. You can also communicate with the Missing Manual team and tell us what you love (or hate) about the book. Head over to *www.missingmanuals.com*, or go directly to one of the following sections.

Missing CD

This book doesn't have a CD pasted inside the back cover, but you're not missing out on anything. And so you don't wear down your fingers typing long web addresses, the Missing CD page offers a list of clickable links to the websites mentioned in this book.

Registration

If you register this book at oreilly.com, you'll be eligible for special offers—like discounts on future editions of *Galaxy Tab: The Missing Manual*. Registering takes only a few clicks. To get started, type *http://tinyurl.com/registerbook* into your browser to hop directly to the Registration page.

Feedback

Got questions? Need more information? Fancy yourself a book reviewer? On our Feedback page, you can get expert answers to questions that come to you while reading, share your thoughts on this Missing Manual, and find groups for folks who share your interest in the Galaxy Tab. To have your say, go to *www.missingmanuals.com/feedback*.

Errata

In an effort to keep this book as up to date and accurate as possible, each time we print more copies, we'll make any confirmed corrections you've suggested. We also note such changes on the book's website, so you can mark important corrections into your own copy of the book, if you like. Go to *http://tinyurl.com/galaxytab-mm* to report an error and view existing corrections.

Newsletter

Our free email newsletter keeps you up to date on what's happening in Missing Manual land. You can meet the authors and editors, see bonus video and book excerpts, and more. Go to *http://tinyurl.com/MMnewsletter* to sign up.

Safari® Books Online

Safari •••> Safari® Books Online is an on-demand digital library that
Books Online lets you search over 7,500 technology books and videos.

With a subscription, you can read any page and watch any video from our library. Access new titles before they're available in print. Copy and paste code samples, organize your favorites, download chapters, bookmark key sections, create notes, print out pages, and benefit from tons of other time-saving features.

O'Reilly Media has uploaded this book to the Safari Books Online service. To have full digital access to this book and others on similar topics from O'Reilly and other publishers, sign up for free at *http://my.safaribooksonline.com*.

Part 1
The Basics and Getting Online

1 The Guided Tour

Your Galaxy Tab is a powerful multimedia, productivity, and communications marvel. The first time you hold it in your hands, you'll immediately want to put it through its paces, browsing the Web, downloading and trying out apps, playing games, watching videos, gathering news, checking your email, and more.

That's as it should be: Your Galaxy Tab can do many remarkable things.

To help you unlock all those powers, though, it's a good idea to get a solid understanding of how the Galaxy Tab works, and a look at all its different parts. You'll want to know where all of its buttons, ports, and cameras are located, for example—not to mention how to get to your Home screen panes, or to a location that will become one of your best friends: the Apps Menu.

Power/Lock Key

On the upper-left rear of your Galaxy Tab as you hold it horizontally, with the small photo lens at the top, you find a small, silver button. It may be only a single button, but it's a hard-working one, and it performs several functions:

- **Sleep/Wake.** When your Galaxy Tab is turned on, pressing and releasing the button puts your Tab into Sleep mode, a state in which the display is turned off and the device uses only a minimum amount of power, in order to save battery life. When the Tab is in dreamland, it doesn't register any taps, so you can't accidentally send an email or delete every picture on your Tab. Pressing and releasing this button wakes up the Tab into its locked mode—you'll see how to unlock it a little later.

 Note In this book, the location of various physical buttons, ports, cameras, and so on, assumes that you're holding the Tab horizontally, with the camera lens at the top.

- **On/Off.** If your Galaxy Tab is turned off, hold down the button, and it springs to life. Simple, yes? If, on the other hand, it's turned on, holding down the button turns it off. When you do so, though, it doesn't immediately shut down. Instead, a screen appears with three options. You can put your Tab into Silent mode, in which it makes no sounds; you can put it into Flight mode (see page 49), in which all of its radios are turned off (but you can still use the device); or you can turn off the power. To do none of that, tap the screen.

Locking the Screen

As described on page 10, when you put the Galaxy Tab to sleep, the screen stops responding to touch. It blacks out, indicating that the screen is locked. Always lock the screen before putting your Tab somewhere like in a bag or backpack to avoid accidental screen taps. In fact, every time you leave the Tab untouched for two minutes, the screen automatically locks itself. (You can change how long it takes to lock; see page 374.)

 Your Galaxy Tab may be Wi-Fi-only, or also have the ability to connect to a cellular network and get a connection that way. Either way, the device looks the same.

While the screen is locked, the Tab still operates behind the scenes, checking email and Facebook and receiving text messages. You get all the usual notifications for all the things you've asked it to notify you about. In fact, in many ways, your Tab works just as hard when it's locked as when it's not.

When you want to use the Tab again, you need to unlock it. Simply put your fingertip on the lock icon on the screen and slide it in any direction. Your Tab is now ready to do your bidding.

 Tip For added security, you can also require that a password be used to unlock your Tab, or even that a specific finger-swiping motion be performed on the keyboard before it can be unlocked. For details, see page 371.

About the Screen

The screen is the Galaxy Tab's center stage—it's where it displays web pages, apps, games, and more, and because it's a touch screen, it's also where you'll tell the Tab what you want to do next. The screen is a roomy 10.1 inches measured diagonally. (For you techies, that's 1280 × 800 pixels with a pixel density of 149 pixels per inch). When you turn it sideways, it switches to a widescreen TV and movie format. As this book went to press, an 8.9-inch version of the Galaxy Tab was being prepared for release. Other than the screen size being smaller than the 10.1-inch one, it works basically the same. So this book shows you how to use that version of the Galaxy Tab as well.

But there's a lot going on behind that pretty display.

 Tip Since you're going to be touching the display with your fingers, it's going to get dirty and streaky. Simply wipe it clean with a soft, lint-free cloth or tissue. The screen is scratch-resistant, but if you're worried about scratches, get a case or screen protector. See Appendix A for ideas.

Built-in Sensors

Underneath its flat black screen, the Galaxy Tab has four sensors that perform a lot of its magic:

- **Ambient light sensor.** This senses the light level and adjusts your screen's brightness to save battery power. So in bright light, it makes the screen brighter so that it can be more easily seen, and in dim light, it makes the screen dimmer, because bright light is not needed.

- **3-axis accelerometer.** As its name implies, this measures acceleration and motion. The Galaxy Tab uses the accelerometer to sense the orientation of the screen and turn it to either landscape or portrait mode. But clever app makers use it for other things as well.

- **Digital compass.** You read that right—it's got a compass built into it.

- **Gyroscope.** Yes, it's got one of these as well, for games and all kinds of motion-sensing apps.

Home Screen

When you turn on your Galaxy Tab, you see its big, beautiful screen, which you can hold in either a horizontal or vertical position.

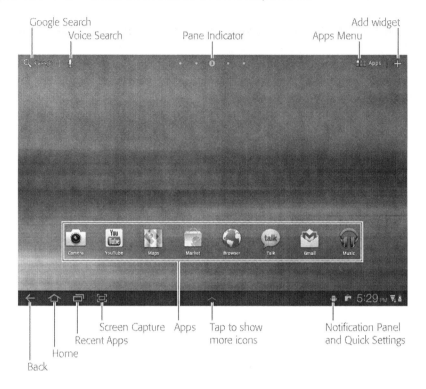

Google Search
Voice Search
Pane Indicator
Add widget
Apps Menu

Screen Capture Apps Tap to show
Recent Apps   more icons
Home
Back

Notification Panel
and Quick Settings

The upper-left portion of the screen is your central location for search. Type a search term, or tap the microphone icon and then speak your search. Either way, you search the Internet as well as your Tab. Over on the upper right, tap the Apps button and you'll open the Apps Menu, displaying all of the apps you've got on the Tab—those that are preloaded as well as any you've installed.

If you've got more apps than can fit on one screen, notice one or more buttons or dots just beneath the apps. Each dot represents another screen that has apps on it. Flick your finger toward the left, and you go to that screen. You see whatever apps you've got there—and if you look to the left of the screen, you see outlines of icons showing you that you've got icons back on the main Apps Menu screen. Flick over to it.

A Honey of an Operating System

Your Galaxy Tab is powered by an operating system from Google called Android; specifically, the Galaxy Tab runs version 3.1 of Android, often referred to as Honeycomb. (Google gives all of its Android versions dessert-related codenames, such as Eclair, Gingerbread, and Froyo, for frozen yogurt.) The Android operating system is constantly getting updated, and those updates are automatically sent to your Galaxy Tab when they're available. So what you see on your Tab may vary slightly from what you see onscreen in this book, depending on the version of Android you have.

Instead of a "pure" version of Honeycomb with no major changes to the interface, the Galaxy tab has Samsung's TouchWiz interface laid on top of Honeycomb. The TouchWiz software helps overcome some bugs inherent to Honeycomb, and includes larger, cooler-looking widgets for your homescreen, as you'll see in the illustrations in this book.

Back on the Home screen, just to the right of the Apps Menu button is a small + button. That's the button you use to add widgets to your Home screen and any of its five—that's right, count 'em, five—panes. More on that later, though. See page 23 for details.

Down at the bottom of the screen are several areas that stay with you no matter where you go: the combination Notification Panel/Quick Settings area on the right, and the four *soft* buttons—onscreen, not physical buttons—on the left. The soft buttons are used for navigation and for taking screenshots of the Tab or using its camera, and the Notification Panel/ Quick Settings area sends any notifications and alerts your way, and lets you change some important Galaxy Tab settings.

Toward the middle bottom of the screen, you'll see a small, upward-facing arrow. Tap that arrow to reveal a half a dozen apps. To make them go away again, tap the downward-facing arrow that appears all the way on the bottom left of the Tab.

The apps include a task manager for managing apps that are running, a calendar, a world clock, a memo-taking program, a calculator, and a Samsung music app that's different from the normal Android music app.

Now it's time to look at some of the Home screen's features in more detail.

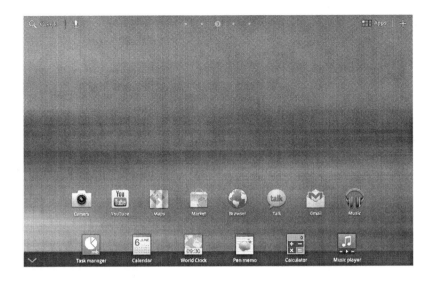

Notification Panel and Quick Settings

The Galaxy Tab makes sure to always keep you updated with information about its current status, and with any news, updates, and information it thinks is important. It does this by displaying a variety of icons in the Notification Panel at the bottom right of the screen. You'll find a variety of icons there, including those that give information about the current state of the Tab, such as Wi-Fi signal strength, 3G or 4G connection status, battery life, and so on. There are also notifications about events, such as a new email or chat message received, a calendar event reminder, and so on.

When a new notification comes in, it briefly appears in a pop-up window with information about it—part or all of a chat message, for example. Tap the notification, and you launch the app that sent that notification. For instance, if the notification is about incoming messages, tapping it will launch Gmail or your email software.

If you miss the notification pop-up, don't worry—the small icon showing you've received a notification stays in the Notification Panel. Tap the icon, and the pop-up appears again. You can then tap the pop-up to head to the app. If you want the notification icon to vamoose, tap the X next to it.

 Even when your Galaxy Tab's screen is locked, you can see all the notifications you have. But don't try tapping them when the screen is locked—they won't respond. You have to unlock the screen first.

You can also see every one of your notifications in one fell swoop, rather than tapping them one at a time. Tap the right side of the Notification Panel, and the Panel expands, showing all of your notifications. It shows not just the notifications about events, but also gives more information about the state of your Tab, such as how much battery life you have left, the name of the Wi-Fi network to which you're currently connected, and so on. It also includes a widget that lets you turn on and off various Tab radios such as Wi-Fi and GPS, turn notifications on and off, and change other settings, such as for sound, brightness, and screen orientation. And it gives you access to all of the Galaxy Tab's settings by tapping the Settings button.

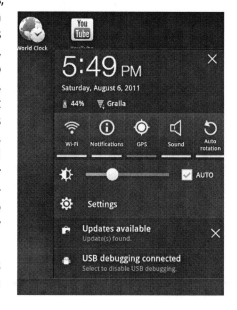

Here are the most common icons you come across in the Notification Panel:

- **Cell signal** . If you've got a Galaxy Tab with 3G or 4G, you see a notification about your cell signal. The more bars you see, the stronger the signal.

- **3G** . This one appears when you're connected via a 3G high-speed broadband service. (It only appears if you have a Galaxy Tab with cellular service.) The little arrows underneath the symbol show when data is being sent and received. Notice that the arrows may turn black even when you think you're not sending or receiving data. That's because the Tab may be checking for email, updates, and so on.

- **Bluetooth connection** . This icon indicates that you've turned on Bluetooth for making a connection to a headset or some other device.

- **Flight mode** . When you use Flight mode, you turn off Wi-Fi and cellular communications so you can keep using your Galaxy Tab's apps without interfering with navigation equipment. See page 49 for more details.

- **Wi-Fi** . Shows that you're connected to a Wi-Fi network, or that a Wi-Fi network is within range.

- **Downloading** . When you're downloading an app or media file, you see this icon.

- **Download complete** . Congratulations—your download was successful.

- **Update available** . One or more of your apps has an update available. Tap the icon to download and install the update.

- **New email message** . You've got mail! See page 304 to learn about reading new email.

- **New Gmail message** . You've got Gmail! See page 280 to learn about reading new email messages in Gmail.

- **GPS** . Your GPS radio is turned on. See page 191 for information about GPS.

- **Upcoming event** . Now you'll never forget your anniversary—or your dentist appointment. The Galaxy Tab alerts you with this icon when you've got an event about to happen.

- **Time** . Shows you what time it is. Say goodbye to your watch.

- **Battery** . Get to know this little icon—it shows you how much battery life you've got. If it's charging, the Tab plays a battery-filling animation and displays a small lightning bolt.

- **USB or USB tethering** . This shows that you've connected a USB device to your Galaxy Tab, or else you've turned on USB tethering in order to give an Internet connection to your PC via the Tab.

- **Google Talk** . You've got a message from someone who wants to chat with you via Google Talk.

- **Music** . You're playing music. Tap the icon and you get a set of mini-controls for the Galaxy Tab's music player.

Quick Settings

As explained earlier, when you tap the Notification Panel, it expands to show you all of your notifications—plus more information, such as how much battery life you've got left, the name of the Wi-Fi network to which you're currently connected, and so on. You also see the Quick Settings Panel, which lets you change a variety of Galaxy Tab settings:

- **Quick Settings widget.** This widget gives you instant access to the Galaxy Tab's most common settings. Tap an icon to turn a feature on or off—green means it's on, no color means it's off. Tap the Wi-Fi icon, for example, to turn Wi-Fi on and off, and Notifications to turn notifications on or off. Slide the widget over to the left to reveal more settings. Most settings are self-explanatory, but a few are worth noting, Auto rotation in particular. Normally when you switch your Galaxy Tab from vertical to horizontal and vice versa, the Tab switches its screen orientation to match the move. Tap this to turn it off, though, and it stays locked in its current orientation.

  Tap the Sound icon and the sounds turns off, and the Tab will vibrate rather than make sounds. You'll find the Flight Mode icon extremely useful. Tap it to turn Flight Mode on or off. Your Wi-Fi, cellular communications, and Bluetooth radios are turned off, so you can still keep using your Tab's apps, but they won't interfere with navigation. See page 49 for more details.

- **Brightness.** Use the slider to make your screen brighter or dimmer. Or just leave it to the Tab to figure out the correct brightness based on your current lighting conditions, and leave it at Auto.

- **Settings.** Tap here to change approximately two zillion Galaxy Tab settings. See Chapter 16 for the rundown.

The Four (and Sometimes Five) Soft Buttons

Down at the bottom left of your screen, you see four soft buttons, which stay with you wherever you go on the Galaxy Tab. From left to right, here's what they do:

Back Button

Wherever you are, tap this button to return to where you just were. The Back button works inside apps as well as in menus. So when you're browsing the Web, for example, it takes you back to the last page you visited. Tapping the Back button also makes the virtual keyboard or a menu disappear if one is currently displayed.

 Note When you're using the keyboard, the Back button turns into a down arrow. After you tap the down arrow to make the keyboard disappear, the down arrow turns back into your old friend, the Back button.

Home Button

Repeat after me, Dorothy: There's no place like home, there's no place like home.... Wherever you are on the Tab, tap the Home button to return to the familiar Home screen. You don't even need to tap your ruby slippers together.

Recent Apps

Here's an amazingly useful button. Tap it, and you see thumbnails of the most recent apps you were running—you even see what was on the screen the last time you were using them. Tap one and you switch right to that app, even if it's closed down. You can scroll up through your most recent apps.

Note Even when you're running an app, all these buttons appear and work. So if you're inside an app and want to switch to another one you were running recently, just tap the Recent Apps button, tap the app you want to switch to, and you're off on your merry way.

Screen Capture/Camera

Tap this button and you'll capture the contents of the Tab's screen. It will be saved in the Gallery. (See page 245 for details.)

The Mysterious Menu Buttons

Every once in a while, when you're inside an app, a fifth button appears at the bottom of the screen, to the right of the other four ▦. It's the Menu button, and it gives you access to more features and options. Tap it to reveal options for that particular app. The options pictured here are for an app called Pandora, which streams music to your Tab.

Other times, the Menu button ▤ appears in the upper-right portion of the screen, such as in the Gmail and Email apps. Tap it, and you see options for the current app. These options often change depending on what you're doing in the app—they're what geeks call context-sensitive. The options pictured here are what appear when you tap the top Menu button when reading a message in Gmail.

Mark unread

Report spam

Mute

Refresh

Settings

Help

Feedback?

Searching

Remember that Search button up at the top left of the screen? Tap it, and a box and keyboard appear that let you type in a search term. As you tap the text you're searching for, your Tab displays matching results. Those on the left are matching and suggested results from the Web, for searching Google, and those on the right are for matching results from your Tab or from your browser's bookmarks. Tap a term on the left, and you search the Internet; tap one on the right, and you launch the appropriate Galaxy Tab app—an app, say, or a contact, or a website, and so on.

If no matches appear, tap your entire search term, and then tap the triangle at the right of the search box. To delete all the text in the search box so you can launch another search, tap the X.

Your Galaxy Tab also lets you do a voice search— instead of typing in your search terms, you can speak them. To do a voice search, hold down the Search key instead of just pressing it, and then speak. The Tab does its best to interpret what you say, and it generally does a good job of it. For more details, see page 349.

Customizing the Home Screen and Panes

Here's one of the many nice things about the Galaxy Tab—it's easy to put your personal mark on it. Wish there were a few more apps on the Home screen? No problem; you can easily add them. Want to change the location of apps, or move around widgets and add new ones to each of your panels and the Home screen? It's a breeze. The rest of this section shows you how. Think of yourself as Picasso and the Home screen as your canvas.

First, a bit of explanation. Your Home screen is actually a whole lot bigger than it looks. At first glance, it appears to be a single panel. In fact, though, there are five panels. To see them, swipe your finger to the left or right along the Home screen. You see two panels to the left of the main Home panel, and two panels to the right of them. The panel indicator at the top of the screen shows you which panel you're currently on. You can also move from panel to panel by tapping the panel's button. This section shows you how to customize any or all of those five panels.

To start, tap the + button on the upper right of the Tab's screen. You see thumbnails of all five of your panels on the top part of the screen. On the bottom part of the screen, you see buttons for widgets, app shortcuts, wallpapers, and more.

 Tip Don't like the idea of tapping the + button? Then simply press your finger against the Tab screen, and the same thing happens.

Tap any of those buttons, and you see all the objects you can add to any of the panels. You'll learn how to add them shortly. But first, here's what each of those buttons means and what they let you add:

- **Widgets.** A widget is an applet that performs a specific task, often grabbing and displaying information from the Galaxy Tab, a Galaxy Tab app, or the Internet. The Galaxy Tab has all kinds of nifty widgets you can add—for example, a widget to display the latest events in your calendar, one to display the latest emails to hit your Inbox, a picture frame that displays your photos and changes them regularly, and so on.

- **App shortcuts.** A shortcut is a quick link to an app or specific task. So, for example, you could create a shortcut to the Pandora Internet radio app, or to your browser. When you tap the shortcut, the app launches.

- **Wallpapers.** Here's where the Picasso part comes in. You can add a wallpaper to the background of any panel, just as you can add wallpaper to your computer. There are three choices here: Gallery, Live Wallpapers, and Wallpapers. *Live Wallpapers* are backgrounds that change, either because they're animated, or because they grab information from somewhere, and then display it as part of the background. The Map live wallpaper, for example, shows your current location on a Google Map as your wallpaper. If you instead choose Gallery, you can take any of your photos and use them as wallpaper. The Wallpaper option lets you use a static wallpaper. No matter what you choose, you get to preview the wallpaper first.

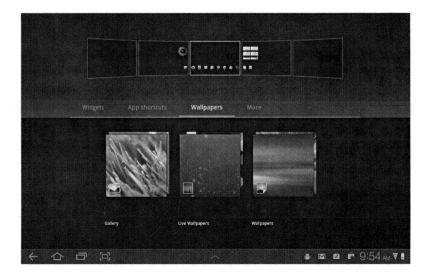

- **More.** You find a hodgepodge of choices here, including app short-cuts, your browser's bookmarks, and more.

 When you add wallpaper to your Home screen, it also shows up as the background on all your panes.

OK, time to go crazy. You can now trick out your Home screen in countless ways. Read on to see how to do it.

Putting Widgets and App Shortcuts on the Home Screen

It's a breeze to put a widget or app shortcut on any of the Home screen's five panels. Here's how to do it:

1. Go to the panel where you want to add a widget or app.

2. Press your finger and hold it, or else tap the + button in the upper-right portion of your screen.

The top of your screen changes to show thumbnails of all of your five home screens, and the bottom shows either widgets, App shortcuts (icons), or wallpapers you can add to any screen. Your current home screen will be highlighted in blue.

3. Tap Widgets to show available widgets, App shortcuts to show app shortcuts, and More for a mix of both of them.

The bottom of your screen shows all of the widgets or app icons you can add to a home screen. Flick left and right through the list to see what's available.

4. When you find the widget or app icon you want to add, tap it. The widget or app icon flies to your current screen, and you'll see a thumbnail of it there.

5. Tap the panel where you've just placed the app or widget. There it is, in all of its Galaxy Tab-like glory!

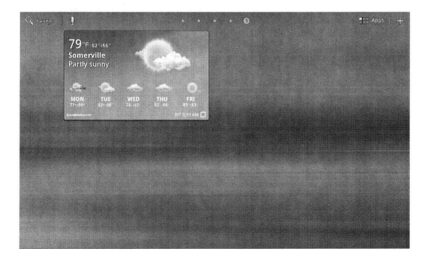

You can add a widget or app icon to as many panels as you want.

Deleting and Moving Widgets and App Shortcuts

Once you've added widgets and shortcuts to your Home screen, you're not stuck with them, or with where you've placed them:

- To move a widget or folder, press your finger on it and hold it. Drag it to its new location and take your finger off it—that's where it stays. You can move it to a different location on the same panel, or to a different panel.

- To delete a widget or shortcut, press your finger on it and hold it for a second or two. The Apps button at the top of the screen turns into a Trash button and the word Remove appears next to it. Drag the widget or app shortcut to the Trash. When you see it turn red, release it—it's gone. Keep in mind, though, that when you delete it, it's gone forever. It's not like the PC's Recycle Bin or the Mac's Trash where it's kept for a while. It's gone, baby, gone.

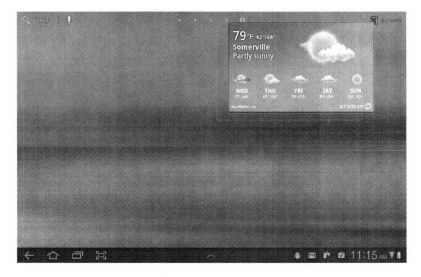

 When you delete a widget or shortcut to an app, you're not deleting the app itself—just a shortcut to it. The app remains. If you want to delete the app itself, you have to delete it from the Apps Menu.

Resizing Widgets

You can resize some, but not all, of your Tab's widgets. After you've placed a widget on a Home screen, hold your finger on it, and then remove your finger. An rectangular outline appears around the widget. A circle appears on each side.

 The only way to know if a widget can be resized is to try resizing it—there are no visible indications whether it's resizable or not.

Drag a circle and release it. The widget will resize, and the outline will still appear around it. Tap the Tab's screen to make the outline disappear.

Changing the Home Screen's Wallpaper

To change your Home screen's wallpaper, you take slightly different steps. Follow the first two steps for putting widgets and app shortcuts on the Home screen, and then:

1. Tap Wallpapers. You'll see the three types of wallpaper you can add: Gallery, Live Wallpapers, and Wallpapers.

2. Tap the type of wallpaper you want to add. For this example, choose Live Wallpapers.

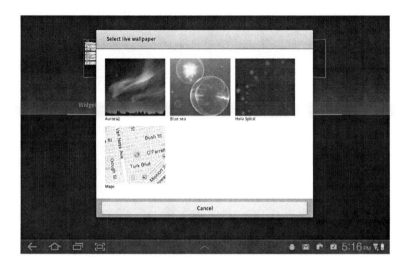

3. Flick through the list until you see one you want to add. Tap it.

   Your Tab's screen fills with the wallpaper. Since you've chosen a live wallpaper, you can change its options by tapping the Settings button. For example, on the Maps live wallpaper, you can choose whether the map should also display traffic and weather.

4. If you decide you don't want to use the wallpaper, tap the Back button to return to the previous screen. If you want to use the wallpaper, tap "Set wallpaper."

   That's it—you've just set your wallpaper. Tap any panel to see it. Note that the same wallpaper will be on all of your Home screen panels. You can have only one wallpaper on all five panels; you can't set different ones for individual panels.

Controlling the Galaxy Tab with Your Fingers

With the Galaxy Tab, your fingers do the walking. They do all the work that you do on a computer with a mouse or keyboard. Here are the eight finger strokes you can use on the Tab's screen.

Tap

Tapping is as basic to the Tab as clicking is to a mouse. This one simple gesture is how you press onscreen buttons, place the cursor for text entry, and choose from menus.

Touch and Hold

Touch an object and hold it for several seconds, and depending on what you're holding, you may perform an action. (For example, when you touch and hold the Home screen, you get sent to the screen that lets you customize it.) You also touch and hold an object as a way to grab onto it if you then want to drag the object somewhere.

Drag

After you've grabbed something, you can drag it with your finger, such as dragging an icon to the trash.

Slide

Slide your finger across the screen to perform some specific tasks, like unlocking your Tab after it's been put into Sleep mode. You also use the sliding motion to move through all of the Home screen panels.

Flick

Think of the flick as a faster slide, done vertically when scrolling through a list, such as a list of your contacts. The faster you make the flicking motion, the faster your screen scrolls—sometimes too fast. You can stop the motion, though, by touching the screen again.

 Flicks seem to actually obey the laws of physics, or at least as much as virtual movement can. When you flick a list, it starts off scrolling very quickly, and then gradually slows down, as if it were a ball set in motion that gradually loses momentum.

To scroll through large lists quickly, you can flick multiple times.

Pinch and Spread

In many apps, such as Google Maps, Mail, Browser, and Photos, you can zoom in by spreading your fingers—placing your thumb and forefinger on the screen and spreading them. The amount you spread your fingers will determine the amount you zoom in.

To zoom out, put your thumb and forefinger on the screen and pinch them together. The more you pinch, the more you zoom out.

Double-Tap

When you're viewing a Google Map, a picture, or a Web page, you can zoom in by double-tapping. In some instances, when you've reached the limit of zooming in, double-tapping again restores the view to its original size.

 Another way to zoom out in Google Maps is to tap with two fingers at once. This trick is unique to Google Maps.

Tilting and Panning

The Galaxy Tab includes some nifty motion settings that let you do things such as reduce or enlarge pictures simply by tilting the Tab while placing two fingers on the screen. When you're in the Gallery (page 249) or using the browser (page 56), put two fingers on the screen (using your thumbs is easiest) and tilt the screen forward to zoom out, and tilt it back to zoom in.

You can also pan from one screen to another by holding down an icon and moving the Tab to the right or left. (In practice, I had problems getting this to work, but you might have better luck.)

You can turn these settings on or off and customize them (for example, changing how tilt works) by tapping the Notification Panel and tapping Settings→Motion Settings.

Using the Keyboard

Tap wherever you can enter text, and the keyboard appears. When you tap in the text-entry box, a blinking cursor appears, indicating that you can start typing text. You can hold the tablet either horizontally or vertically to use the keyboard.

The Galaxy Tab doesn't use the normal Android keyboard. Instead, it uses one devised by Samsung. And as you'll see later in this chapter, you can also use a very nifty keyboard called Swype that lets you input text quickly by swiping your finger along the keyboard, instead of tapping keys.

Using the keyboard is straightforward; tap letters and characters to input them. As you tap you'll feel just the slightest vibration to let you know that the Tab has input the character you tapped.

There are a few special keys, though, that you should know about:

- **Shift** ⬆️. There's one on either side of the keyboard. Tap one and it changes to blue, and the letters all change to uppercase on the keyboard. Tap any key, and it gets entered in uppercase. After you tap the key, though, the keyboard changes back to lowercase. If you want to type multiple uppercase characters in a row, there's a nifty way around the problem: Keep your finger on the Shift key as you type. As long as you hold your finger there, you type in upper case. Remove your finger, tap a key, and you're back to lower case.

- **?123** . As the label implies, this key reveals punctuation marks and numbers. When you tap it, you see a whole keyboard full of them, and the same key now reads ABC. Tap it to return to alphabetic typing.

  When you switch to the numbers and punctuation keyboard, the Shift key turns into a key indicating that there are several more keyboards available to you ▪ 1/3 . Tap it, and you can then display the second numeric and punctuation keyboard—one with special characters and symbols such as the trademark symbol, several types of brackets, the symbol for euros, and so on. Tap it again and you'll come to a keyboard filled with emoticons and smiley faces. Tap it one more time to get back to the first number and punctuation keyboard.

- **Return** ◄┘. This key works exactly as you would expect: Tap it, and you move on to the next line, just as on a computer.

- **Settings** ◉. Tap here to change a variety of settings, such as the input language and how to handle autocorrection.

- **Insert** ▪. You'll find this key quite useful. Tap it and you'll be sent to the Galaxy Tab's Clipboard (see page 40), where you can insert anything that you've pasted there. What you can paste will vary according to the app you're using. For example, in email, you can't paste pictures, while in the Galaxy Tab's built-in Pen Memo app, you can.

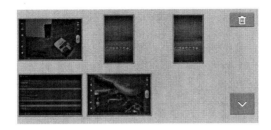

Using the Swype Keyboard

The Galaxy Tab also includes a very nifty keyboard called Swype. With this keyboard, you don't tap individual keys when you want to enter text. Instead, you tap a key, then drag your finger over each letter in the word you want to input. Swype enters all the letters in the word, using built-in intelligence to figure out what you're entering. It's much faster than tapping individual letters. Yes, it takes some getting used to, but you can master it in a few minutes. Once you get used to the Swype, you may never go back to the standard keyboard.

The Swype keyboard takes a few minutes to get used to, but once you do, you'll be amazed at how much faster you can enter text with it than the traditional keyboard. So put aside your trepidations and give it a try. Switch to it by tapping the Notification Panel, selecting Settings, and then choosing Language and input→Current Input method, and then tapping Swype.

There's another way to switch to the Swype keyboard. Whenever you're using the Galaxy Tab's keyboard, a keyboard icon appears in the Notification Panel. Tap the icon and you'll come to a screen that lets you select which keyboard you want to use. Tap Swype.

The Swype keyboard looks similar to the multitouch keyboard, although with some differences. The real difference, though, isn't in the keyboard—it's in the way you input text. Rather than tap each letter individually, you put your finger on the first letter of the word, and then with a single motion, move your finger from letter to letter of the word you want to input. As you do so, you'll see the path you've traced. Don't worry too much about accuracy, because Swype does an exceptional job of interpreting the word you want to input, using its dictionary. Just try to get near each letter; it's okay if you're off a little bit. When you've finished tracing the word, lift your finger.

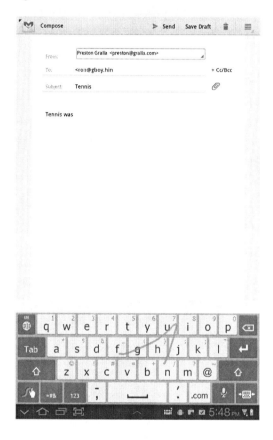

There are times when Swype might not know precisely what you're trying to trace, and the trace might match multiple words. If that happens, Swype pops up a Word Choice window.

 Note If you're entering numbers or special characters with Swype, you'll have to tap on them, just like you have to with the multitouch keyboard. You won't be able to move your finger across the keys in order to input them.

Tap the word you want. Press the arrow key at the bottom of the pop-up to see more choices. If you want to go with the first word on the list (the most likely choice), simply press the space key. If none of the words match, tap the X and start over. And remember, you can always tap the Swype keyboard in the same way that you can tap the multitouch keyboard if you simply can't get Swype to recognize a word.

The Swype Key

The Swype's keyboard is laid out a bit differently than the normal keyboard. The basic keyboard is the same, although some special keys are in different locations. The real difference, though is in the Swype key . This key does double-duty. Press and hold it, and a screen appears with a tip about Swype on it. If you just tap the key, it highlights the word directly to the left of the insertion point and brings up the Word Choice menu, so you can correct the word if you want. If you tap the key in an empty input box, it brings up a tip.

Autocorrect, Word Choice, and the Swype Dictionary

Swype uses its own dictionary for recognizing words and presenting them in the Word Choice pop-up screen. You can't add words to this dictionary or delete them in the same way you can with the multitouch keyboard. The two dictionaries don't share information.

Swype takes a much more aggressive approach to correcting your tapping than does the multitouch keyboard. As you drag your fingers across keys, it either enters a word from the dictionary—the closest match to what it thinks you want to type—or pops up Word Choice and presents a list of words from the dictionary. So if you carefully drag your finger across the letters t-h-i-m-k, Swype doesn't enter "thimk."

But what if you really do want to enter thimk? Simply tap the letters individually. Do that, and two things happen: The word is entered onscreen, and the word is added to the dictionary. Next time you drag your fingers across t-h-i-m-k, Swype dutifully enters thimk into the text box. And thimk also starts appearing in the Word Choice balloon.

If you don't particularly think that having thimk in the dictionary is a good idea, you can remove it. Highlight the word onscreen by tapping it twice. The word turns blue, bracketed by two triangles. Tap the Swype key, and you're asked if you want to delete the word from the dictionary. Tap OK.

Tips for Using Swype

Swype is a surprisingly full-featured little app. Here are some useful tips for getting the most out of it.

- Don't use the space key. After you enter a word using Swype, lift your finger and enter another word. Swype automatically puts a space between the two words.

- Swype usually recognizes when you want to add accented characters. Slide your finger across the letters, and the proper accent generally appears, as in the word café. However, you can still add accented characters if Swype doesn't automatically recognize them. To add an Ö, for example, hold down the O key, and a menu of accented characters appears above the keyboard. Choose the character you want to use.

- Circle or scribble for double letters. If you want to enter the word "tennis," then when you get to the "n," make a circle on the key with your finger, or scribble back and forth across the key. Then glide with your finger to the next letter.

 Swype offers an exceptional number of ways to customize how it works—for example, how long to display the Swype trace path onscreen, how to balance speed of word recognition versus accuracy, and so on. To customize Swype, press the Swype key and at the bottom of the help screen, tap Options. Then customize to your heart's content.

- Work quickly. Don't slow down in an attempt to be more precise. Swype is built for speed. Move your finger quickly; you'll be surprised at how well Swype recognizes words.

Moving the Insertion Point

Once you get the hang of entering text, you have another challenge—moving the insertion point to go back and edit, delete, or add words or letters. You can tap where you want to place the insertion point, but that's not always effective. Even with fine-tuned hand-eye coordination, it can be difficult to tap in the precise spot where you want the insertion point.

There's a better way. Tap anywhere in the text, and a large blue polygon appears beneath a blinking insertion point. Drag the polygon to move the insertion point wherever you want it to go, then remove your finger.

Copying and Pasting Text

What's a computer without the ability to cut, copy, and paste? A computer at heart, the Tab lets you do all that, even though it has no mouse. For example, you can copy directions from Google Maps into an email to send to a friend, paste contact information into a note to yourself, and so on. You copy and paste text using the same basic techniques you use on a PC or a Mac. You select it, and then copy, cut, or paste it.

 This technique works only in areas where you enter or edit text, such as in email messages you're composing, text messages you're creating, contact information, and similar locations. You can't copy and paste text from an incoming email. You can, however, copy and paste text from a web page, although using a different technique. See page 68 for how to do it.

There are several ways to select text in an input box, depending on how much text you want to cut or copy:

- **Double-tap.** Double-tap the first or last word in a selection of text that you want to cut or copy. The word is highlighted and bracketed by polygons—those are the handles. Drag each to include all the text you want to select, and then release.

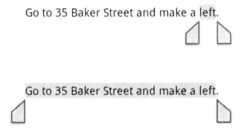

- **Hold.** Press your finger on a word and hold it there. The word is highlighted, but not bracketed by polygons, so you can't expand the selection.

- **Select all.** Whenever you select text, a Text Selection toolbar appears at the top of your screen. Tap Select all to select all the text in the text box, the body of an email message, and so on.

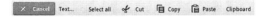

Once you've selected text, it's time to do something with it. That's what the Text selection toolbar is for:

- **Select all.** Selects all the text in the text box. It overrides you if you've selected only some of the text in the text box.

- **Cut.** Cuts the text you've selected and puts it onto the Galaxy Tab's clipboard, so you can later paste it somewhere if you want. The clipboard works just like the one on your PC or Mac—it holds things you've copied until you want to paste them later. Unlike the PC or Mac, though, this clipboard holds multiple clips, not just a single one.

- **Copy.** Copies the last piece of text you've put onto the clipboard, so that you can paste it somewhere.

- **Paste.** Pastes the last piece of text you've put on the clipboard and replaces whatever text you've selected. So if you've selected all text in the text box, Paste deletes all that text, and replaces it with the last thing you put on the clipboard. If you've selected only a word or a few words, it deletes them and replaces them with the latest from the clipboard.

- **Clipboard.** This shows you all the clips you've placed in the clipboard, including text as well as pictures. Tap the clip you want to insert. Note that in emails, you'll only be able to insert text clips, not any pictures. Other apps, such as the built-in Pen Memo app, let you insert pictures from the Clipboard.

 Here's an easy way to paste the last piece of text in the Clipboard anywhere you want. Tap where you want to paste text. The familiar blue polygon appears. Wait a second or so until the word Paste and an icon appears above the insertion point. Tap the icon and you'll paste the last piece of text from the Clipboard into that location.

Accented and Special Characters

You can easily type in accented characters (such as é, Ö, Ü, and so on) with the Galaxy Tab keyboard. Press any one of a number of keys, and keep your finger on it for a second or so. A palette of accented characters appears. Tap the one you want to use, or tap the X to make the palette of characters go away. The following chart shows which keys let you enter special characters.

Key	Accented and Special Characters
A	ā, ã, å, æ, â, à, á, ä
C	ç
E	ê, è, é, ë
I	ì, í, î, ï
N	ñ
O	ø, õ, œ, ò, ô, ö, ó
U	ù, û, ü, ú

Changing and Customizing the Keyboard

The keyboard that the Tab uses right out of the box isn't the one built into Android. Rather, it's a special Samsung keyboard. What's so special about it? It's equipped with *predictive text*—that is, as you type, it guesses what word you're typing, and suggests common words to insert. You can then select a word from the options displayed. This feature can save you plenty of time, although some people find it distracting.

As a general rule, predictive text doesn't work when you first turn on your Galaxy Tab. Instead, you have to turn it on. To turn it on:

1. Tap the Apps Menu and select Settings.

2. Tap Language and Input→Configure input methods.

3. At the bottom of the screen, a "Samsung keypad settings" entry appears. Tap Settings.

4. Turn on the "XT9 Predictive text" checkbox.

From now on, your keyboard will be your best friend and recommend words for you. To turn predictive text off, head to this same location and uncheck the box.

You can configure how predictive text works; for example, you can control whether it corrects your spelling. To configure it, after you've turned on predictive text, tap "XT9 advanced settings" just below the "XT9 predictive settings" checkbox. You can then fiddle with the settings to your heart's content.

Once you've turned on predictive text, your Samsung keyboard will go to work, suggesting words and text as you type. The words and text appear just above the keyboard. Tap any to paste it into the text area where you're typing.

You can make your keyboard even smarter, and have it recognize words it doesn't know yet. As it suggests words or text, you'll notice a small down arrow all the way on the right. Tap that arrow and an "Add word" box appears. Tap that box, and in the screen that appears, type in your word and then tap Done. From now on, your keyboard will suggest that new word when you're typing the appropriate letters.

What if you don't like the Samsung keyboard and would prefer to use the one built into Android? It's a snap to switch:

1. Tap the Apps Menu and select Settings.

2. Tap Language and Input→Configure input methods.

3. Tap "Current input method."

4. From the screen that appears, select "English (US) Keyboard (Android Keyboard)."

From now on, you'll use the built-in Android keyboard.

Instead of the Android keyboard, you can choose other keyboards, including the Swype keyboard (see page 35) and the TalkBack keyboard, which is designed to allow people who are blind or who have low vision to use voice input to use the Tab.

Headphone Jack

If you hold your Tab horizontally, with the small photo lens at the top, you find a 3.5-millimeter headset jack right smack dab on top. You can plug in headphones or even external speakers and enjoy the Tab as a music machine (it offers full stereo). Notice that it's a head*set* jack, not just a garden variety head*phone* jack. It doesn't just let you listen; it can send outgoing sound as well. That's so you can plug an earbud headset (or another kind of headset) into it and use it along with a voice or video chat program like Google Talk. (See page 133 for more details.)

Charger/Accessory Port

Down at the bottom edge of the Galaxy Tab if you're holding it horizontally, with the small photo lens at the top, you'll find a port for charging your Tab and for connecting it to a computer for transferring music and files. (For details, see page 227.) The Tab comes with a special cable, one end of which connects to this port, and the other end of which connects to a computer via a USB connection. The Tab can connect to both Macs and PCs.

If you often use power-hungry features like video and GPS, you may have to charge your Tab every night. If you use it less often, you might be able to get by with every other day.

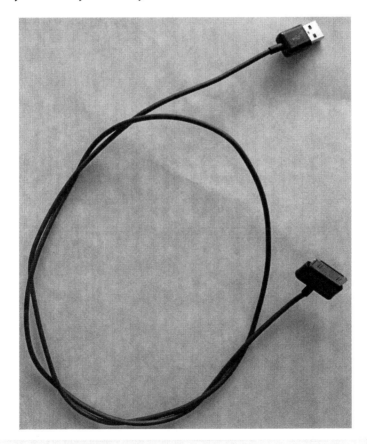

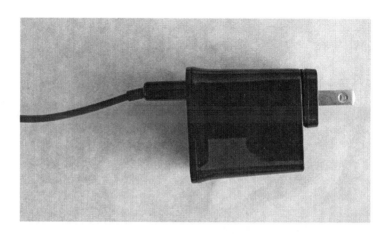

Maximizing Your Battery Charge

If you use a lot of power-sucking features, your Galaxy Tab may not even get through a whole day without having to recharge. In addition to turning off the screen when you're not using it (page 11), you can do a lot to make your battery last.

- **Be smart about email fetching.** The more often the Tab checks for and retrieves email, the faster the battery runs down. Either check email manually only when you need to, or increase the interval at which the Tab checks. Launch the Email app, press the Menu button, and then tap your email account. In General Settings, you see an entry for "Inbox check frequency." Tap it to change the interval from anywhere between every 5 minutes and every hour. You can also have it never check, so that you have to check manually.

- **Turn off antennas you're not using.** If you're not using a Bluetooth headset and don't need Wi-Fi services at the moment (or 3G or 4G connection if you have a Tab with those capabilities), by all means, turn them off. They use up tons of power. Use Flight mode to turn them all off. Turn them off individually from the Wireless and Networks Settings page (page 361).

- **Watch out for power-sapping apps.** Some apps, such as 3D games, can use serious amounts of juice. If, after installing an app, you notice your battery running low quickly, consider deleting it or running it only when necessary.

Microphone

That tiny little hole at the bottom edge of the Galaxy Tab—to the right of the Charger/Accessory port if you're holding the Tab horizontally with the small camera lens at the top—is the Tab microphone. Yes, it's small, but it does the job very nicely.

Volume Key

Is your ringer too loud? Too soft? Get it just right by using this key. It's at the top left of the Galaxy Tab if you're holding it horizontally with the small photo lens at the top. The key is the large one, just to the right of the small Power Lock key. Press the right side to make the volume louder and the bottom one to make it softer. When you press either key, a ringer volume app pops up on your screen, showing you how much louder or softer you're making the ring.

Cameras

Your Galaxy Tab includes not just one but two cameras—one facing front, and the usual back-facing one as well. Why two cameras? One you use for taking photographs, and the other you use as a webcam, for video chatting, for example. The one for taking photographs is 5-megapixels. Its lens is located on the back of the Tab and there's a flash right next to it. As you'll see on page 265, there's no physical button for taking photographs; instead, you press a button on the Tab screen itself.

The webcam lens is right at the top of the Tab in the middle as you hold it horizontally with the small camera lens at the top. It's a 2-megapixel camera.

Speakers

On the back of your Galaxy Tab, you find a pair of stereo speakers. So if you want to listen to music without using a pair of headphones, you're all set. You can also plug a pair of external speakers or headphones into the Tab's headset jack.

2 Getting Online: Wi-Fi, 3G, and 4G

Your Galaxy Tab is filled with plenty of nifty features, but it really comes to life when you take it online. With it, you've got the whole Internet laid out in glorious, full-screen color. Whether you need to search, get maps and directions, watch YouTube videos, or do pretty much anything else on the Internet, your Honeycomb tablet lets you do it.

But first, of course, you need to get connected. You'll get the rundown on how to do that in this chapter.

How the Galaxy Tab Gets Online

Your Galaxy Tab is built to hop onto the Internet via its Wi-Fi connection, and if you've got one with a 3G connection (or 4G connection) built in, you can get onto the network that way as well. 4G stands for *fourth generation*—the fourth generation of cellphone standards. The difference between 4G and 3G networks is simple: 4G is much faster. The term 4G is sometimes used interchangeably with a standard called *LTE* (Long Term Evolution), such as Verizon's LTE network. In fact, an LTE network doesn't quite meet all of the geek specs of a 4G network, but the differences are too small to worry about.

If you've got a 3G or 4G tablet, connecting to the Internet is as easy as turning the thing on. Whenever your 3G or 4G network is available, the tablet uses it—you can tell by the 3G or 4G symbol in the status bar. Both 3G and 4G networks were built for data and the Internet—delivering email attachments, downloading music, and playing video.

Connecting via Wi-Fi—which is usually even faster than 3G or 4G—takes a little more work.

Connecting via Wi-Fi

When you connect via a Wi-Fi hotspot, you've hit the mother lode of connection speeds. Wi-Fi hotspots can be as fast as a cable modem. If you've ever taken a laptop on the road, you may already know where the best Wi-Fi hotspots are. Some coffee shops and hotels offer free Wi-Fi, while others make you pay for it. More and more, you find Wi-Fi coverage in airplanes, libraries, and even entire cities. In fact, if you connect your computers to the Internet at home using a wireless router, you have your own Wi-Fi hotspot, and you can connect your Tab to the Internet via your home network.

Your connection speed varies from hotspot to hotspot. At a public hotspot, you're sharing the connection with any number of other people, so if the hotspot isn't set up to handle that many connections, your speed may suffer. Also, Wi-Fi isn't a good bet when you're in motion. Hotspots have a range of only about 300 feet, so you and your Tab can move right past them. Your 3G or 4G connection is a better option when you're moving.

 When you're connected to a Wi-Fi hotspot, your Galaxy Tab uses it for more than just Internet access. It also uses Wi-Fi for finding your current location in apps like Google Maps (unless you turn on GPS, as described on page 18). The Tab uses a clever technology that finds nearby Wi-Fi networks and employs fancy algorithms to determine your location. It's not as precise as GPS, but it's still pretty good.

Depending on how your Galaxy Tab is set up, Wi-Fi may automatically turn on when you turn on your Tab, or you may need to turn it on manually. Here's how:

- **Turn off Flight mode.** When you're in Flight mode (there's a small airplane icon in the Notifications Panel), all built-in radios, including Wi-Fi, are turned off. To turn off Flight mode and turn on Wi-Fi, tap the Notifications Panel, and in the panel with widget icons, flick to the right until you see the Flight Mode widget. Tap it to turn it off. Tap it again to turn it on.

- **Turn on Wi-Fi.** You can turn on Wi-Fi without having to muck around with flight mode. If Wi-Fi is turned off, tap the Notifications Panel, and then tap the Wi-Fi widget to turn it on. Tap it again to turn it off.

Now that you've got Wi-Fi turned on, a Wi-Fi icon appears in the Notifications Panel when a Wi-Fi network is nearby, and the Wi-Fi Settings screen appears. You'll see a list of nearby Wi-Fi networks under the words "Wi-Fi networks." The list tells you the name of each Wi-Fi network and also whether it's an open network (that is, it doesn't require a password) or password protected.

Tap any network on the list, and a connection screen appears. Tap Connect if it's open, or, if it's protected, type the password. After a few seconds, you make the connection. The network to which you just connected appears in your list with the word "Connected" underneath it. A blue Wi-Fi indicator also appears in the Notifications Panel.

 Tip If you find yourself getting disconnected from Wi-Fi networks, try this technique. On the Wi-Fi Settings screen, tap "Wi-Fi sleep policy." From the screen that appears, select "Never." Now, your Wi-Fi antenna doesn't go to sleep when your Galaxy Tab's screen turns off. Select "Never when plugged in," and Wi-Fi doesn't go to sleep when your Tab is plugged in.

Disconnecting and Reconnecting

To disconnect from a Wi-Fi network, turn off Wi-Fi. If you want to disconnect from the network but keep Wi-Fi on, go back to the screen that lists the nearby Wi-Fi networks, tap the network to which you're connected, and then tap Forget. Boom—you're disconnected.

There's a downside to disconnecting this way, though. Normally, whenever you connect to a Wi-Fi network, your Tab remembers that connection, so it automatically connects (password and all) the next time you're in range.

If you tap Forget, though, the Tab can't log you in automatically the next time you're in range.

 The Notification Panel tells you that there's a nearby Wi-Fi network if that network is an open one—that is, one that doesn't use security. If you want to stop being notified when an open network is available, on the Wi-Fi settings screen, turn off the "Network notification" checkbox.

Connecting to For-Pay Wi-Fi Networks

Some Wi-Fi hotspots make you pay a fee to use them. In those cases, you have one more step when connecting. First, make the connection in the usual way. Then launch your Tab's web browser. A screen appears, delivered by the network, asking you to register and pay.

Some free Wi-Fi networks require you to agree to terms of service before you can use them. In that case, those terms appear when you launch the browser. So if you're connected via a free Wi-Fi hotspot but can't get an Internet-based app like Pandora to work, it might be because you haven't yet launched your browser and agreed to the terms of service.

 In some instances, you must enter a password into your Galaxy Tab's Wi-Fi connection screen to connect to a Wi-Fi network. In that case, whoever runs the for-pay hotspot can give you the password.

Connecting to an "Invisible" Network

For security reasons, some people or businesses tell their network not to broadcast its name—its *Service Set Identifier* (SSID). That way, the network may appear invisible to people passing by. (Dedicated hackers, though, can easily detect it.)

If you need to connect to a network that isn't broadcasting its SSID, you can still connect as long as you've been provided with its name, the type of security it uses, and its password. From the Home screen, tap the Notifications Panel, tap Settings, and tap Wireless and Networks→Wi-Fi settings→Add Wi-Fi network. From the screen that appears, type the network's SSID, choose the security type, type the password, and then tap Save to connect to the network.

Managing Wi-Fi Networks

The more you use your Tab, the more Wi-Fi networks you're going to connect to. Over time, that means you may have a long list of networks to which you automatically connect—and maybe you don't want to always connect to so many of them. You may want some control over your connections.

It's easy to tell your Tab to "forget" the connections to which you don't want to connect. From the Home screen, tap the Notifications Panel, tap Settings, and then tap Wi-Fi. At the bottom of the Wi-Fi settings screen, beneath "Wi-Fi networks," you see a list of all the networks to which you automatically connect. Tap any you don't want to connect to automatically, and then tap Forget. From now on, you don't automatically connect when you're within range, and you have to make the connection manually.

 Think you're in range of a Wi-Fi network, but it isn't showing up on the Wi-Fi settings screen? You can tell your Tab to re-scan the area and look for networks. On the Wi-Fi settings screen, tap the Menu icon on the upper right, and then select Scan. The tablet re-scans and lists any networks it finds.

Setting Up and Managing Your Google Account

Now that you're connected, feel free to browse the Web. But if you want to do more than Web browsing—for example, use Gmail, Google Calendar, or some other Google services—you also need to be signed into a Google account.

When you first turned on your Galaxy Tab, you were likely prompted to log into your Google account, or if you didn't have one, to set one up. If you didn't do that when you first turned on your shiny new Tab, don't worry; you can do it at any later point—and there's no time like the present.

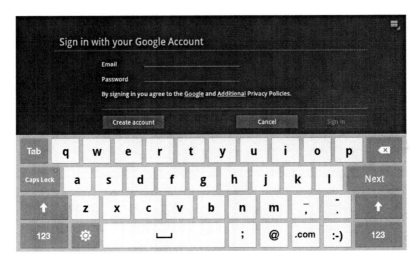

Tap the Gmail icon on the Home screen, and you come to a page that prompts you to sign into your Google account. (You can instead tap Create Account if you don't already have one.) After you sign in, your Tab talks to the Google servers, and soon you're ready to go. A screen appears, asking if you want to back up your apps and settings (which include your browser bookmarks and Wi-Fi passwords). Backing up is a good idea. As you'll see on page 69, it lets you keep your browser bookmarks in sync on your Tab, your computer, and any Android phones you have. And of course, backing up means your information and settings don't get lost if there's a problem with your Tab. Make sure the box next to "Keep this device backed up with my Google Account" is turned on. Tap Done, and you're ready to go.

 Have more than one Google account? Make sure that the first one you enter is the primary one you plan to use. After you do that, you can create new Google accounts. To do it, from Settings, tap Accounts and Sync→Add Account.

There are plenty of ways you can customize the way your Google account works, for example, to sync your mail and calendar. For details, see page 383.

3 Navigating the Web

Once you've used your Galaxy Tab to research a vacation destination online, check out an online menu before you choose a restaurant, or find a magazine to read on the train, you may wonder how you ever got along without having the Web in such easy reach. The screen is big, clear, and high resolution, so you get a top-notch Web experience. With more and more web designers making their sites look and work great on devices like the Tab, you may find yourself using the browser more than any other app.

The Galaxy Tab's Browser

To access the Web, tap the Browser icon on the Home screen.

The Galaxy Tab's Android browser looks a lot like Google's Chrome browser, which runs on the PC and Mac (and Linux). It's a full-fledged browser, with everything you expect in a browser—like tabs for browsing multiple sites simultaneously, bookmarks, autofill for web addresses, cookies, password memorization…just about the whole nine yards. You can also share pages with friends and even browse the Web privately. It looks and works a lot like computer-based browsers, so you don't have much of a learning curve. Here are the main controls you need to know about:

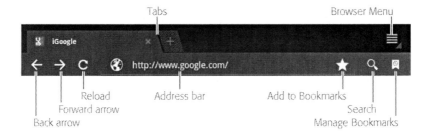

Tabs   Browser Menu

Reload   Address bar   Add to Bookmarks

Forward arrow   Search

Back arrow   Manage Bookmarks

- **Back and Forward buttons.** As expected, these buttons take you backward or forward one page in your Web travels.

 You can also tap the Tab's normal Back button at the bottom of the screen to move back a page.

- **Reload/Stop loading.** Tap to refresh your current page. If a page is in the process of loading, this button appears as an X—tap it to stop it from reloading.

- **Address bar.** Enter the URL (the web address) for a page you want to visit. It also does double-duty: Type a search term, and the browser does a Google search for you.

- **Tabs.** Tap the + sign, and you open a new separate tab so you can visit multiple sites at the same time. Switch among open tabs by tapping the one you want to switch to.

- **Add to Bookmarks.** Tap to save the page to your Bookmarks list.

- **Search.** Tap, type your search terms, and you launch a Google search. Since you can just type your search term into the address bar, this search box is somewhat superfluous, but it's there because old habits die hard.

 When you search the Web using the browser, you search using Google. But you can change your preference to another search site, like Bing, for example. For details, see page 81.

- **Manage Bookmarks.** Tapping the star at the end of the address bar adds the current page to your Bookmarks list. To use or edit your Bookmarks, tap this icon instead.

 Geeks may want to know that although the Galaxy Tab's browser looks very much like Chrome and is based on the same WebKit V8 JavaScript engines, it doesn't use the same code as Chrome. It's one of those rare instances in which something looks like a duck, walks like a duck, and quacks like a duck…but isn't actually a duck.

- **Browser menu.** As with many other apps, there's a Menu button tucked all the way in the screen's upper-right corner. Tap this button to get to a variety of the browser's features, like sharing the page, changing your settings, or opening an "incognito" tab that lets you browse the Web in privacy.

Navigating a Web Page

You'll spend approximately zero time learning basic navigation on the Galaxy Tab's browser, because in almost all respects, it works just like your computer's browser. To go to a web page, tap the address bar, and then type the URL you want to visit. Use the Forward and Back buttons as you do on a computer's browser. Tap the circular icon to the right of the Forward button to refresh a page. When a page is loading, that button turns into an X; to stop the page from loading, tap the X. To scroll up and down and sideways on a web page, use the same flicking and dragging gestures you do everywhere else on your tablet.

You can also perform some navigational tricks with your Tab—zooming, scrolling, and switching page orientation—that you can't easily do on your home computer:

- **Rotate your Tab.** Turn it 90 degrees to the left or right. Hold it horizontally for a wide view of your page or vertically for a narrower one. Simply choose the best view for the page's layout and content.

 Some websites can find out what type of device is accessing them and deliver a different-looking page based on that device. However, some sites think your Galaxy Tab is a smartphone—and pages built for smartphones don't always display well on your Tab's roomy screen. Changing your Tab's orientation can help solve that problem.

- **Use the two-finger spread.** Put two fingers on the Tab's screen on the areas where you want to zoom in, and move your fingers apart. The web page stretches and zooms in. The more you spread, the greater the zoom. Pinch your fingers together to zoom back out. You may need to do the two-finger spread and pinch several times until you get the exact magnification you want.

- **Double-tap.** Double-tap with a finger on the section of the page where you want to zoom. Double-tap again to zoom out. You can't control the zoom level as finely with the double-tap as you can using the two-finger spread.

Double-tap

Using and Managing Tabs

Tabs are one of your Galaxy Tab's handiest browser features. With them, switching among multiple sites is a breeze!

To open a new tab, tap the + button at the top of the browser; a new tab opens up to the right of the rightmost open tab. It starts out on your home page, but you can use it to go to any site you want. Your other tab stays open; it's like being in two places at once. You can keep opening multiple tabs, and they keep opening up to the right. To switch to another tab, simply tap it. To close any tab, tap the X on it.

Tap here to open a new tab
Tap here to close a tab

Tip If you like taking the slow lane rather than the express, there's another way to open a new tab: Tap the Menu button, and then select New Tab.

If you open up more than three tabs, you can't see them all at the top of your browser—just flick your finger across the tabs, and the tabs move, uncovering the ones that are hidden. Bear in mind that when you flick, the tabs across the top move, but the actual tab you're viewing doesn't move. In other words, the tab showing at the top of the page doesn't match the page you're on. You can tap the Globe button to move the tabs back into their original locations (or just flick them back).

Flick this way to reveal hidden tabs to the left

Web Pages Designed for Mobile Devices

As you browse the Web, you may come across sites that look significantly different on your tablet than they do on a computer. That's because web designers design pages specifically to be viewed on tablets and smartphones, taking into account that these devices have smaller screens than computer displays.

CNN and Boston.com, for example, have sites designed especially for mobile viewing. Head to the same site at the exact same time of day with a smartphone and a computer, and you see very different pages, even though the *content* of those pages is the same.

Pages formatted for the small screen often don't include complex layouts, and instead present articles and other information in scrollable lists. They generally don't let you zoom in and out; you navigate primarily by scrolling and clicking links. That's good news for smartphone jockeys, but not necessarily good news for Galaxy Tab owners like you. Your 10.1-inch screen is generally capable of viewing the same web pages intended for computers. Because pages built for smartphones may leave out graphics, videos, and fancy layouts, you may end up being frustrated by what you see.

Over time, this may become less of an issue. Web designers will eventually start designing three types of pages for each website: one for computers, one for smartphones, and one for tablets. When that day comes, you'll always see a page optimized for whatever device you're using to connect to the Internet.

If you come across a page that displays for a smartphone and it doesn't look good on your Tab, you can try a few things. Try changing the orientation; sometimes that works. You may also want to look around the page to see whether there's a link you can click to display the full version of a page, rather than the smartphone version. The techie news site *Techdirt.com*, for example, includes a link like that. If you're feeling in a super-techie frame of mind, you can perform some browser magic on your Tab and force websites to display their pages as if they're on a computer. For details, head to this Computerworld blog entry describing how to do it: *http://bit.ly/ectyru*.

A Few Words about Flash

Many web pages use Flash animation technology to deliver videos and multimedia content. Unlike the iPad, the Galaxy Tab has Flash capability. However, if you were one of the first people to buy a Galaxy Tab, Flash may not be installed on it yet. So if you have a problem viewing videos and multimedia on web pages, a lack of Flash may be the problem. To install it, search the Android Market for Flash (page 90), or have your Tab download the latest operating system fixes (page 392).

The Address Bar

The address bar is the box at the top of the browser where you type the URL of the website you want to visit. To type a URL into the address bar, first tap the bar; the current URL is highlighted in green. Then use the keyboard to type an address. As you type, the Tab displays sites you've visited that match the letters you type. So when you type the letter *C*, for example, it might display Computerworld.com, CNN.com, and so on. Just tap the site in the list to go to there. A very small glowing bar above the address bar shows you how much of the page has loaded (in blue).

You may notice that the URLs in your list don't necessarily start with the same letter you typed. If you've previously visited a site about the international opera star Cecilia Bartoli, you may see that site come up when you type *C*. That's because the Tab's browser looks through your browsing history and Bookmarks list (see page 66) and looks for *all* matches to that letter, not just in URLs but also text in the page's title. When it displays its list as you type, it includes both the page's title and the URL.

As you continue to type, the list narrows down, and matches only those sites that match *all of the letters* you're typing. So, for example, if you type *com*, CNN.com no longer appears on your list, but Computerworld.com (*http://computerworld.com*) does. When you see the site you want to visit, tap its listing.

If there's no match on the list, you have to type the entire URL.

 Note Don't bother to type the *http://* part of a web address. Your Galaxy Tab knows to put that in for you. You do, however, need to type the .com or other ending, such as .edu. Of course, as you saw on page 65, you don't need to tap out *.com*— just tap the .com button on the keyboard.

You can also use the address bar to search the Web. Just type your search term, but *don't* add a .com ending. Your browser searches the Web for the term using Google (or whatever primary search engine you've chosen; see page 81).

When you tap the address bar to enter text, the Favorites button vanishes and is replaced by a right-facing triangle ▶. Tap the triangle after you've entered the URL or search term to head to the page or complete the search.

Playing Peekaboo with the Address Bar

Every once in a while you may notice that the address bar and navigation tools play peekaboo—the bar vanishes, along with the navigation, Reload, Search, and Favorites buttons. In their place is a down arrow. This arrow appears when you've scrolled deep into a web page. Just tap the down arrow to get your address bar and buttons back, lickety-split. (They also reappear when you scroll back up to the top of the page, but why go to all that trouble?)

Tap here...

...and the Address Bar and buttons return

Bookmarks

Just as with computer-based browsers, your Tab's browser lets you save your favorite sites as *bookmarks*—sites you can easily visit again without having to retype their URLs. In fact, before you even use your browser, it has bookmarks for few popular sites, like eBay, CNN, the Weather Channel, and others.

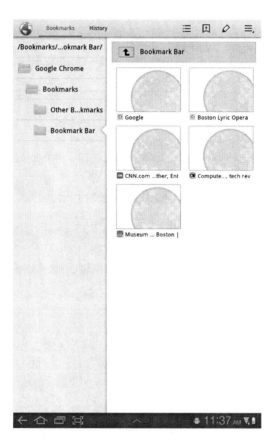

To see your bookmarks, tap the Bookmarks button. You see all your bookmarks displayed as a group of thumbnails so that you can distinguish them visually. To see them as a list, tap the list icon at the top of the screen—it's the fourth icon from the right. You'll see your bookmarks as a list, and the list icon turns into a thumbnail icon. Tap the thumbnail icon to see your bookmarks as a list.

No matter which view you use, to go to a bookmarked site, tap the site. Voilà—you're there.

When you're viewing your bookmarks, to return to the browser, tap the small ⊕ icon in the upper left of the screen.

Adding a Bookmark

Whenever you visit a web page you want to add as a bookmark, tap the star-shaped Bookmark button. The name of the page (what your Galaxy Tab calls a *label*) and the address are already filled in. Tap OK, and the page is added to your bookmarks.

If you want, you can change the name of the label, and even the address (although if you change the address, of course, then you add a different page from the one you tapped). In the Name box, type a different name if you want one, and in the Location box, type a different location. Then tap OK.

You can also add a bookmark when you're not on a web page. From the Bookmarks list, tap the Add bookmark icon, and then fill in the form that appears.

> **Note** When you visit a page that you've bookmarked, the Bookmark button displays as all yellow, rather than transparent.

Managing Bookmarks

Your tablet lets you do more than just go to Bookmarks. You can delete them, share them, edit them, and so on. To do so, head to Bookmarks, and then press and hold your finger on the bookmark you want to work with. A menu appears with the following choices:

⊘ Boston Lyric Opera	blo.org
Open	
Open in new tab	
Edit bookmark	
Add shortcut to home	
Share link	
Copy link URL	
Delete bookmark	
Set as homepage	

- **Open.** Opens the bookmarked site in the current window. So if, for example, you're at *www.google.com*, open your bookmarks, and then choose *www.cnn.com* from your bookmarks. Now, *www.cnn.com* opens in the window where *www.google.com* had previously been open.

- **Open in new window.** Opens the bookmarked site in a new tab, even though the menu says it will open in a new window. So if you're at *www.google.com*, open your bookmarks, and then choose *www.cnn.com*, *www.cnn.com* opens in a new tab.

- **Edit bookmark.** Brings up a page that lets you edit the name and location of the bookmark. It looks much like the page for adding a bookmark.

- **Add shortcut to home.** Tap this option, and a shortcut to the book-marked page is added to your Home screen. When you tap the book-mark, it opens the browser to that site. You can move and delete the icon after you add it (page 23).

 If you add a shortcut to your Home screen, and then delete the shortcut, the book-mark still remains in your browser's Bookmarks list.

- **Share link.** Tap to share the link of the bookmark by email or text message.

- **Copy link URL.** Tap to copy the bookmark's URL to the clipboard so you can then paste it somewhere else, like into a document or email.

- **Delete bookmark.** Deletes the bookmark. After you tap it, you get a warning that you're about to delete the bookmark, just in case you want to reconsider, or if you tapped this option by accident.

- **Set as homepage.** Tap this, and from now on whenever you open a new window, it opens to that site.

Reordering Bookmarks and Adding Folders

You can also change the order of your bookmarks and add new folders. To do it, tap the Edit icon at the top right of the screen ✐. A toolbar appears that lets you add a new folder, or change the order of your bookmarks. In addition, empty boxes appear next to your bookmarks. To delete bookmarks, check the boxes next to those you want to delete, and then tap Delete, which appears at the top of the screen.

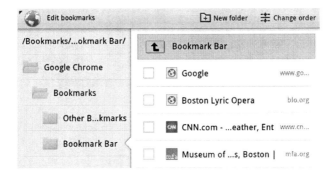

Syncing the Galaxy Tab's Bookmarks with Your Computer's

If you use the Chrome browser on your PC or Mac, your Galaxy Tab can perform a very useful bit of magic: It can synchronize the bookmarks between Chrome on your computer and the bookmarks on your Tab. No more will you have to recreate the bookmarks that you have on your computer on your Tab, or vice versa. When you're on your Tab, when you add (or delete) a bookmark, that bookmark is also added to the bookmark on Chrome on your computer—and when you're on your computer and add or delete a bookmark, it's added or deleted on your Tab.

Here's how to do it:

1. Tap the Menu button, and then select Settings→General.

    The browser's General Settings screen appears.

2. Tap "Sync with Google Chrome."

   A screen appears that lets you perform the sync.

3. Tap "Add bookmarks to Google Account. "

   If you instead want to delete the existing bookmarks on your Tab, tap "Delete bookmarks." And if you're feeling squeamish about the whole thing (no reason to, though—buck up!), tap Cancel.

4. Tap Next.

   You get a confirmation of the step you're about to take—for example, deleting the bookmarks on the Tab and synchronizing with your main Google account. Tap Done.

   After that, your bookmarks synchronize between Chrome and the Tab's browser—that's all it takes!

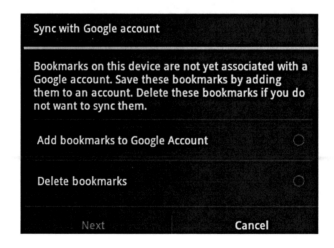

Most Visited and History Lists

When you go to your bookmarks, you find two more ways to browse sites that you've been to before—Most Visited and History. Your Galaxy Tab's browser keeps track of sites you've visited, and puts these two lists together based on that. They're great ways, in addition to Bookmarks, to head back to sites you've visited before without having to type—or even remember—the web addresses.

To see the History list, tap the word "History" at the top of the Bookmarks screen. To see the Most Visited list, tap "Most visited" at the top of the History list. These lists work much like the Bookmarks list—tap the site you want to visit. Notice one difference between these lists and the Bookmarks list: The sites all have stars to the right of them, and the stars are either outlines ☆ or all yellow ★. A yellow star indicates that the site is on your Bookmarks list; a transparent one indicates it's not. Tapping a transparent star adds that site to your bookmarks (and turns the star yellow). To remove a site from your Bookmarks list, tap a yellow star. It turns gray, and the site gets removed from your Bookmarks list.

The History list shows you not just sites you've visited today, but yesterday, in the last seven days, and in the last month. Rather than show you all the sites you visited before today, your Tab shows you your options ("Today," "Yesterday," "Last 7 days," "Last month"). Tap the arrow next to one of these, and you see the full list of sites for that time period.

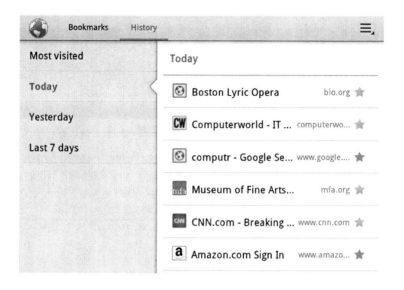

Editing and Managing the Most Visited List

Just as with Bookmarks, you can edit and manage the Most Visited list. Hold your finger on the site you want to edit or manage, and a menu appears, similar to the one for managing Bookmarks.

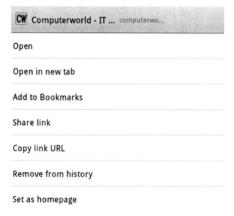

The lists are nearly identical, with a few minor differences:

- **Add to Bookmarks** is included in the Most Visited menu so you can add the site to Bookmarks.

- **Remove from history** removes a site from the Most Visited list as well as from your History list.

Editing and Managing the History List

You can do one thing to your History list that you can't do with either the Bookmarks list or the Most Visited list: You can clear your entire history. If you feel guilty about visiting sites for any reason, you can get rid of them all. While in the History list, press the Menu key, and then select "Clear history." Your slate is wiped clean.

Tapping Links

When it comes to links, your Galaxy Tab's web browser works largely like any computer browser, except that you tap a link rather than click it. Tap the link, and you get sent to a new web page.

http://www.computerworld.com/s/
article/9218933/6_tools_to_help_tame_Twitter_

Open

Open in new tab

Save link

Copy link URL

Select text

 Sometimes when you tap a link, instead of loading a web page, your Tab may take a different action. For example, if the link is to an email address, it opens the Email app with a new message addressed to the link's email address.

But this is a Galaxy Tab, so you can do a lot more with links than just tapping them. Hold your finger on a link, and a menu appears with these options:

- **Open.** Opens the linked page in the current window.
- **Open in new tab.** Opens the linked page in a new tab.

- **Save link.** Saves the linked page to your Tab. To view the page after it's been downloaded, when you're in the browser, tap the Menu button, select Downloads, and you come to a Downloads screen with a list of all the pages (and graphics) you've downloaded. To view a page or a graphic, tap it. To delete it, tap the box next to it so a green checkmark appears, and then tap Delete from the menu that appears at the bottom of the page.

 If you hold your finger on a graphic that's also a link, a "Save image" option appears, which lets you save the graphic. There are more options as well—see page 75.

- **Share link.** Lets you share the link via email or text message.

- **Copy link URL.** Tap to copy the link's URL to the clipboard, so you can paste it somewhere else, such as in a document or email.

- **Select text.** Lets you select text for copying—go to page 39 for details on what to do next.

Other Nifty Things to Tap

Your Tab is smart enough to take actions based on what you see on web pages, without even having to use links:

- When you see an address on the Web and want to see a map of its location, tap it. Google Maps launches, centered on the location.

- When you see an email address, even if the address hasn't been created as a link, tap it, and the Email app opens, with a new message already addressed to that address.

Saving Online Images

When you're browsing the Web, sooner or later you come across a picture you'd like to save. For example, if a friend posts a picture from your birthday party on Facebook, you can save it on your Tab and then share it with others.

The Tab gives you a quick and easy way to save that image. Hold your finger on the picture for a second or two, and a menu appears with the following three options:

- **Save image.** Downloads the picture. See the next section to learn how to go back and view all the pictures in this folder.

- **View image.** Opens the image in its own page. As a practical matter, this option doesn't do much, because it doesn't make the image any larger or smaller—you're seeing the same image, just on its own rather than on a web page.

- **Set as wallpaper.** Tap and—presto!—the image becomes your Tab's wallpaper.

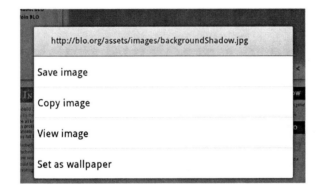

 If the picture is also a link, the menu shows the usual options for bookmarking the link, saving the link, and so on.

Viewing Images and Downloaded Pages

Now that you've got graphics saved on your Galaxy Tab, how can you view them? When you're in the browser, tap the Menu key, and then select Downloads.

You come to a list of all your pictures. They're listed by file name, which may or may not give you a clue to their contents. If you see something like Serena_Williams.jpg, then you know it's a photo of the tennis great Serena Williams. But if you see something like _5HABau-IVgrZ2QWCTqil.jpg, you won't have a clue what it is.

Downloads - Sorted by date

Today

backgroundShadow.jpeg
blo.org
Complete   4.94KB   1:16 PM

IBM_launches_new_services_model_for_city_planners.htm
www.computerworld.com
Complete   131KB   1:12 PM

google-plus-logo-120.jpeg
www.computerworld.com
Complete   5.16KB   1:12 PM

Amazon_Web_Services_reports_outage_in_the_U.htm
www.computerworld.com
Complete   134KB   1:12 PM

twitter.gif
www.computerworld.com
Complete   6.54KB   1:12 PM

Sort by size

Underneath the name, you see the address of the site you downloaded it from, along with the file size and, to the right, the date of download or the time, if you downloaded it today. The downloads are sorted by the date you downloaded them, with the newest first. If you'd prefer to sort them by file size—the largest first—tap "Sort by size." To sort them again by date, tap "Sort by date."

Tap any picture to view it. It opens in the Gallery, and you can handle it like any other picture in the Gallery. For more details about the Gallery, turn to page 245.

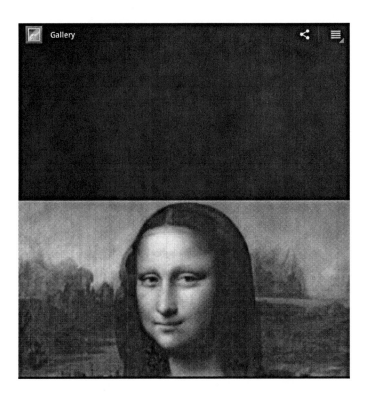

Reading PDF Files

The Web is filled with PDF files that often have complex layouts combined with graphics. Your browser can't read these files directly—but your tablet can. When you tap a link to a PDF file, it gets downloaded to your tablet, and a small download notification appears in the Notification Panel. Tap the panel, and a notification pops up to tell you that the download is complete. Tap the notification, and you open the PDF in QuickOffice, an app on your Galaxy Tab that displays Word, Excel, PowerPoint, and PDF files. (See page 346 for more details.) To dismiss the notification, tap the X on it. The PDF is stored in the Downloads area, so you can always go back and read it.

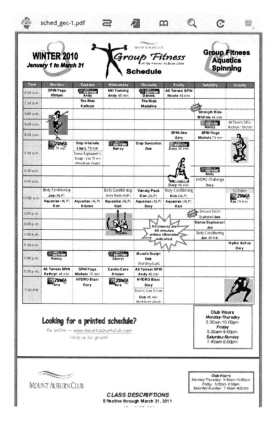

Copying Text, Finding Text, Getting Page Information, and More

When you browse the Web, you may be on a mission of sorts—looking for a specific piece of information. You might be looking for a particular word or phrase within a web page, and you may even come across text on the Web that you want to use elsewhere, say in an email or a document.

Your Galaxy Tab's browser can do all that and then some. To copy text, hold your finger down in a block of text. The text menu appears at the top of the page, and text selectors appear. In addition, you'll see a magnifying glass that magnifies the text you selected. Drag them around the text you want to copy, and then tap Copy. It copies to your Tab's clipboard, and the text menu disappears. Once the text is in the clipboard, you can insert it somewhere, and share it with others—anything you can normally do with copied text. (For more details about copy and paste, see page 39.) If you want to copy all of the text on the page to the clipboard, instead of using the text selectors, tap "Select all" at the top of the page.

You can do plenty of other fancy tricks while visiting any web page as well. Tap the Menu button on the upper right of the screen, and you get a menu of options that lets you do any of the following:

- **New tab.** Opens a new tab. This command does the same thing as tapping the + button on an empty tab.

- **New incognito tab.** Don't want anyone to know which web pages you've been visiting? This option opens a tab that keeps your Web travels secret—pages you visit aren't listed in the History list, for example.

 The incognito tab works just like Chrome's incognito mode on your desktop computer. See page 82 later in this chapter for more details.

- **Find on page.** Looking for text on a page? Tap this option, and a search box appears at the top of the page, with the keyboard at the bottom. Type the text or phrase you're searching for, and the Tab finds the text, sends you to its location on the page, and highlights it in green. To find the next occurrence of that text, tap the right arrow. To find a previous mention of it on the page, tap the left arrow. To abandon the search, tap the X to the left of the search box.

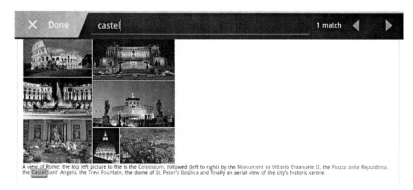

A view of Rome: the top left picture to the is the Colosseum, followed (left to right) by the Monument to Vittorio Emanuele II, the Piazza della Repubblica, the Castel Sant' Angelo, the Trevi Fountain, the dome of St. Peter's Basilica and finally an aerial view of the city's historic centre.

- **Share page.** Tap to share the page via email or Bluetooth. If you opt to share it via email, the URL appears in a newly opened email message. You can then select an email address and add explanatory text to the message. This message doesn't share the page itself, just a link to it. If you select Bluetooth, your Tab scans for any nearby Bluetooth devices and then connects you to any you choose. In this case, you're sending the entire web page, not just the URL.

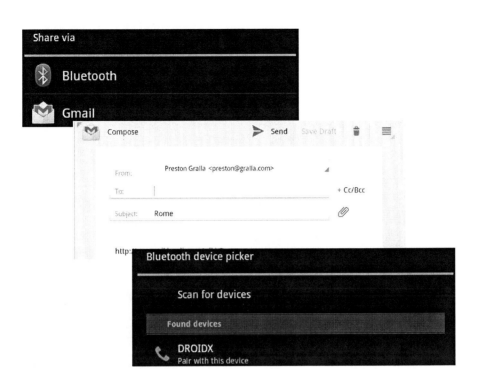

 Note Make sure that device you want to save the page to has Bluetooth turned on and is discoverable (page 364). If it's not, you can't send the page.

- **Page info.** Tap to see basic information about the page: title and web address.

- **Downloads.** Brings you to the Downloads area. If you've saved pictures or other items here, then you see a list of them.

- **Print.** Select this, and you can print to a Samsung printer set up for remote printing.

- **Settings.** Here's how you can change countless browser settings, including the size of the text displayed, your default search engine, and so on.

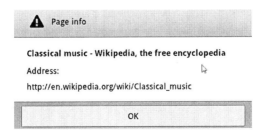

Online Privacy and Security

Whether you browse the Web with a computer or with your Galaxy Tab, there are potential security and privacy dangers out there—cookies, pop-ups, and malicious websites. The browser, just like its big brother browsers on computers, includes the tools you need to keep you safe and protect your privacy when you browse the Web.

Incognito Tab

As explained in the previous section, if you want to keep your Web browsing safe from prying eyes, you can open up an incognito tab, and browse in that tab by selecting "New incognito tab" from the menu. This tab starts out showing you basic information about how incognito works. You can tell the tab is an incognito one by the incognito icon.

You've gone incognito. Pages you view in this window won't appear in your browser history or search history, and they won't leave other traces, like cookies, on your computer after you close the incognito window. Any files you download or bookmarks you create will be preserved, however.

Going incognito doesn't affect the behavior of other people,servers, or software. Be wary of:

- Websites that collect or share information about you
- Internet service providers or employers that track the pages you visit
- Malicious software that tracks your keystrokes in exchange for free smileys
- Surveillance by secret agents
- People standing behind you

When you browse in an incognito tab, the pages you visit won't appear in your browser history or search history. They also won't leave other traces of your travels, such as cookies. (When you create bookmarks in incognito mode, though, those bookmarks will remain.)

> **Note** When you open an incognito tab, only the visits you make in that tab are kept incognito. Your other tabs show up in your browser and search histories and leave behind cookies.

Pop-up Blocker

What's top on your list of web annoyances? Gotta be those *pop-ups* and their cousins the *pop-unders*—ugly little windows and ads that get in your face by opening up over (or, more sneakily, under) your browser window.

Sometimes pop-ups and pop-unders are malicious; if you tap, them they attempt to install harmful software or send you to a dangerous website.

Sometimes they're merely annoying ads. Other times, though, they may actually be useful, like a pop-up that displays a seating chart when you're visiting a ticket-buying site. Your Tab's browser includes a pop-up blocker, and like all pop-up blockers, it can't necessarily distinguish between bad pop-ups and good ones, so it blocks them all.

However, if you're at a website with pop-ups that you want to see, you can turn off the pop-up blocker. Press the Menu key, select Settings→ Advanced, and then tap the green "Block pop-up tabs" checkbox to turn it off. When you leave the site and want pop-ups blocked again, go back to the setting and tap to turn the checkmark back on.

 When you turn off the pop-up blocker, it stops blocking pop-ups in *all* your browser windows, not just on one site. So be careful when you browse other places on the Web when the pop-up blocker is turned off.

Cookies

Cookies are tiny bits of information that some websites store on your Tab for future use. When you register for a website and create a user name and password, the website can store that information in a cookie so you don't have to retype it every time. Cookies can also remember your habits and preferences when you use a website—your favorite shipping method, or what kinds of news articles you're likely to read. But not all cookies are in-nocuous, since they can also track your web browsing from multiple sites and potentially invade your privacy.

The Tab's browser gives you control over how you handle cookies—you can either accept them, or tell the browser to reject them. Keep in mind that if you don't allow cookies on your Tab, you may not be able to take advantage of the features on many sites.

To bar websites from putting cookies on your Tab when you're in the browser, press the Menu key, select Settings→Privacy and Security, and scroll down to the Cookies section. Turn off the green checkbox next to "Accept cookies." You can always turn cookies back on again, if it causes problems with web browsing.

While you're in Privacy Settings, you can also delete all the cookies that sites have placed on your Tab so far. Tap "Clear all cookie data." You get a warning that you're about to toss your cookies. Tap OK to delete them, or Cancel if you change your mind.

Privacy Settings

You can do more in the Privacy and Security section of the browser's settings screen to make sure your privacy isn't invaded. For example, you can clear your browsing history so that others who use the browser can't see where you've been. Tap "Clear history" to do it.

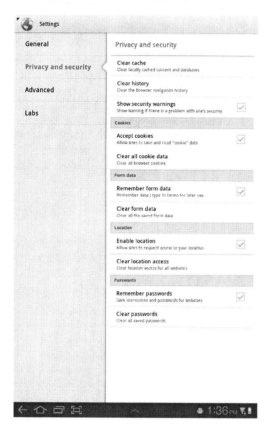

You can also tap "Clear cache" to clean out website information your browser has stored on your Galaxy Tab. A *cache* is information the browser stores on your Tab so it doesn't have to re-retrieve that information the next time you visit that site. The cache speeds up browsing, since it's faster to grab the information—a website image, for example—from your Tab than from the Web. Tap "Clear cache" if you want to clear all that information out, if you worry that the information there poses a privacy risk.

For another example, at many websites, you log in by typing a user name and password, and other information such as your address. Your Tab's browser remembers those user names, passwords, and other information, and fills them in for you automatically when you next visit. That's convenient, but it also presents a privacy risk, because someone else using your Tab can log in as you.

If that concerns you, you can take two actions. First, in the Privacy section, turn off the green checkmark next to "Remember form data." When you turn it off, the browser doesn't remember user names, passwords, and other information you type into forms. You can always turn it on again. To delete all the information already stored on your Tab, tap "Clear form data." Next, go to the Passwords area and turn off the "Remember passwords" checkbox. To clear out saved passwords, tap "Clear passwords."

As you browse the Web, your Tab can notify websites of your location. That way, the site can serve up information specific to your location—local restaurants, interesting places to visit, and so on. If you worry about the privacy implications, go to the Location area, and turn off the "Enable location" checkbox. Then tap "Clear location access" to kill the stored location information about you.

4 Downloading and Using Apps

Apps, apps, and more apps. One of the main reasons you bought that shiny new Galaxy Tab is so you can get your hands on apps that do just about everything under the sun—and a few things that seem beyond the range of the solar system. In this chapter, you'll find out how to download and use those apps, as well as how to uninstall and troubleshoot them.

Android's Free and Easy Approach to Apps

Unlike the iPad, the Galaxy Tab, along with all other Android devices, takes a wide-open approach to apps. Google doesn't step in to say what you can and can't download. You're free to choose from tens of thousands of apps, with thousands more being written every month. There are apps for tracking expenses, chatting with people, playing games, using social networks like Twitter, finding new friends, tuning your guitar, viewing maps of the night sky—even making your Tab work better.

 Note Some Android apps cost money, but many more are free. So whenever you find a for-pay app, search around to see whether you can find a free one that does the same thing.

These apps tie in to the Tab's unique hardware and software. One even automatically detects potholes as you drive, using your Tab's various sensors to measure sudden movements. The app then uses the Tab's positioning software to locate exactly where the pothole is, and creates a text file with all the relevant information so you can send it to your local Department of Public Works. (Unfortunately, no app has yet been developed that will get your local Department of Public Works to actually fix the pothole.)

Apps and Multitasking

Your Galaxy Tab is great at multitasking—running more than one app at a time. Your Tab can browse the Web while you listen to music, receive email, and have Facebook updates delivered to you, all without breaking a sweat.

You usually don't notice that Android is multitasking, though, because unlike in Windows or Mac OS X, you can't resize app windows and see the underlying desktop while you're using an app. But you have a simple way of seeing many of the apps that you're currently running, or apps that you've been running recently: Tap the Recent Apps button at the bottom of the screen and a list with big thumbnails of all of the apps you've recently run pops up. Tap any item to switch to it.

Note The apps you see aren't necessarily running right now. The apps you've most recently quit show up, too.

When you switch between the app you're running and another app, that first app is still running in the background. If it's a music-playing app or a radio app, it keeps playing until you close it. With many other apps, though, at some point Android notices that you haven't used it in a while and closes it down. You won't even notice that your Galaxy Tab has closed it.

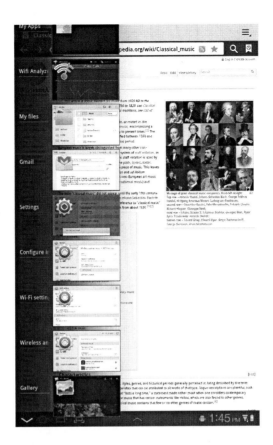

To make *sure* that you close an app when you switch away from it, try this: Press the Menu key at the upper right of your screen ☰ and see if there's a choice for closing the app. Not all apps offer this choice (or even a Menu key), but that's OK; Android closes the app when it's no longer needed.

Tip You can find apps called *task killers* that claim to speed up Android by automatically closing apps when they're no longer needed, or by letting you manually close those apps. Most everyone agrees that these apps are superfluous—the Android operating system does an excellent job of closing apps when they're no longer needed. In fact, many task killers don't even run with Honeycomb.

Where to Get Apps

Your Galaxy Tab offers you not just one, not just two, not just three, but four different ways to download and install apps:

- **Android Market on your Galaxy Tab.** Here's the primary way that most people get apps. Tap the Market button right on your Home screen. From here you can search for apps, read about them, and buy them.

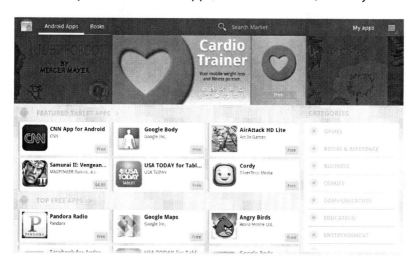

- **Android Market on the Web.** You can head to the Web on your computer, and search for and download Android apps to your Tab. Yes, that's right—you can use your PC or Mac, not the Tab itself. When you do it this way, you can also have that same app downloaded to any other Android devices you have, and manage apps for all of your Android devices from a central location. Get there by going to *https://market.android.com*.

- **The Web.** You can download and install apps from websites. Visit the site on your Tab, and download from there.

> **Tip** In a few cases, you can download an app to your PC or Mac, and it's installed on your Tab when you connect it to your computer. Generally, this happens if you've downloaded an app that works with your PC or Mac, as well as with Android.

- **Using a bar code scanner.** Of all the amazing tricks your Tab can do, this is one of the coolest. A free app gives the Tab the power to scan bar codes and QR codes. (*QR codes* are a special kind of bar code used by smartphones, cameras, and other devices.) After you've installed this app, you can use your Tab to scan a QR code to download other apps.

When you're browsing the Web with your PC or Mac and come across a bar code for downloading, just point your Tab's camera at it, click a button, and the magic begins. The Tab grabs and installs the software from the website. For more on bar code scanning, see page 101.

Voice Search

Search widget

 The QR in "QR code" stands for *quick response*. QR codes were designed to be scanned at high speeds. They were initially created by a subsidiary of Toyota as a way to track the auto manufacturing process, but are now used for many other purposes, especially in Japan.

Using the Android Market

Tap the Market icon, and you get sent to the Android Market, which has tens of thousands of apps you can download, with more added every month. The apps are either free or very low cost—typically under $4, although some business-related apps can cost up to $30:

- **Categories** (more than two dozen of 'em) are listed on the right side— Books & Reference, Business, Comics, and so on. Flick to see them all.

- **Featured, top-selling, and other popular apps** are listed to the left of the categories. Tap any to view more information and, if you're interested, download the app.

- **A featured list** is near the top. It's a mix of free and for-pay apps.

- **A navigation bar** at the very top includes search (tap it to type in a search), a "My apps" button that reveals the apps you've downloaded, and a Menu button. On the left of the navigation bar, you can see your current location in the Market (Games, for example), or if you're at the top, it shows a Books link for downloading books. (For more information about downloading books, see page 201.)

Tip If you're somewhere deep in the Market and want to return to the top, tap the shopping bag icon on the screen's upper left.

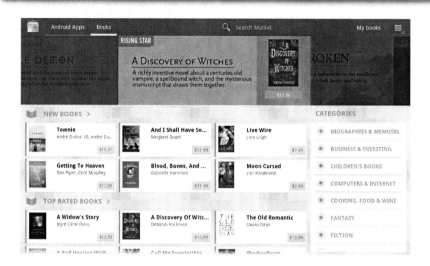

Browsing by Library Divisions and Categories

Tap any category, and you come to a screen showing the most popular apps in that category, typically sorted by Featured Tablet Apps (that is, paid for) status, Top Free Apps, and Best Selling Apps. You can tap that text to go straight to apps of that description. You also see subcategories listed on the right. So, for example, in Games, you find subcategories like Arcade & Action, Brain & Puzzle, Cards & Casino, and so on. Tap any subcategory, and you come to a list of all the apps in that subcategory, typically sorted by "top free" and "best selling." You see the name of the app, the maker, whether it's free, and, if it's paid, its cost.

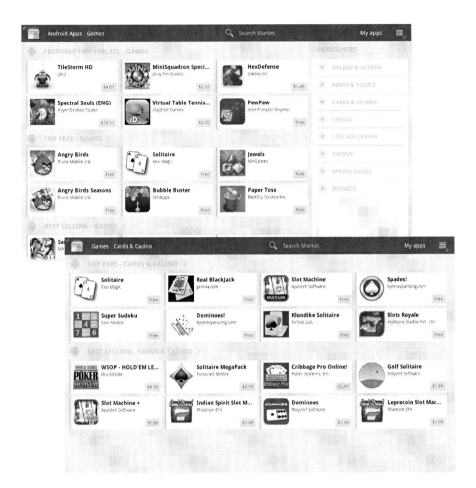

 Note Many Android apps were written for smartphones, and so don't take advantage of your Galaxy Tab's larger size, more powerful processor, and Honeycomb operating system. A *tablet app*, on the other hand, is one specifically written for a tablet like the Tab—like a 3D game.

Searching the Market for Apps

Browsing is well and good when you've got the time to scroll leisurely through lists. But often you're on a mission: You know the type of app you want, and you want to find it fast.

In that case, you want to search. You can search by the type of app, the name of the program, the name of the software company that created it, and by keyword. (For example, the word *car* would be a keyword for searching out a racing game.) Tap Search, and a keyboard and search box appear. Type what you're looking for, and then tap Enter. You see a list of programs associated with what you're looking for.

 The Market remembers what you've searched for in the past, so as you type, it shows you results that match previous searches. If that annoys you, tap the Menu key, and then select Clear Search History.

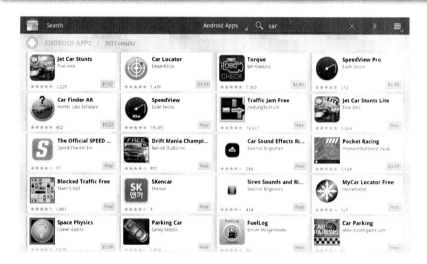

 In some instances, the Android Market doesn't show every single Android app available. For example, it doesn't list any apps that can't run on your Tab, like an older Android smartphone app that can't run on Honeycomb.

Getting Info About an App

Whether you're browsing a list or scrolling through search results, you eventually want to see more details about an app and possibly download it. In that case, tap the app's name, and you come to a page with a great deal of information, including a description, version number, size, number of downloads, ratings, price, screenshots, and individual user reviews. If the developer has made other apps, you see those as well, along with their star ratings and number of reviews. You also often see More buttons that reveal more information, such as a longer description.

A Share button also appears, which lets you share the app via email or Bluetooth.

Tip Be careful when using the star ratings as a guide to download and pay for an app. In some instances, that star rating may be based on just a rating or two (the info screen shows you how many). Any star rating based on a few ratings may not be particularly accurate, especially since the ratings may come from the developer's friends. If there are a dozen or more user ratings, the results are more trustworthy. So read the reviews, and note how *many* ratings each app has gotten.

Downloading and Installing Apps

Say you've read all about an app, and you've decided to take the plunge. You're ready to download. What's next? Depending on whether you have to pay for the app or not, you do things a bit differently.

Note When you're looking at a list of apps, you may notice some with buttons for Open or Manage instead of Install or Buy. In that case, you've already installed that app on your Tab. Tap Open to run the app, or Manage to change its options, such as whether to allow auto-updating, or to uninstall it.

Installing free apps

If the app is free, you see an Install button in the screen's upper-left corner, near the app's name and average rating. Tap it. The next screen tells you what information and features the application needs access to, such as your location, your Tab's storage, and so on. Typically, applications ask only for information they need to function—after all, a GPS app can't do its job without access to your Tab's GPS features. Still, if you're concerned about what you're asked to reveal, don't download.

Tip If an app wants to access information that it shouldn't need to do its job, you may be downloading a privacy invader. If, for example, if you're downloading a puzzle game designed to be played alone, and it says that it's going to access your contacts, that should raise a red flag.

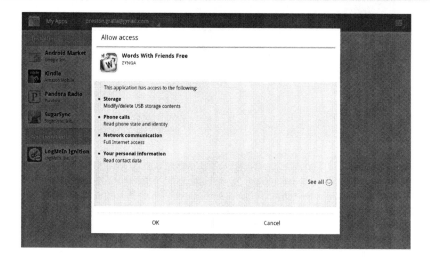

Next, click OK. The app immediately starts downloading in the background. The Notification Panel shows you the download's progress. Meanwhile, you can use your Tab any way you want. Soon a checkbox appears, indicating that the download is complete.

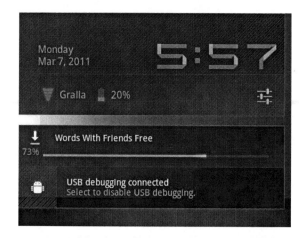

Tap the notification to run the app. You can also find the app's icon in the Apps Menu.

Installing for-pay apps

If the app is a for-pay one, you need a free Google Checkout account. Simply set one up ahead of time on the Web at *https://checkout.google.com*.

With that done, you can buy the app. Tap the Buy button. As when you're downloading a free app, a screen tells you what kind of features and information the app uses. It also shows the payment details, including how much the app costs, and which credit card you're using. (If you want to use a different credit card than the one showing up on the screen, tap the triangle next to the credit card. You can choose a different card already on file in your Google Checkout account, or pay with a new one.)

At the bottom of the screen, tap the OK button, and the download proceeds the same way as for free ones. You also get a receipt notification in the Notification Panel. Tap it to view your email receipt (in Gmail) for the purchase of the app.

After the app downloads, the icon for running it shows up in two places—on your Home screen, and in the App Menu. If you don't want the icon on your Home screen, delete it by holding it down until the Trash button appears and dragging it to the trash. (You're not deleting the app; only the icon.)

 If you drag the app's icon *from the Apps Menu* to the Trash you *will* delete it, so make sure not to drag it from there, unless you're sure you want to delete the app itself.

Downloading Using the Android Market on the Web

Your Galaxy Tab can perform a bit of magic—you can download apps to it even when you're not using it. Go to the Android Market on the Web (*https://market.android.com/*), and you can browse and search for apps, just as you can on your Tab. You can then download apps to your Tab without *using* the Tab. And even better, you can manage the apps on all of your Android devices from one place.

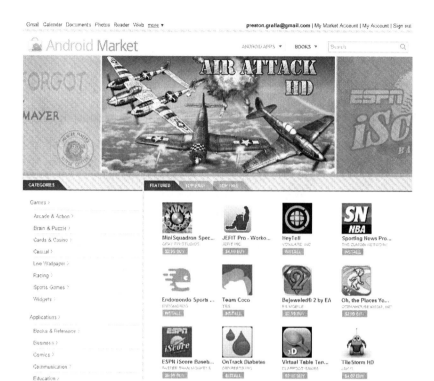

When you go to the Market on the Web, sign in with your Google Account. You can browse, search, and get information about apps in much the same way as on the Tab. When you come across an app you want to download, click the Install or Buy button. If you have more than one Android device, you'll find the Market does a very nifty trick.

When you click Install or Buy, you get the usual information about what access the app has to your Tab. You also see a Send To button. Click it, and you see a list of all of your Android devices, including your Tab. Select the device to which you want to download, and then click Install. You get a message that the app will be downloaded to your device the next time it's turned on and connected to the Internet via 3G, 4G, or Wi-Fi.

Not all apps in the Market work with all Android devices—some might work only on certain tablets, others only on certain phones, and so on. When you tap the Send To button and the list of your devices appears, any devices that cannot run the app are grayed out so that you can't choose them.

When you're browsing and searching through the Market, notice that apps you've already downloaded don't have an Install or Buy button—instead they show an Installed button (if the app was free), and a Purchased button (if the app was paid for). Click the Installed button, and you see which device it's installed on. You can also install it on another device; click the drop-down list next to the "Send to Another Device" button, and it's installed to that device.

The Market has one more handy feature—you can see a list of every app installed on every one of your devices. Click the My Market Account at the top of the page, and you come to a My Account page that has a list of all the apps you've installed. From here, click any app, and then click the Installed or Purchased button; you can see where it's installed, and also install it on additional devices.

On the My Account page, you can also edit information about all of your Android devices, such as changing the name that appears in the drop-down box. Click Settings to do so.

Downloading from the Web

You're not limited to getting apps from the Android Market on your Galaxy Tab or the Web—you can download them directly from other websites. You can either visit the developer's website to download the app, or head to one of the many web libraries that house and rate multitudes of apps.

 When you install apps from the Web, they haven't been through the same kind of vetting procedure as those in the Android Market. So be careful about what you download. It's a good idea to download apps only from well-known developers or trusted download libraries.

Downloading from the Web takes a bit more work than downloading from the Android Market. It's a several-step process, rather than being straightforward and all-in-one like the Android Market:

1. Go to a website using your Tab and search for an app, or go directly to a developer's site.

2. Download an installation file to your Tab.

3. Install the app using the installation file.

Unless you know a specific app you want to download and the URL of the developer's website, your best place to start is one of the many Android download libraries. The Android Freeware site—*www.freewarelovers.com/android*—is one good place, as is the Android download library run by PC World. To get to the PC World Android library, go to *www.pcworld.com/downloads/downloads.html*, click the Apps link, and then follow the Android Apps link. You can find other good download libraries as well. The download library *www.download.com* also has an Android area—find it in the site's Mobile Apps area. And *www.appbrain.com* is good, too.

Once you find an app you want, tap the link to download the installation file. You see the progress on a Downloads screen. After the file is downloaded, you see an odd file name—Astro_File_Manager_2.5.2.apk, for example. (Android apps end in the extension *.apk*.)

 Note At some websites, when you tap a link to download an app, you're sent to the Android Market, where you can download and install the file.

After the file downloads, tap it to install it. When you're done installing the app, you don't need the installation file any longer.

 Note For security reasons, your Tab may block installation of any apps found outside the Android Market. If that's the case, then you have to change the settings so you can install your downloaded apps. On the Home screen, tap the Notifications Panel, and select Settings→Applications. Tap the checkbox next to "Unknown sources." You can now install apps from outside the Android Market.

Downloading and Using a Bar Code Scanner

Here's an even slicker way to download apps from the Web—scan a bar code. All you need is your PC or Mac and a free bar code app on your Galaxy Tab. You then browse the Web, and when you come across a file you want to download, point your camera at the onscreen bar code, and the app downloads to your Tab.

First you need to get one of the many bar code scanner apps. One highly rated, popular app is called Barcode Scanner, from Zxing Team—and it's free, as well. (Barcode Scanner does a lot more than just let you download apps. It can also scan a bar code on a product, identify the product, and send you to web pages with more information about it, including reviews and places to buy.)

After you install the scanner app on your Tab, you're ready to go. Many web-based Android libraries and developer websites have bar codes next to the app descriptions, so you can easily download them.

When you come across a bar code for downloading an app, run Barcode Scanner, and then point your Tab's camera at the bar code, centering it in the window in the middle of the viewfinder. The app quickly recognizes the bar code and shows you the information it contains, including the web page's URL. At the bottom of the screen, tap "Open browser," and the file downloads just as if you'd tapped a download link. You can then install the app in the usual way.

 Tip You can also share the link to the app with others by tapping either "Share via email" or "Share via SMS." If you do that, you don't send the app or the bar code, but a link to the page.

Updating Apps

Apps are often updated, and the nice thing about the Galaxy Tab is that it tells you when your apps are ready for updating—and then updates them with a single tap. When an update is available, an icon appears in the Notification Panel. Tap the notification icon, and you see a list of all the apps that have available updates.

Tap any update you want to download, and you see the description page you normally see before downloading an app, except that the buttons at the bottom have changed. Tap Update to update the app, and Uninstall to uninstall it. When you tap Update, you get a warning that the new, updated app will replace the existing app. Tap OK, and you see the features and information the app will use. Tap OK again, and your Tab downloads the app in the background. You see its progress as it downloads, but you don't have to watch it unless you really want to.

Managing, Sharing, and Uninstalling Apps

After a while, you may suffer from app overload: You've downloaded so many apps you don't know what to do with them. It's time to get them under control.

A single location helps you do that. From the Home screen, tap the Notification Panel and then select Settings→ Applications→Manage applications. You see a list of your apps, including their names and file sizes, categorized in three tabs:

• **Downloaded.** Apps you've downloaded and installed.

• **All.** The mega-list of your Galaxy Tab's apps, both built-ins and those you've downloaded.

• **Running.** Apps currently running on your Galaxy Tab.

 You can sort the app list either by alphabetical name or size. Tap the "Sort by size" and "Sort by name" buttons to change the way they're sorted.

Tap any app, and you come to a screen chock-full of information about it—its version number, its total size, the size of any data associated with it, the size of the program itself, and, toward the bottom of the screen, information about what kinds of features and data it uses.

You can uninstall the app by tapping the Uninstall button. You can also share the app with others via email or text message, although you don't actually send the app itself. Instead, you send information about the app including its description, size, and where it can be downloaded. Just tap the Share button. If a friend expresses curiosity about an app you use, this is the way to clue him in.

If you see that an app is running and you want to close it, tap the "Force stop" button. (That button is grayed out if the app isn't currently running.)

Putting an App on the Home Screen or Panes

When you download an app, its icon automatically shows up on your main Home screen. But you may have deleted the icon and want it back—or want to put it on one of your other Home screens. That way, you can run it without having to open the App Menu. Here's how to do it:

1. On any of the Home screens, press your finger and hold it, or else tap the + button in the upper-right portion of your screen.

   The top of your screen changes to show thumbnails of all five of your Home screens, and the bottom shows either widgets, App shortcuts (icons), or wallpapers you can add to any screen.

2. In the middle of the screen, tap App shortcuts.

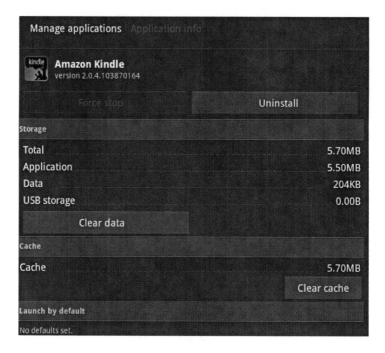

   The bottom of your screen shows all of the app icons you can add to a Home screen.

3. Drag an app icon to any screen, and the app icon moves there. To move the icon to a different position on the Home screen where you added it, open that Home screen, and drag it where you want it to be.

> When you drag the icon to a Home screen, the original icon stays in the App Menu as well.

What if you want to delete the icon but still keep the app? Put your finger on the app's shortcut icon and hold it there until a trash can appears. Drag the icon to the Trash. The icon disappears, but the app remains, and is accessible from the Apps Menu.

Troubleshooting Apps

In a perfect world, apps would never misbehave. Unfortunately, it's not a perfect world. An app may quit the moment you launch it, or cause your Galaxy Tab to restart, or do any number of odd things. If that happens, try these steps:

- **Launch the app again.** There's no particular reason why this should work, but it often does. When you launch the app again, it just may work properly.

- **Uninstall and reinstall.** There may have been an oddball installation problem. So uninstall the app, and then reinstall it. That action some-times fixes the problem.

- **Restart the Galaxy Tab.** Just as restarting a computer sometimes fixes problems for no known reason, restarting the Tab may have the same effect. Power it down by pressing and holding the Power/Lock key, and then press and hold the Power/Lock key again to restart.

- **Reset the Galaxy Tab.** If an app causes the Tab to stop responding, then you have to reset the tablet. See page 400 for details.

If none of this works, then it's time to uninstall the app. Don't fret; there are plenty more where it came from.

The Samsung Apps Store

Samsung also has an app store of its own. To use it, you need to first reg-ister with Samsung. From the Apps Menu, tap Samsung Apps. From the screen that appears, select your country. Read the terms and conditions, and tap Accept. You may next see a screen that warns that your tablet can't download apps outside the Android Market. In order to download from the Samsung store, you'll need to change that setting. Tap Settings, and from the screen that appears, check the box next to "Unknown Sources."

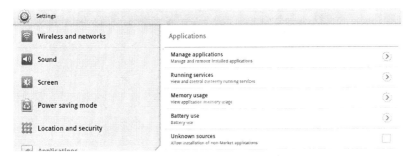

Now continue installing Samsung apps. When the installation is done, launch the app. You'll now be able to browse and download apps from a store powered by Samsung.

5 Ten Great Android Apps

I n the previous chapter, you learned how to download apps. Now it's time to put that knowledge to good use. You can get plenty of great apps, with more written every day—everything from games to productivity tools, entertainment, information, and more.

This chapter introduces you to 10 of the hottest ones around. Don't stop there, though—after you give these a try, go out and find your own new favorites. You may be the first to discover the next Angry Birds phenomenon!

Games

Angry Birds

Anyone'll tell you: Angry Birds is the most addictive game you can download to your Galaxy Tab. It may well be the biggest productivity-killer since Solitaire for Windows 95. Once you start playing it, you'll have a hard time stopping. "Just one more level," you'll keep telling yourself. An hour later…

An international phenomenon, the app is said to have been downloaded 100 million times and counting. Among the many who play the game, according to the *Wall Street Journal,* are British Prime Minister David Cameron and the famous literary novelist Salman Rushdie, who in a radio interview boasted that he is "something of a master at Angry Birds."

It's not only good enough for one of the most powerful politicians on the planet and a potential candidate for the Nobel Prize in literature; the game has even begun to expand beyond the world of tablets. You can already buy Angry Birds plush toys, and Mattel has an Angry Birds board game in the works. Angry Birds executives have also been in touch with Hollywood for possible TV show and movie adaptations.

So how do you play the game? The premise is deceptively simple. Nefarious pigs have stolen some birds' eggs, and the birds want revenge on the porkers. You help the birds get their revenge by flinging the birds at pigs, who are protected by a variety of Rube Goldberg-type structures put together with wooden planks, stones, glass, and other assorted junk. A bird is placed in a slingshot, and you pull back the slingshot and release, aiming at the pigs.

As you move up the levels, the structures get more complex, and the pigs harder to destroy. To combat that, you get a variety of birds to fling, who do things such as separate into multiple birds en route to the target when you tap the screen—think of them as the multiple independently targetable reentry vehicles (MIRVs) of the avian world. (Whenever a bird with new destructive capabilities is introduced, you get an onscreen tip showing you how to use it.)

The game is so popular for many reasons. For one thing, you can easily play it in short bursts, so it's ideal for brief spurts of time-killing—like when you're on hold or waiting in line. And the game's onscreen physics are spectacular—objects seem to behave with lifelike accuracy when they hurtle through the air, roll on the ground, and so on.

But there's a bigger reason it's so popular: It's just plain fun.

Get it in the Android Market—there are multiple versions available, because Rovio, the developer, constantly releases updates. And, at this writing anyway, they're all free.

AirAttack HD

For a more elaborate game that really gets your heart pumping, try AirAttack HD. It has various versions, including free and for-pay ones. (But almost everyone who tries AirAttack wants to upgrade to the for-pay version after sampling the free one.)

As the name implies, it's a combat game, in which you fly a fighter plane against planes, tanks, cannons, and other assorted enemies. It's all beautifully realized in full 3D. Drag your fighter around the Tab's big screen; there's absolutely no lag time, and gameplay is spectacular. There's a heart-thumping sound track and plenty of action…what more could you want in an action game?

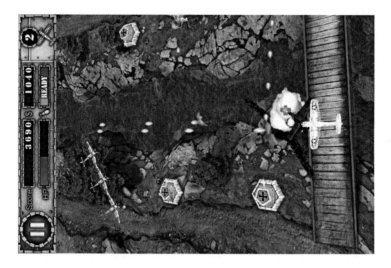

Productivity

SugarSync

Here's one of the all-time great productivity tools for Galaxy Tab owners. With it, your Tab gets full access to files on your PC, Mac, and Android devices. Similarly, your PC, Mac, or Android device can access the files that live on your Tab.

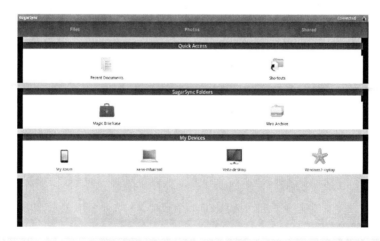

First, install SugarSync on any computers and devices whose files you want to access with your Tab. For example, you can use it with two PCs, a Mac, and a Droid X. Next, on each of those computers and devices, tell SugarSync which files you want to back up, synchronize, and share.

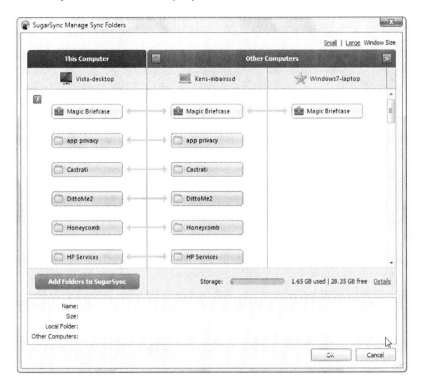

On your PCs and Macs, you can synchronize all those files and folders with each computer. So, for example, say you have a Mac and a PC. You choose which folders and files to synchronize among them. Now, suppose you edit a Word file on your PC that's in a folder you've chosen to synchronize. SugarSync automatically changes it on your Mac as well. So when you go to work on it on your Mac, the latest version is available.

Better yet, SugarSync also backs up all those files to its servers, providing you with a backup as well. If your computer's hard disk dies, you can get those files back as long as you can get to a computer connected to the Internet.

 Note The SugarSync service offers 5 GB of backup space free. If that's not enough, you can pay for more space. How much you pay varies according to how much space you need. For $50 a year, for example, you get 30 GB of space, and for $100 a year you get 60 GB. And if you really, really, *really* need a lot of backup space, you can get 250 GB for $250 a year.

So where does the Galaxy Tab come in? Install SugarSync on it, and you can use it in a few different ways. You can browse through all the folders that you've chosen to back up through SugarSync on all of your PCs, Macs, and other Android-based devices. You can download and view all the files you've backed up as well. So as long as you have your Tab and you're using SugarSync, all of your important files are within easy reach.

Here's how: Tap the name of the computer or Android device whose files you want to view. You can then browse through the folders, looking for files. Tap the file you want to view, and it gets downloaded to your Tab. Then, you can use whatever apps you have on your Tab to work with that file. For example, if you download an Office document such as a word processing file or spreadsheet, you can view it in the QuickOffice app that comes on the Galaxy Tab or in a similar app that you've downloaded.

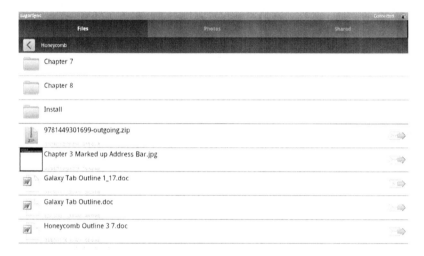

SugarSync also backs up files from your Tab and lets you take a photo from your tablet and store it in a Mobile Photos folder.

For even more features, tap the Menu button at the bottom of the screen. You can check your file transfer status, manually upload a file to the SugarSync servers, take a photo for your mobile photo gallery, and more.

Evernote

If you suffer from information overload, here's your medicine. Evernote does a great job of capturing information from multiple sources, putting it in one location, and then letting you easily find it—whether you're using your computer, your tablet, or another Android device.

Not only that, it's free.

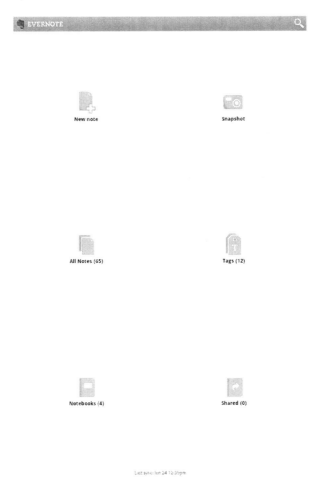

You organize all your information into separate notebooks. You can then browse or search each notebook, search through all notebooks, and so on.

No matter where you capture or input information, it's available on every device on which you install Evernote. So if you grab a web page from your PC and put it into a notebook, that information will be available on your Tab.

You can capture information from the Web, you can take photos and include them, you can dictate notes, and you can import existing documents. You can also type in notes.

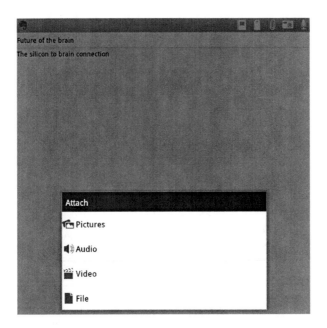

The upshot of all this? This is the best app you'll find for capturing information and making sense of it all.

ASTRO File Manager

If you're not a geek, don't read any further. But if you're ready to let your geek flag fly, this app's for you. ASTRO File Manager is just what it sounds like—a file manager for your Galaxy Tab. Normal people who have no desire or need to understand their Tab's file-and-folder structure and move or manage those files have no use for it. But if you're the kind of person who doesn't feel comfortable using any computer or device, including a Tab, without knowing what's under the hood, you probably already have ASTRO installed.

Launch the program, and you see the underlying folder structure of your Android Galaxy Tab. ASTRO looks and works much like any computer file manager—like Windows Explorer or the Mac Finder. To browse the files and subfolders in any folder, tap the folder to open it. The navigation buttons at the top of the screen are also useful, along with buttons for tasks like setting your view, sorting files and folders, setting your preferences, searching for files, and so on.

Tap a file to open it, if it can be opened (for example, a document file, a photo, and so on). Hold your finger on a file to perform a variety of actions on it, like editing it, opening it, sending it to someone else, or viewing details.

Tap the Menu button at the bottom of the screen for even more options, including bookmarking files and folders, backing up, creating a new folder, and so on. This section provides just a small sample of the geeky goodness this app has in store.

 Note ASTRO File Manager displays ads as you do your work. If you want to eliminate the ads, you can get the Pro version for $3.99. There's also an "SMB module" you can download that lets you browse to files on a PC, although only if the PC is connected to a Windows server or a SAMBA server.

Music and Pictures

Pandora

Wish you had a personalized music station that played exactly the kind of music you love, without obnoxious radio announcers and interruptions? Wish that station could switch to any kind of music you want at the tap of a button—rap for one mood, techno for another, jazz for another, opera for another, and so on? And what if it played not just stuff you already know, but music you haven't yet heard but would most likely enjoy?

Time to stop wishing. You've got Pandora. This free music service may forever change the way you think about and listen to music.

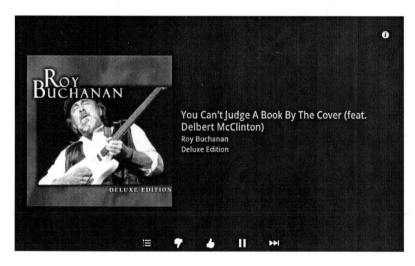

You may already know Pandora from the Web; it started life as a web-based music service. But it's expanded into Android as well, and you can use it on your Tab. Just download the app and sign up for an account. If you already have an account, just sign in once you've downloaded and installed the Pandora app.

Once you've got your account, the fun begins. Tap the Menu button at the bottom of the screen, and then select Create Station. Type the name of an artist, a song title, or a composer that's most similar to the kind of music you want to listen to. As you type, Pandora lists possible matches. Tap a match, or else type the full name. Pandora then creates the station for you and starts playing the music.

As the music plays, the app displays a graphic of the album from which the song is taken, along with the album and song titles, and the name of the artist. At the bottom of the screen is a set of buttons that control Pandora.

The buttons are fairly self-explanatory. The leftmost button brings you to a list of all of your stations. The Thumbs-Down button tells Pandora that you don't like the current song. When you tap it, the song stops playing, and Pandora learns something about your musical tastes. Based on that, it stops playing songs with some of the characteristics of that particular song. The Thumbs-Up button tells Pandora that you like the current song, and so it plays more songs with its characteristics. The next two buttons are the usual buttons for controlling pause, play, and skip.

 Note Because of licensing restrictions, only people in the U.S. can use Pandora. If you live somewhere else, you're out of luck.

Want more information about the current artist playing? Tap the little Information button at top right, and Pandora gives you a great deal of information about the artist. If you want to know why Pandora thinks you'll like a particular song, tap the Song button. You may or may not understand what it's telling you, but it's worth checking out. For example, when playing the Tom Petty Song "Love is a Long Road," Pandora might say it chose the song because it "features rock song structure, a subtle use of vocal harmony, a vocal-central aesthetic, extensive vamping, minor key tonality, electric rhythm guitars, a dynamic male vocalist, and many other similarities identified in the Music Genome Project."

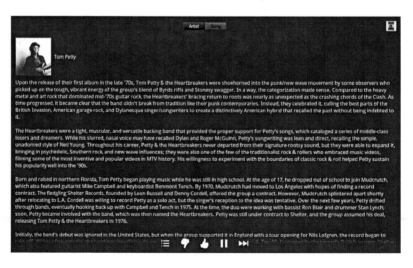

Note The Music Genome Project is an endeavor to understand music at its most fundamental level, based on its core musical components. It's the core of Pandora's technology.

To switch to another Pandora station, tap the leftmost button on the bottom of the screen. A list of all of your stations appears; tap any to play it. If you have a long list, scroll through it. If you want a mix of all of your music instead of any individual artist, tap the Quick Mix button.

Pandora is free, and to help fund it, ads appear as the music plays. Tap the small X at the top of an ad to make it go away. But when you do that, a new ad pops up. If you want ad-free Pandora, you have to pay for it.

Google Music Cloud Player

The Google Music Cloud Player pulls off a remarkable trick: it lets you play music on your Galaxy Tab that isn't actually on the device itself, and instead lives in what's called the "cloud"—basically, big Google computers called servers that store your music and stream it to your Tab, or any other device, for that matter.

To use it, you need to first install the software on your PC or Mac—whichever computer houses your music collection. You then tell the software to upload the music to the cloud. After that, you install the Google Music player on your Tab (or other Android device). At that point, you can listen to your music from the cloud, as long as you have a 3G, 4G, or Wi-Fi connection, of course.

The Music player isn't a separate application; instead it integrates directly into the Google Music player on your Tab. (It doesn't integrate with the Tab's Music Hub, though.) When you go to the Android Market, search for Google Music, and then download an upgrade. The cloud player will be installed.

Mostly, the cloud player looks and works just like the normal Google Music player. There are a few differences, though. For example, at times, your music won't be available from the cloud—whenever you're not connected to the Internet. So you can choose whether to hide streamed music at that point. You can also set a variety of other options, such as whether to only stream music when connected via Wi-Fi rather than via 3G or 4G.

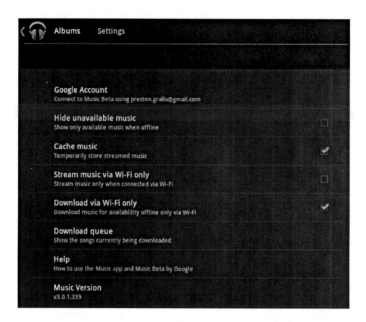

At this writing, the cloud player is still in beta, and may not yet be available for your PC or Mac. But as soon as it is, grab it, and then update the music player on your Tab—this is one fabulous player.

Little Photo

Not happy with normal photos you take on your Tab? Want to add special effects? Then you want the free Little Photo app. With it you can add many kinds of special effects to any photo, such as "vintage paper," "angel kiss," "B&W film," and many others.

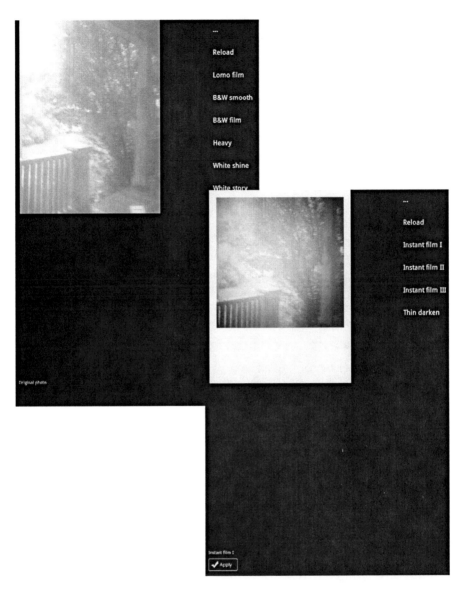

You can also add frames around the photos and layer effects on top of effects. Just be prepared to spend plenty of time with the app, not because it's hard to use, but because it's so simple and fun that you won't be able to stop yourself from adding so many effects.

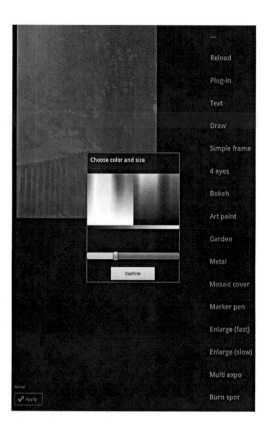

Information

Google Body

Want to see the human body in all its glory? (Calm down, not *that* kind of glory!) Then go download Google Body. This remarkable free app was developed by Google not just for educational and information purposes, but to show off all of the remarkable capabilities of Honeycomb tablets like the Galaxy Tab.

Launch the app, and you see a graphic of a human being. Nicely drawn, you may think, but not overly impressive. See those small icons at the top of the screen? They let you display various overlays of the body—the muscular system, the skeletal system, the nervous system, internal organs, and so on. Tap any, and you see just that aspect instead of the full body.

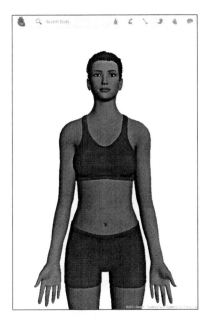
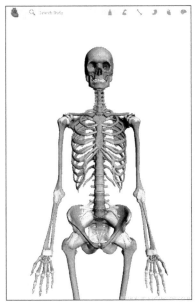

Now the fun begins. Zoom in, rotate, spin the body, travel through it—it all happens instantaneously.

Want to find a particular object in the body? Go to the Search box at the top of the screen and type your search term. As you type, Google Body shows suggestions. Tap any, and you're on your way; Google Body immediately displays it in full 3D.

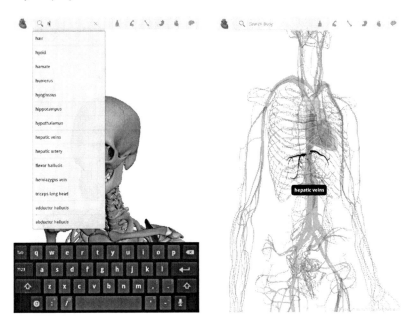

What's more, when you're looking at the body, you can tap any part, and Google Body identifies it for you.

Google Goggles

Google Goggles might just be the most amazing app of all time. It brings together everything remarkable about a Galaxy Tab and its relationship to the physical world and the world of information.

Launch Google Goggles, and then use it to take a photo of something…a landmark, a work of art, a product, a menu, a bar code, a book cover, a sign in a foreign language, a logo, or just about anything imaginable.

After you take the photo, Google Goggles does its best to recognize what that thing is and then tells you what it knows. For example, if the thing is a menu or sign in a foreign language, Google Goggles translates for you. If it's a piece of artwork, the app does a Google search on that artwork so you can get more information. It may also include links for buying prints.

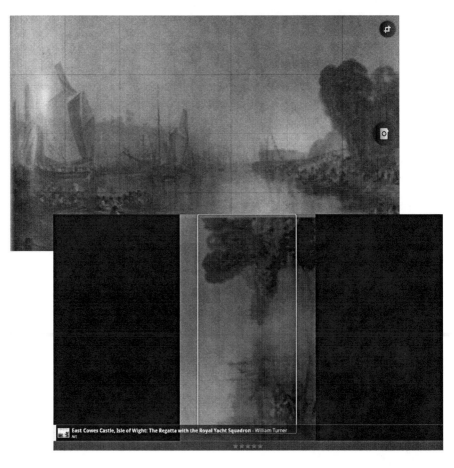

East Cowes Castle, Isle of Wight: The Regatta with the Royal Yacht Squadron · William Turner
Art

Also useful is that it saves all of the photos you've taken so that you can go back and view old information as well.

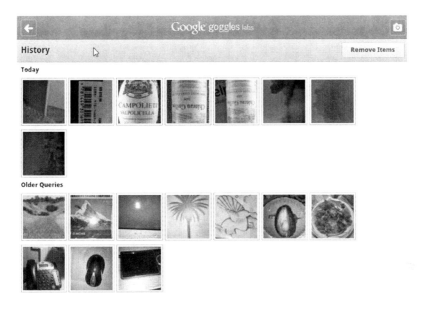

Part 2
Getting Social and Finding Your Way

6   Contacts, Chat, and Video Chat

Your Galaxy Tab may not include a phone, but that doesn't mean it's not a great communications device—it is. With its big keyboard, it's great for text chats. With its microphone and speakers, it's great for voice chats. And with its two cameras and big, beautiful screen, it's superb for video chats. And it's also great for keeping track of all of your contacts.

As you'll see in this chapter, the Tab is a great way to keep in touch with friends, family, and coworkers.

How You Chat

You use your Galaxy Tab to chat in much the same way that you chat on a computer or phone. You type text, speak into a microphone, and possibly use the Tab's webcam if you want to go full-bore into video.

You can do all this with Google Talk, built directly into the Tab. It's front and center; the app's icon is right there, waiting for you on your Home page. And Google Talk is integrated so deep into the Tab that you find it even inside Contacts, and you can launch chat sessions from there. (You're not locked into using Google Talk, though; this chapter clues you in to other chat applications as well.)

Starting Google Talk

To launch Google Talk, tap its button on your Home screen. If you're not logged in, tap the Sign In button that appears, and then type your login information. Your Google Talk login is the same as the one you use for Gmail and all other Google accounts. In fact, when you tap Sign In, your Galaxy Tab probably doesn't ask for login information. Instead, it uses the Tab's primary Google account to log you right in.

preston.gralla@gmail.com   ⊗   Sign in

One you're signed in, you see two panes. In the left is a list of all of your Google Talk friends—those you've chatted with before in Google Talk, or those you've added to your Google Talk friends list.

At the top of the list, you see yourself and your account information. You've got four main options there:

- **Status message.** When people see that you're available on Google Talk, they see your name. But if you want, you can also have them see a status message—"Finally dug out from work!" for example. Many people use the status message to post playful notes about themselves or current events. To enter a status message, tap the Status Message gray box. From the input box that appears, type your message, and it appears as your status.

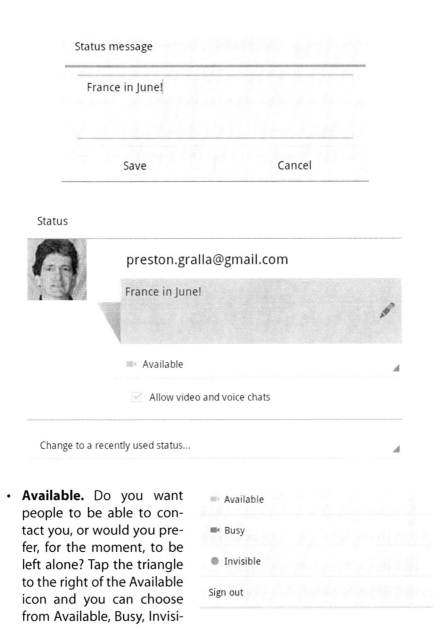

Status message

France in June!

Save   Cancel

Status

preston.gralla@gmail.com

France in June!

Available

Allow video and voice chats

Change to a recently used status...

- **Available.** Do you want people to be able to contact you, or would you prefer, for the moment, to be left alone? Tap the triangle to the right of the Available icon and you can choose from Available, Busy, Invisible, or Sign out.

Available

Busy

Invisible

Sign out

Tip When should you use Invisible, and when Sign out? In Invisible mode, you're still signed into Google Talk, so you can still see other people's availability and status, and you can initiate chats. When you sign out, though, you can't see any of that. With either choice, people don't see you as being available.

- **Allow video and voice chats.** Do you want to be available to chat via voice as well as video? If so, make sure that this box is turned on.

- **Change to a recently used status.** This straightforward-sounding selection is actually a bit more confusing than it seems. Tap the triangle, and you see a list of your recently used status messages and availability. What's odd is that you might see on the list availability messages ("Having lunch," "Reach out and call me," "Not now, I have a headache") that you've never chosen. How do they end up there? Those selections and several others are available from Google Talk on the Web, but not Google Talk on the Tab. So they show up here, even though you can't choose them from the Availability selection box, and even if you've never used them. Go figure.

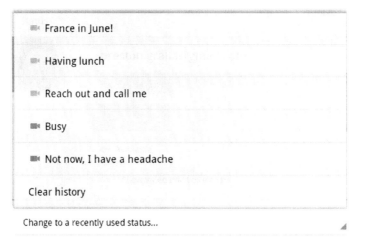

Change to a recently used status...

 Note Some of your contacts in Google Talk have photos next to them, and others don't. That's because Google Talk hooks into your Contacts list. If you've put a photo of someone in your Contacts list—or the photo has been added by a social networking app—you'll see the person's photo in Google Talk. If not, you see a generic face icon.

On the left side of the screen, you see all of your Google Talk contacts, along with indications of your communication status or history with them. The colors of the button also mean something: Green indicates people who are signed in and available, orange means they're signed in but not actively using Google Talk at the moment, red means they're signed in but busy, and gray means they're not signed in. These icons show up not only next to your Google Talk contact, but next to your icon as well, both on Google Talk on your Tab, and whenever someone sees your availability wherever they use Google Talk.

Here are the common buttons and what each means:

- (green dot) Signed into Google Talk; available for a text chat.
- Signed into Google Talk; available for an audio chat.
- Signed into Google Talk; available for a video chat.
- Signed into Google Talk, but away and not active.
- Signed into Google Talk, but busy and not available for a chat.
- Signed out of Google Talk.
- (gray dot) Signed into Google Talk, but invisible and so appearing signed out to other people.

 The Invisible indication doesn't appear next to the names of other people when you look at them—instead you see the Signed Out button. In the same way, when you're invisible, people don't see the Invisible button next to your name. Only you see the Invisible button next to your name. After all, if people saw the Invisible icon next to your name, you wouldn't be invisible, then, would you?

Tap any of your Google Talk contacts, and you see a recent history of your chats. If you've had text chats, then you see the back and forth of all of your recent conversations. If you've had a video or audio chat, you don't see the video or hear the audio; you just see when your audio or video chats ended.

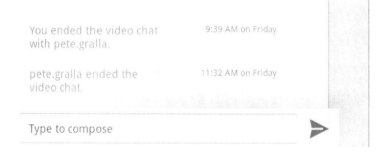

Starting a Chat Session

Want to chat with someone? It's quite easy to do. You have several different ways to start a chat:

- **Tap the person's name in Google Talk and compose your message.** Look at people's availability. If you see that someone is available for a chat, tap his name. You see the history of your chat sessions with him, and at the bottom of the screen, a text input box. Type your text, press the arrow next to the text box, and you've just started a chat.

  If you prefer to initiate an audio or video chat, rather than typing text into the box, tap the Video button ◼ or Audio button 🎤 on the right side of the Google Talk screen.

- **Send an invitation.** At the top right of the Google Talk screen, there's an icon of a person with a + button 👤₊ . Tap it, and a box appears that lets you send a chat invitation to someone. She gets a chat invitation via email. If she already has Gmail and a Google Talk account, then she can simply click a link to start chatting with you. Otherwise, she may need to go through an intermediate step or two: for example, first setting up a Google Talk account.

Chat with preston.gralla@gmail.com

preston.gralla@gmail.com to me   show details 9:24 AM (7 minutes ago)   Reply ▾

9:24 AM   **preston.gralla**: Finally! The Sox won a game. Better yet, it was against the Yankees in the home opener.

↩ Reply   ➡ Forward   Reply by chat to preston.gralla

- **Start a chat from your Contacts list.** Your Contacts list tells you when someone is available for a chat—there's a green button next to the person's name. There's also an IM (instant messaging) entry for the contact, along with the other contact information such as email address and phone number, so you know what kind of chat they can do. Tap in the IM entry area. You go to that contact in Google Talk and can initiate a chat in the usual way.

Responding to a Chat Invitation

When someone sends you a chat message, a notification pops up from the Tab's Notifications Panel. It shows you the first few words of the message, and also indicates whether the message is the first one in a chat, or the second, third, and so on. Tap the notification, and you get sent to Google Talk, with the full message showing. You can type a response at that point.

If you don't immediately see the notification, or decide not to respond to it for the moment, the notification goes away, but a Google Talk icon remains in the Notification Panel. Tap that icon to see the first few words of the chat in the pop-up panel, and then tap it again to open the message in Google Talk. You can then type a response.

If you're invited to a video or audio chat, when you tap the notification, you see an invitation instead of a message. Tap Accept to start the video or audio chat; tap Decline to cancel it.

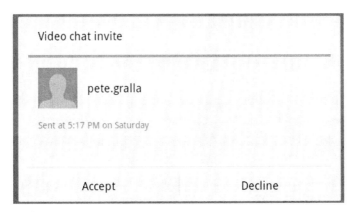

How to Chat

Whether you initiate the chat, or someone else does, once you start chatting, it works the same.

Text Chat

Text chatting is quite intuitive. If you've used instant messaging or text messaging, then you know how it works. Someone types messages to you and they appear; you type messages back, and they appear on his screen. It's designed for quick, ad hoc messages.

Given that this is a Galaxy Tab, though, it's no surprise that it has some fancy tricks built into it. Look on the right-hand side of the screen; you see four icons stacked vertically. Here's what each does:

- **Leave chat.** 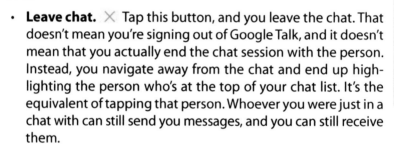 Tap this button, and you leave the chat. That doesn't mean you're signing out of Google Talk, and it doesn't mean that you actually end the chat session with the person. Instead, you navigate away from the chat and end up high-lighting the person who's at the top of your chat list. It's the equivalent of tapping that person. Whoever you were just in a chat with can still send you messages, and you can still receive them.

- **Switch to video.** Tap this button, and if the person with whom you're chatting is video-enabled, then you initiate a video chat. He has to agree to participate.

- **Switch to audio.** Tap the button, and if the person with whom you're chatting is audio-enabled, then you initiate an audio chat. She has to agree to participate.

- **More Options.** Tap here for a host of more options for chatting. You'll learn about those in the next section.

Note All these icons only show up if you're actively chatting with someone. If you tap someone's name and you're not chatting with her, then the Leave Chat and More Options buttons show up, but no others.

More Chat Options

Here's all you can do when you tap the More Options button:

- **Go off the record.** No, this doesn't turn you into an ace investigative reporter, using your derring-do to track down government evils. Instead, anything you and your chat friend type after you go off the record doesn't get saved by Google Talk. Normally, you can see a history of all your chat conversations in Google Talk. Use this option for any part of a conversation you don't wish to show up later. After you tap it, the button changes to "Stop chatting off the record," and your chat from that point on continues to be recorded. So think of this as the "What happens in this chat *stays* in this chat" option.

- **Friend info.** Launches a screen that gives basic information about the friend, including his email address and Google Talk capabilities (video-enabled or not). From the screen, you can tap "View in Contacts" and be sent to his full information in your Contacts app.

- **Block friend.** Is this "friend" really not so much of a friend, and annoys you to no end? Then tap this to banish her from your Google Talk list. You always show up as offline in her Google Talk list. And if she's very pushy and sends you a text message, you don't receive it.

 After you've blocked a friend, you can always unblock him. See page 147 for details.

- **Remove friend.** Removes the friend from your Google Talk list, but doesn't block the person from seeing your presence or sending you messages.

- **Add friend.** Sometimes, when it comes to chat, the more the merrier. If you want to include more people in your chat, tap this, send an invitation, and if they accept, you've got a *talk-a-trois*.

- **Clear Chat history.** Removes all the chat history between you and the selected friend. It doesn't affect the history of other chats.

Video Chat

When you invite someone to a video chat and she accepts, or if she invites you and you accept, your screen comes to life. Most of the screen gets taken up by the live video of the person with whom you're chatting. Down at the bottom right, you can see a snapshot-sized video feed of yourself— this is a smaller version of what your chat friend is seeing. You see a red light at the top of the Tab, telling you that your video is being captured live. As for chatting, it's as easy as it gets. Talk. Gesticulate. Emote. Wave your hands if you want. Your friend sees and hears everything you say and do. And you see everything she says and does.

> **Tip** When you video chat, you can also receive and send text messages. The messages are displayed at the bottom of your screen. See page 146 for details on how to send a text message during video chat.

Are you Ready for Your Closeup?

If you look at the small video window that shows you, you see a set of controls just above it—a slider bracketed by two hands. This slider controls whether the video should be a closeup of you, and also whether the video frame should be locked or move as the Tab moves. The changes you make here are reflected not just in what you see in the snapshot, but in what your chat friend sees—remember, whatever is in that snapshot is what he sees.

When video chatting, don't look down at your little image in the lower right as you chat—if you do, your chat partner will see an unflattering view of you, with your eyes looking as if they're closed. It's better to look at the image of your friend, or at the red light.

Move the slider by holding it with a finger and dragging it. You can move it to four positions. The position at the far right makes your image smallest on the screen. Move the slider over to the next position to the right, and it zooms in on you. So next time you feel like saying, "I'm ready for my closeup, Mr. DeMille," here's where to move the slider. Now slide it over one more position, and you still have the closeup, but the video of you in the frame can move—if you move the angle of the Tab, you notice that your image floats inside the frame, surrounded by a black box. (**Why** you'd want to look as if you're floating around in a box is entirely up to you.)

Using Video Chat Options

Tap the screen during a video chat and four icons appear on the upper right. Here's what each does:

- **Leave video chat.** ⊠ Tap this button, and you leave the video chat and end the video chat session.

- **Microphone off.** 🎤 Tap this button, and you turn off your microphone, so that the person with whom you're video chatting can't hear what you're saying. When you tap it, the slash on the microphone turns red, to show that the microphone is off. Tap it again to turn the microphone back on.

- **Send a text message.** ▤ When you're video chatting, you can send and receive text messages as well. Tap this button, and you go back to the text chat view. Tap in your message and send it on. When you're doing this, your camera isn't live—your chat friend sees a static image of you, the last image captured before you switched to send a text message. The image on her screen also has a Pause button on it, to show that your image is not live. To switch back to video chat, tap the video icon on the right side of the screen that shows when you're in text chat.

- **Switch cameras.** 📷 Tap this, and you switch the camera from the one pointing at you (called the front-facing camera), to the one on the back of the Tab (the one you normally use for taking photographs or videos). Why do this? Say, for example, you're somewhere in the great outdoors, and you want your chat partner to see the remarkable scene at which you're looking. Tap this button, and the camera switches to show the view you see. Tap the button again, and it switches to the camera that looks at you.

Audio Chat

Audio chat is very much like video chat, with a few minor differences. Most obviously, there's no video involved—it's just talk. Your screen looks almost identical to the text chat screen, so you can type as you talk. You have only two buttons available to you on the right-hand side of the screen—one for ending the voice session, and another for muting your microphone.

Managing Google Talk

When you're on the main Google Talk screen, or when you're text chatting or audio chatting, you see a Menu button on the top right of your screen. This button lets you manage how your friends are displayed, and dig deep into changing Google Talk options. When you tap it, here's what you can do:

Most popular
Close all chats
Sign out
Settings
Help

- **Most popular.** Tap this, and on the Google Talk main screen, you see only those of your friends with whom you frequently chat, and not every one of your Google Talk friends. When you tap it, this option changes to "All friends." Tap it to display all your Google Talk friends, not just those who are the most popular with you.

 You can force Google Talk to always show one or more of your friends in the "Most popular" view, even if you haven't chatted with them a lot. When you've high-lighted a friend, tap the Menu button to the right of the chat window, and then tap "Friend info." When the "Friend info" screen appears, tap the "Show in chat list" button, and then select Always.

- **Close all chats.** Just like it says, this closes all your chats.
- **Sign out.** Signs you out of Google Talk.
- **Settings.** Lets you change a whole lot of options, ranging from whether to sign you in to Google Talk automatically when you launch the app to your notification ringtone, whether to display notifications, and more. Pay particular attention to the Account section. From there, you can unblock your blocked friends.

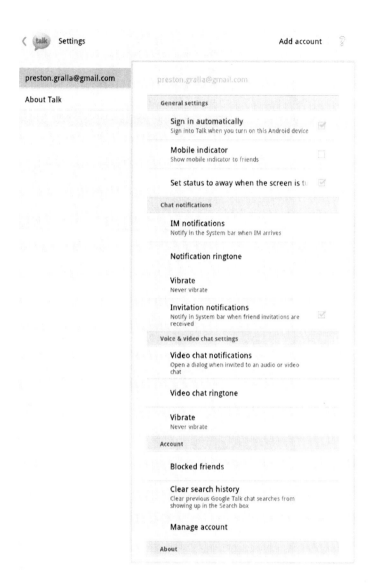

preston.gralla@gmail.com

About Talk

preston.gralla@gmail.com

General settings

Sign in automatically
Sign into Talk when you turn on this Android device

Mobile indicator
Show mobile indicator to friends

Set status to away when the screen is t

Chat notifications

IM notifications
Notify in the System bar when IM arrives

Notification ringtone

Vibrate
Never vibrate

Invitation notifications
Notify in System bar when friend invitations are received

Voice & video chat settings

Video chat notifications
Open a dialog when invited to an audio or video chat

Video chat ringtone

Vibrate
Never vibrate

Account

Blocked friends

Clear search history
Clear previous Google Talk chat searches from showing up in the Search box

Manage account

About

- **Help.** Launches your browser and opens to a Google Mobile help page. You can search to get the help you need.

Searching Google Talk

Remember back when you had a text chat with an old friend about the birth of his second child? It's time to send a birthday present, but you can't quite recall the kid's name—Jared, Jason, or John?

With Google Talk, you never have to worry about forgetting what was said in a text chat. Tap the Search button at the top of the screen, type in the text or person's name and let Google Talk do its magic. It displays all the results it finds, sorted by date, and shows you the relevant section of the chat. It even shows you the time. You can also initiate a Chat session, send a reply by Gmail, or forward that part of the conversation to someone else. Just tap the appropriate button.

Other Chat Apps

Google Talk is built right into your Galaxy Tab, and it's a great chat app. But it's certainly not the only chat app that your Tab can use; there are plenty of others as well, as you can find by doing a search in the Android Market.

Why might you need other chat apps? Well, one problem with chat apps is that as a general rule, every chat app is an island. Let's say you use Google Talk, and a friend of yours doesn't use Google Talk, but does use AIM (formerly called AOL Instant Messenger). That discrepancy means that the two of you can't chat, because your chat apps don't communicate with one another.

So if you want to do more chatting than you can with Google Talk, here are a few other chat apps you might want to consider:

- **AIM.** Use this if you want to chat with friends who use AIM. It also lets you chat with Google Talk friends—but given that you've got Google Talk on your Tab, you don't need it for that.

- **Meebo.** Think of this as a universal chat app. From one central interface, you can chat with friends who use AIM, MSN Messenger, Yahoo Instant Messenger, Google Talk, Jabber, and ICQ.

- **KakaoTalk.** This South Korean chat app is available in English, Japanese, and Korean. Most people who use it are in Korea, with quite a few in Japan as well.

- **Skype.** This service is much more than a chat app, and has a massive worldwide following based on PCs and Macs as well as on Android devices and iPhones. People use it largely to make phone calls over 3G or Wi-Fi. You can talk to other Skype users for free, but you can also use it to make phone calls—yes, actually call people from around the world from your Tab. To do it, you have to pay, but the rates are low.

Contacts

The Galaxy Tab does a lot more to help you keep in touch with people than just by chatting. It also keeps track of all of your contacts.

To see your contacts, tap Contacts from the Apps Menu. You see all your contacts listed in alphabetical order. Notice something odd and potentially annoying—the Tab arranges your contacts alphabetically by first name, not last name. So if you know a lot of Joes and Marys, you're going to possibly spend a little more time than you'd like scrolling. (There is a way to sort them alphabetically by last name. See page 157 for details.)

If you use Gmail, then the Tab automatically imports its contacts into the Contacts list. You can also add contacts directly to the Tab, as you'll see later in this section. The Contacts list is more than just a place for you to go to find contact information. It feeds other apps as well, such as Google Talk.

Most likely, you know more than a screenful of people, and you can navigate through the list in several ways. First, you can flick through the list. You can also put your finger on the list and drag it. That moves you more slowly, but also more precisely.

 Tip Wonder how big your Contacts list is? Scroll up to the top of the list, and it tells you your total number of contacts.

You can also search through the list. Just tap in the search box on the upper left of the screen and type in your search. As you type letters, the list gets pared down, hiding everyone whose first name, last name, company name, words anywhere in their contact entry, or title doesn't match what you've typed. It's a great timesaver for quickly narrowing down a big list. As the list gets pared down, you also see the number of contacts that meet your search criteria.

 Tip If you can't remember someone's name, you can search by whatever detail you can remember, like place of work. You'll see a list of all of your contacts who work at that company, which you can then scroll through to see if any names ring a bell.

When you've gotten to a person's contact listing, tap the person's name. You see all the information you have about the person—phone numbers, email addresses, home and work addresses, and any notes you've written about the person. Some of this information will have an icon next to it. Tapping that icon performs a task:

- To send an email, tap the email icon ✉.
- To contact the person via Google Talk, tap the Google Talk icons ● ●.
- To view the location of an address on Google Maps, tap the location icon ♀.

Integration with Facebook and Twitter

If you use Facebook or Twitter (see page 159), you'll find that those social networking apps integrate with your Contacts list. That's a good thing, but it can also be somewhat confusing.

First the good news: People's profile photos from those social networking apps will show up in your Contacts list, so rather than seeing a generic gray outline of a person, you actually see the person's face. Also, you see people's latest updates from Twitter and Facebook right inside Contacts. And if you want to see someone's Facebook profile, you can jump to it from within Contacts as well.

Now the confusing part: Facebook and Twitter also add their own Contacts entries. So, for example, if you have a Facebook friend who's *not* in your Tab's Contacts, his Facebook information shows up in your Contacts list anyway. Even more confusing, if you have a contact who is also a friend on Facebook and someone you follow on Twitter, you'll have three listings for her—the original contact, plus one imported from Facebook and one imported from Twitter.

Managing Contacts

If you use Gmail, the Galaxy Tab thoughtfully imports all of your Gmail contacts into your Contacts list. And it's not just a one-time transfer of contacts; it happens every time you add, edit, or delete a contact. Whenever you change or add a contact in Gmail, those changes are synced to your Tab, and vice versa.

Adding a Contact

It's easy to add a contact right on your Tab. Tap the "Add contact" button at the top of the screen, then choose whether you want the contact you add to be added to and sync with your Google account, or to live only on the Galaxy Tab. After you do that, fill out the screen that appears, and tap Done.

To edit a contact, tap the pencil icon 🖉 , edit the contact, and then tap Done.

Working with Groups

Your Contacts app probably contains a long list, and even though the Galaxy Tab lets you zip through it quickly by flicking, it can still be tricky to find the person you want. There's a simpler way—Groups. The Tab lets you put contacts in various groups—for example, Family, Work, and so on—making it easier to find the person you want. You can view just the group rather than the entire Contacts list.

Adding someone to a group couldn't be easier. When you fill out the form to create a new contact, you see an entry for groups. Simply type in the name of a group—Family, let's say—and that group gets created, and the contact is put in that group. To see a list of all of your existing groups, tap the small triangle at the right of the Groups field. Tap the name of any group on the list, and it gets added. A contact can be part of more than one group. Just select or type in as many groups as you want.

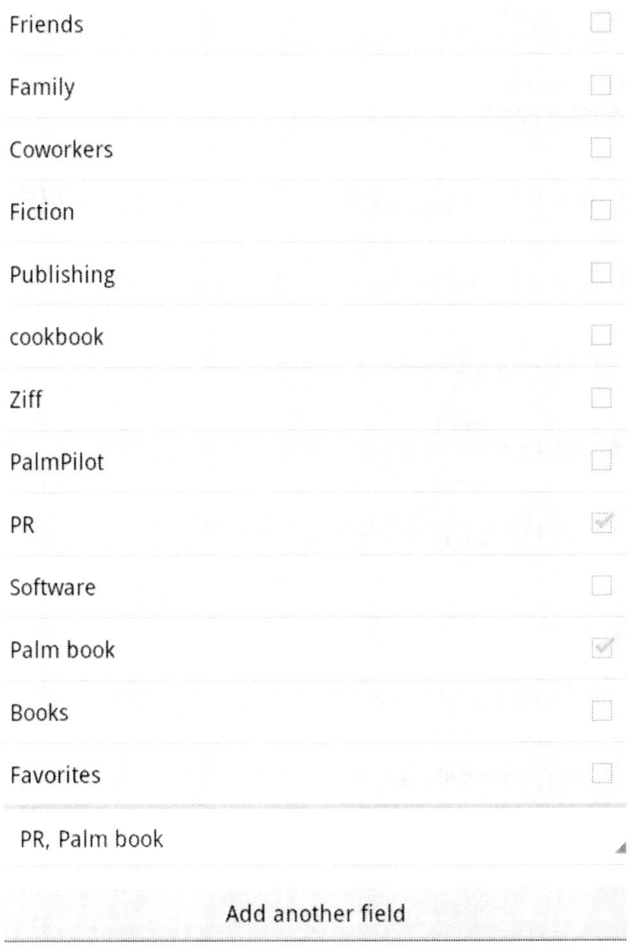

Friends	☐
Family	☐
Coworkers	☐
Fiction	☐
Publishing	☐
cookbook	☐
Ziff	☐
PalmPilot	☐
PR	☑
Software	☐
Palm book	☑
Books	☐
Favorites	☐

PR, Palm book

Add another field

When you're viewing your entire Contacts list and want to see only people in a specific group, tap the Groups button at the top of your screen, then tap the small triangle in the text box at the upper left of your screen, in the field that reads Not Assigned. You'll see your list of groups. Tap any list and you'll see only people in that group.

Fancy Tricks with Contacts

The Galaxy Tab has a few more tricks up its sleeve when it comes to working with contacts. To see them, open a contact, and then press the Menu key. Here are the choices you see, and what each does:

- **Edit.** Brings up a screen for editing the contact.

- **Delete contact.** Displays a screen in which here are empty boxes next to all of your contacts. Put check marks next to the contacts you want to delete, and then tap delete to delete them.

- **Get friends.** Lets you import contacts from services such as Twitter and Facebook.

- **Sync contacts.** Syncs your contacts with your Google account.

- **Import/Export.** This option lets you export your contacts by saving them to a USB flash drive attached to your tab, or import them from a USB flash drive attached to your tab.

 When the Galaxy Tab was first released, it couldn't recognize USB flash drives, so the Import/Export feature via USB didn't work. That problem may or may not be fixed by the time you read this.

- **Join contact.** If you have contacts listed multiple times, for example, if you have them in your Google Account and on Facebook, you can use this option to combine multiple listings of the same contact into a single listing.

- **My profile.** Lets you create a profile with information about yourself that you can then share with others by sending the information via Email, Gmail, or Bluetooth. It creates a file in the vCard format (with the extension .vcf) that can then be imported into contact software. Most recognize and import .vcf files.

- **Set default.** Sets a default main contact—it should be you.

 You can also get some of these same choices by holding your finger on a contact's listing. But if you hold your finger on a contact imported from Twitter or Facebook, the options won't be available.

- **Send namecard via.** This lets you send a vCard to someone via Email, Gmail, or Bluetooth, with information about a contact.

- **Print namecard.** This will print contact information about a contact to a Samsung printer setup for wireless printing.

- **Settings.** Tap this, and you can sort the list by last name rather than first name. If you're really a contrarian, then when you tap a contact, you can have the Tab show the last name first, rather than the first name first. You can also choose to display only contacts with phone numbers, and only contacts from a particular service—for example, only Twitter, only Google, or only unsynced contacts on your Tab.

7 Facebook, Twitter, and Other Social Apps

Your Galaxy Tab has everything you need to keep in touch with friends, family, and others throughout the world via social networking apps like Facebook and Twitter. It not only connects to the Internet, but it also has GPS so you can let folks know where you are (if you wish), a big beautiful screen where you can read your updates, and a camera or two so you can share photos and videos. This chapter shows you how to run your Tab like the mean, lean, social networking machine it is.

How Do I Get Social?

You Galaxy Tab doesn't have social networking apps built right into it, because the standard version of Android 3.1 Honeycomb doesn't include them. So you have to download social networking apps from the Android Market.

When you read descriptions of social networking apps in the Android Market, you may notice that they refer to "phone" rather than tablet. Don't worry—the same app that works on a phone works on your Tab. If you see more than one app from a social networking service in the Market, read the descriptions for both of them, in case one was written for a tablet.

 Tip Samsung may decide to put social networking apps on the Tab at some point. So check the App Menu before downloading new versions.

Using Facebook

To use Facebook, download and install the Facebook app. (For details about how to find and install apps, see page 90.) Make sure it's the official app, with Facebook listed as the author on the description page.

After you install and run the app for the first time, you have to agree to the usual license agreement that you've seen, ignored, and agreed to countless times before. After that, either log in to your existing Facebook account, or, if you're one of the seven people left on the planet without a Facebook account, click the Sign Up button to create a new account.

Either way, after a moment or two, you're logged in. Tap Finish. Voilà— you're there!

 Note You must be connected to the Internet in order to use the Facebook app.

The first screen you come to asks whether and how you want to synchronize information between the Contacts on your Tab and your Facebook friends. When you sync data between the two, information from Facebook gets shuttled into your Contacts. So, for example, you'll see friends' Facebook profile pictures and status messages in your Tab Contacts. Your friends' contact information from Facebook goes into your Tab Contacts as well.

You get three choices:

- **Sync all.** Puts all of your friends' information from Facebook into your Galaxy Tab Contacts, including people who you haven't yet put into your Tab Contacts.

- **Sync with existing contacts.** Syncs Facebook information only with people already on your Contacts list. So if you have Facebook friends who aren't in your Galaxy Tab Contacts, you won't see their information in your Tab contacts.

- **Don't sync.** As it says, no syncing is done.

Make your choice and then tap Finish. After a few seconds you come to the main Facebook page—your news feed page. You see your Facebook friends' updates, uploaded photos, shared links, and so on, just like when you visit Facebook on the Web.

Scroll through the feed by flicking and dragging. When you get to the bottom of the screen, you see an Older Posts button. Tap it, and older posts appear. You can keep pulling up more posts as long as you want. If you've got a lot of friends, there seems to be no end to the eternity of postings.

 Note This chapter assumes that you already have some familiarity with Facebook on the Web. If you want to become a real pro, check out *Facebook: The Missing Manual.*

To make sure that you're seeing the most up-to-the-minute news from every one of your friends, tell the Facebook app to check for any new postings. To do so, tap the Menu button at the bottom of the screen ▦ and then tap Refresh. If anyone else has posted an update, you see it at the top of the page. The app regularly checks for updates on its own, of course, but if you absolutely, positively must see the latest updates from any one of your 400 closest friends on the planet, the Refresh command is the way to make sure you're seeing them the instant they're posted.

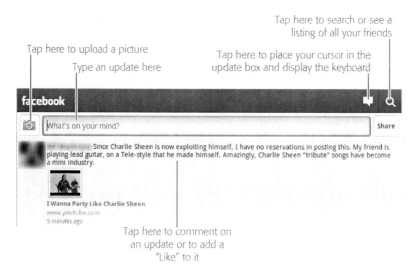

Tap here to search or see a listing of all your friends

Tap here to upload a picture

Type an update here

Tap here to place your cursor in the update box and display the keyboard

Tap here to comment on an update or to add a "Like" to it

 Note The official Facebook application that you use may look and work a bit differently than what you see pictured here. That's because the app may have been updated since this book was published.

To post an update, either tap the "What's on your mind?" box, or tap the Talk button ▣. The keyboard appears. Type what you want, tap Share, and the world sees the all-important news about your cat's recently changed sleeping position.

To "like" (give a virtual thumbs-up to) or comment on a friend's update, tap the update, and you come to a page that lets you do both. Simply tap "Like" or write your comment at the bottom of the screen. When you tap in the text box at the bottom, the Tab's keyboard appears, along with two buttons—Comment and Clear. Type your comment, tap Comment, and off it goes. Clear it if you want to start from scratch again or have decided not to comment.

When you're on the screen for making a comment or adding a Like, you can view the profile of the person whose update you're reading. Press the Menu button at the bottom of the page, and then select View Profile.

Adding Friends

If you want to search for people on Facebook, find new friends, or browse through your friends, tap the Search button 🔍 . From the screen that appears, to search to see if someone you know is on Facebook, tap the Everyone tab, type the name, and then tap the Search button. A matching list appears—and the list includes people on Facebook who are already your friends, as well as those on Facebook who are not your friends.

The Facebook app may crash once in a while. It has had problems running on Android 3.1 Honeycomb, although by the time you read this, Google may have fixed the problem.

When you find the person you want to add as a friend, tap her name, and you come to a page—much like the one on the Facebook website—that shows the person's picture, name, location, hometown, activities, interests…the whole Facebook nine yards. Tap "Add as a Friend," and a box pops up so that you can add a message if you want. Tap Send, and your friend request goes on its merry way.

If someone sends you a friend request, you'll get a notification, but to see it, you have to go to the page where you perform a search. So tap the Search button, and then look at the bottom of the page. You'll see a Requests button. Tap it to see all your friend requests.

Viewing your Friends' Walls, Info, and More

Back on the Search page, if you want to scroll through a list of all your friends (and their Facebook information), or search for a friend and see her information, first tap the Friends tab. You come to an alphabetical list of all your friends—by first name, not last name, in true Facebook fashion.

Tap any friend, and you get sent to her Wall, where you can see her most recent updates and post a message by typing into the Write Something box. You can also include a photo, as described on page 162. Or you can comment on and Like any individual posts by tapping them.

Tap Info to see the info your Facebook friend has shared (education, work, and so on). Tap Photos to browse albums of pictures.

 Tip If a friend has shared an email address on the Info page, you can easily send an email. Tap the small Email button to the right of the address, and your email program opens, with a blank, preaddressed email message. If you have more than one email account, you're asked to choose one.

Uploading Photos

Want to upload a picture to Facebook from your Galaxy Tab? Simple. Tap the Photo button on the Facebook app's main screen [📷] and a screen appears asking whether you want to upload a photo already in your Gallery, or whether you want to take a new photo and upload it.

Upload photo

Choose from Gallery

Capture a photo

If you chose Gallery (page 245), choose the picture you want to send, and you come to a Facebook page that shows the picture you're uploading. Beneath it, you can write a caption. Tap Upload to upload the photo and caption. They get sent to your Facebook Mobile album, which is your photo collection on Facebook for posting photos from your Tab, cellphone, and so on.

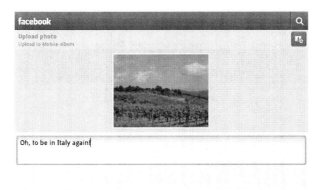

If you want to send it to a different Facebook album, tap the small Album button on the top right of the screen, and you come to a screen that displays all your Facebook photo albums. Choose the album to which you want to upload the photo. Tab sends you back to the previous screen, where you can then send the photo.

If you choose to take a new photo, you're sent to the Galaxy Tab's camera app. Take a photo as you would normally (page 265), and Tab sends you to the uploading screen.

Facebook Notifications

Facebook uses your Galaxy Tab's Notifications Panel to let you know when something important has happened—someone responded to a friend request, wants to chat, or whatever. Tap the notification to open it and take action.

> **Note** The Facebook app doesn't include all of Facebook's considerable features, so if you want to get at everything it has to offer, you have to go to the Web. Still, the app lets you do most of the important stuff.

Add a Facebook Widget

If you want to see Facebook updates at a glance, you don't need to run the Facebook app. Instead, add a Facebook widget to one of your Home screens. The widget is a great and easy way to use Facebook on your Tab, because it lets you see updates at a glance and do a few simple Facebook tasks without firing up the full app.

To add a widget, on your Home screen, tap the + button. On the bottom half of the screen, tap Widgets. Then flick through all the available widgets until you come to the Facebook widget. Drag it to the Home screen where you want the widget to appear.

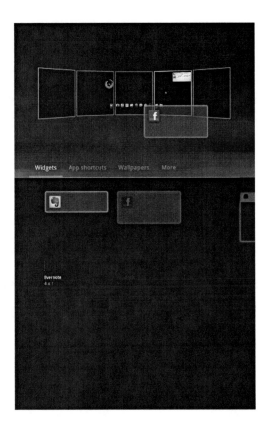

Now you can see your friends' status updates right on that Home screen. The widget constantly refreshes itself.

 You may have some problems getting the widget to work. If that happens, you may have to wait for Facebook to release a new app and widget to fix the bugs.

Twitter

Are you one in the vast army of tweeters? If so, you'll be pleased to see that you can use your Tab for Twitter. As with Facebook, you must first download and install the Twitter app. (For details on installing apps, see page 95.)

 Note When you download the Twitter app, make sure it's the official one from Twitter. You can tell because Twitter is listed as the author on the app's description page.

Once you install it, log into your existing Twitter account. As with the Facebook app, if you're one of the few people on earth without a Twitter account, you can click the Sign Up button to create a new account.

After a moment or two, you're logged in. Tap Finish.

When you come to the main Twitter screen, look across the top—that navigation bar is Twitter central for your interactions:

- **Tap the leftmost button** to see tweets from all the people you follow.

- **Next to it, the At button** @ brings you to a screen that shows retweets of your tweets.

- **Tap the button that looks like an envelope** ✉ and you see private messages that you've exchanged with others.

- **The Lists button** ▤ on the right sends you to a screen with a variety of lists, such as tweets that you've retweeted, Favorites, and more.

Just above those four buttons are two buttons:

- **A button for** searching Twitter 🔍.

- **A button that** lets you create and send a tweet ✎.

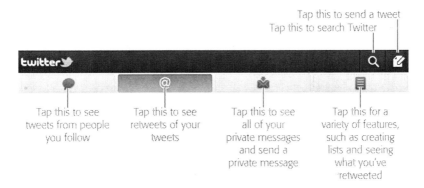

Tap this to send a tweet
Tap this to search Twitter

Tap this to see tweets from people you follow

Tap this to see retweets of your tweets

Tap this to see all of your private messages and send a private message

Tap this for a variety of features, such as creating lists and seeing what you've retweeted

Note You must be connected to the Internet to use the Twitter app.

Creating a tweet is straightforward. Tap the Tweet button, tap in your message, and then tap Tweet to send it. As you type, you see an indication at the top of the screen of how many characters you have left, so you can stay within Twitter's 140-character limit.

But there's a lot more to it than that. Look along the bottom of the screen, and you see four buttons:

- **The leftmost one** @ brings up a list of all the people you follow. Tap one, and your tweet goes directly to him.

- **The button that looks like a camera** 📷 lets you take and send a photo as part of the tweet. It launches the Camera app (page 265), where you can take a photo that gets included in the tweet.

- **The button that looks like camera film** 🖼 launches the Gallery, where you can take an existing photo and attach it to the tweet.

- **The GPS button** ◉ attaches GPS location information to your tweet.

Taking Action on Tweets

Reading tweets and messages is straightforward. You see a list of tweets, along with the person's Twitter ID and picture, as well as how long ago the tweet was made. Small icons give more information about the tweet—for example, whether it's a retweet, a message, or whether the tweet has a photo attached. Press any tweet and hold it, and a bar appears with five icons:

- **The leftmost button** 🗨 puts the tweeter's @ address in front of a message so you can send the person a message.
- **The Retweet button** 🔁 lets you retweet the post.
- **The Star button** ☆ adds the post to your Favorites.
- **The Information button** 👤 brings you to a page with a bio of the person who wrote the tweet, and other information, such as how long the person has been a Twitter member, the number of people he follows, the number of people following him, and so on. From this page, you can follow or unfollow the person. You can also tap a small gear icon to perform more actions, such as sending him a message, adding him to a list, blocking him, or reporting him as a spammer.
- **The Share button** 🏴 lets you share the post in a variety of ways, including Email, Bluetooth, and Facebook.

Similarly, if you tap the tweet, you come to a screen that shows the tweet with four buttons across the bottom. They're the same buttons that appear if you press and hold on a tweet, except that the Information button is missing.

A List of Lists

When you tap the Lists button 🗒 at the top of a Twitter screen, you come to a screen with a series of lists. Tap any to see what they contain:

- **Favorites** includes all of the tweets you've marked as favorites.

- **Suggested users** brings you to a list of many categories, such as Books, Entertainment, Health, Music, Science, and so on. Click any category, and you come to a list of people that Twitter thinks you might be interested in following. You can take actions on them, just as you would on any other post.

- **Create new list** lets you create a new Twitter list; for example, the favorite authors or singers you follow.

Changing Twitter Settings

The Android Twitter app is chock-full of settings you can change, including how often to check for new tweets, whether to notify you about new tweets, whether to notify you about mentions of you on Twitter, and so on. To access them, press the Menu button at the bottom of the Twitter screen, and then select Settings.

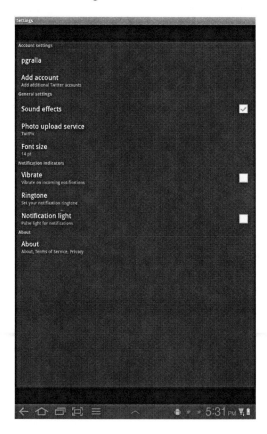

The settings are self-explanatory—just put checkmarks next to those you want to turn on, uncheck those you want to turn off, and so on. For example, tap "Notification ringtone" to select a ringtone to notify you of a new Tweet, and uncheck the box next to Notification if you don't want to receive any notifications of new Tweets.

Editing Your Twitter Profile

You can also use your Tab's Twitter app to view and edit your profile. Tap the Menu button at the bottom of the Twitter screen, and then select My Profile. Read what you've got there, and tap Edit Profile to change it or add what you'd like.

Twitter Notifications

Twitter uses your Tab's Notification Panel to let you know when something important has happened—you have a message, you've been retweeted, and so on. Tap it to open it, and take any action needed.

 The Twitter app doesn't include all of Twitter's considerable features, so if you want to get at everything it has to offer, then you have to go to the Web. Still, the app lets you do most important things.

Twitter and Your Contacts

When you install Twitter on your Tab, its power extends beyond Twitter itself. It also integrates with your Contacts (page 153), which makes them much more useful.

People with whom you've established a relationship on Twitter automatically show up in your Contacts list, and they bring over their information as well. So if you follow someone on Twitter, her information shows up in your Contacts, including her email address and other information. And if she has Twitter photos, those photos show up in Contacts as well.

Contacts also merges information from Twitter into existing contacts. For example, if you have a contact whom you also follow on Twitter, then you see her tweets right inside her contact information on the Tab.

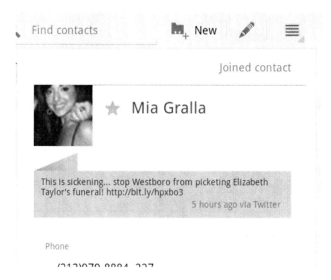

Other Social Networking Apps

Facebook and Twitter are just two of the most popular social networking apps—there are plenty more out there, many of which have nifty apps for your Tab. To find them, head to the Android Market, and go to the Social category.

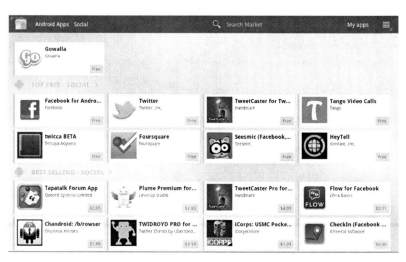

Here are just a few you might want to try:

- **Foursquare.** This app is designed for mobility from the ground up. Share your location information, share pictures, get discounts, and so on.

- **TweetDeck.** This software isn't a separate social networking site; it serves as a front end for Twitter. Many people prefer it to Twitter's own app. You need a Twitter account to use it.

- **HootSuite.** A front end to multiple social networking services, including Twitter, Facebook, and Foursquare.

- **Seesmic.** Like HootSuite, it lets you manage multiple social networking services.

- **LinkedIn.** Think of LinkedIn as Facebook for business. It's buttoned-down and strictly for work. At this writing, an Android tablet version is being developed; by the time you read this, it may be ready to go.

8 Maps and Navigation

Think of your Galaxy Tab as The Great Navigator. It's got the spectacular mapping app, Google Maps, built into it, and more amazing still, it's got a full-blown GPS navigation system as well. Wherever you are, the Tab can lead you to your destination with ease. Read on to find out more about these two great apps.

Using Google Maps

Google Maps on your Galaxy Tab is the mobile version of the renowned Google Maps website (*http://maps.google.com*). In fact, the Tab's Maps app is even more powerful than the Web version, since it can incorporate GPS information. And your Tab has full 3D graphics, so you see eye-popping three-dimensional views as well.

Type any address or point of interest in the U.S. (or many places all over the world), and you see a map. You can choose a street map, an aerial satellite photo, or a combination of the two. You can also find nearby businesses, points of interest, and traffic congestion. Maps can also give you turn-by-turn directions, even including public transportation in some cities.

 The Maps app on your Tab may vary somewhat from what you see explained here. Google frequently updates Maps. The Maps app described here is the latest version as of the writing of this book. So if you have an older or newer version of Maps, it may vary.

Browsing Google Maps

Tap the Maps icon in the Apps Menu, and Google Maps launches. At first launch, if it finds your location, it shows a map of your neighborhood with a pointer to your location. As you walk, drive, bicycle, or otherwise move, the blue arrow moves as well. The arrow changes direction to show the direction in which you're moving. If it can't find you, then you probably see a map of the United States. You can get all the way down to street level. Navigate the map by dragging or flicking.

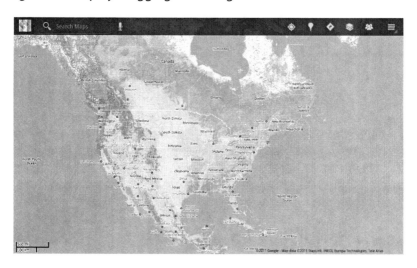

Indicator shows your location

Zoom out by spreading your fingers or tapping the screen once with two fingers (the amazing, little-known two-finger tap). Zoom in by pinching your fingers or tapping the screen twice with one finger (the slightly better-known one-finger tap).

 Note Google Maps doesn't work if you don't have a Wi-Fi or data connection.

As you zoom in on the map, you see locations of interest—museums, libraries, schools, parks, and so on. Tap any, and the name pops up in a balloon. Tap the balloon, and a screen appears with more information, which lets you get directions to the location, search for nearby businesses, see reviews of it, share information about the location by email, text message, or direct Bluetooth file transfer, and more.

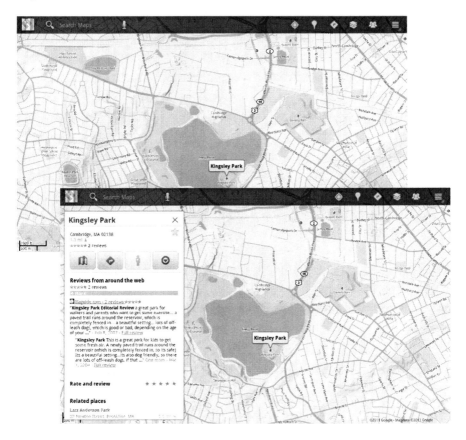

Getting More Information

Just being able to zoom in and out of a map down to the street level, or all the way out to the continent level, is pretty amazing. But that doesn't even begin to get at all the amazing things you can do with Google Maps.

To get at these amazing things, tap one of the icons at on the upper right of the screen. Here's what each does:

- **Compass button** 🔘 shows a map of your current location, with an indicator in the center showing where you are. So if you're viewing a map halfway across the world and you tap this button, you go back home. Think of it as the ruby slippers button.

- **Places button** 💡 brings up a list of places you can have displayed on the map, including restaurants, coffee shops, hotels, gas stations, and more.

- **Directions button** ◈ brings up a menu that lets you get directions from your current location to somewhere else—or, in fact, from anywhere to anywhere. You can get walking, driving, biking, and public transportation directions.

- **Layers button** ≋ brings up a menu of other types of information you can have superimposed on your map, such as terrain, traffic, and more.

- **Latitude button** 👥 lets you use Google Latitude, a social networking service that shows your friends where you are, and shows you where your friends are.

- **Menu button** ▤ brings up the Google Maps menu, which offers a variety of miscellaneous settings and features, such as clearing the map and getting help.

Using Places to Find Businesses and Contacts

Using Places, Google Maps can easily find local businesses. Any business that you can find with a Google search, Google maps can find, too. But Maps can also find the home and business addresses of your friends, which it does by tying into your Contacts list.

If you want to search for a business near your current location, tap the Places icon. A screen appears, listing various types of businesses, such as restaurants, coffee shops, bars, hotels, attractions, ATMs, gas stations, and so on. Tap the icon of the type of business you want to display, and Google Maps displays all of those types of business near you. To see a cross-section of places, tap Explore Nearby.

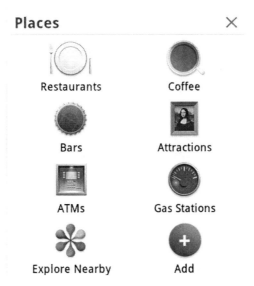

Places　　　　　　　　　　　　✕

Restaurants　　　　　Coffee

Bars　　　　　　Attractions

ATMs　　　　Gas Stations

Explore Nearby　　　　Add

Alternately, you can do a search for a type of business by typing into the top-left search box—*pharmacy*, for example, or *bakery*.

When you choose a type of business from the Places menu, you see push-pins on the map, each of which represents a business in the category you've chosen. A pane also appears with information and reviews about the closest ones to you. Tap any review in the pane for more information about that place.

Tap any pushpin on the map, and the business's name appears above it. Tap the name, and you see far more detail about it, depending on whether the business has been reviewed by any users of Google's content partners, such as Yelp.com, Urbandaddy.com, Citysearch.com, Zagat.com, and others. If it hasn't been reviewed, you can share information about the location, type a Buzz (page 190) about it, add it as a contact, and more, as you'll see in the next few paragraphs.

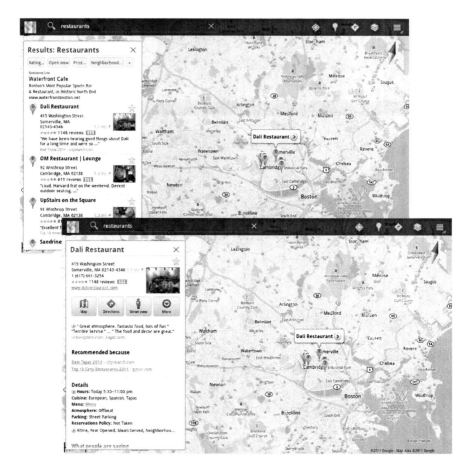

When you get details about a business, you see four buttons near the top of its information. The leftmost one 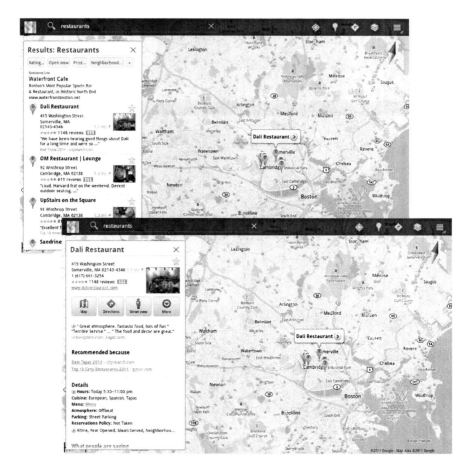 brings you back to Google Maps and shows you the location of the business on the map; the next one gives you turn-by-turn directions to the business; the next one brings up Street View, which shows you a photographic street view of the location—an amazing piece of technology that you'll learn more about on page 193; and the rightmost one brings up a menu with many more selections, such as sending a Buzz and sharing information.

What if you come across a business you like and want to be able to return to it later? Simple—when you're viewing details about a business, look for a small gray star at top right. Tap it, and the star turns gold. You've just put that location on a Starred Items list so you can easily find it again. You can see the star on the map or, to see the list, tap the Menu key in Google Maps, and then tap Starred Places. To take a business off the list, when you're viewing its description, tap the gold star to turn it back to gray.

 Tip Your map can quickly fill up with pushpins that become very distracting. You can delete them all in a single swoop. Press the Menu key, and then tap Clear Map.

Locating the address of your friend's home or business on a Google Map is easy—if the address is in your Contacts list. In Google Maps, search for the friend's name. If you have an address for the friend, it appears in the search results. Tap it, and you see the location on a map.

You can also do it straight from the Contacts list. Find the person in your Contacts list (see page 153). Next to the person's address or addresses, you see pushpins. Tap a pushpin to go to the location on Google Maps, complete with another pushpin at the address.

Getting Directions

You've heard the old cliché: Ask a Maine resident for directions, and the answer is inevitably, "Can't get there from here." Fortunately, Google Maps is much more helpful. Ask it the same question, and you get to choose how you want to get there: driving, walking, biking, or public transportation. Google provides directions for all four, or as many as it can find. (Not all types of directions are available for all places; you have more choices in major metropolitan areas.)

You can get directions in many places throughout Google Maps, and throughout your Galaxy Tab, because that capability is embedded very deep in the tablet. So expect to find directions in many different places— for example, when you search for a business, find the location, and then look at the page that gives you information about the business.

One surefire way to get directions anywhere in Google Maps: Tap the Directions button. A screen appears, with a starting point, ending point, and icons for finding directions via car, public transportation, bicycle, and on foot.

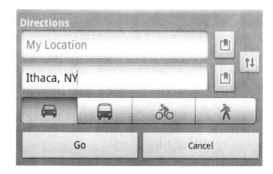

If the Tab knows your current location, then it uses that as the starting point, and puts the words "My Location" in the starting point box. If you want a different starting point, then type an address into the My Location box, or instead tap the little icon to the right of the box 🕮 . If you tap the icon, you can choose to have Google Maps use your current location as a starting point, to tap a point on the map to be your starting point, or to create a starting point from an address in your Contacts list.

Next, choose your destination—what Google Maps calls an **end point**. As with the starting location, you can type a location, or tap the icon and choose an endpoint on the map, your current location, or a contact's address. Once you've set the starting and ending points, you're ready to go. Tap which kind of directions you want, and then tap Go. You see a summary of your starting point, your ending point, the distance, how long it's expected to take, and turn-by-turn (or step-by-step) directions for how to get there.

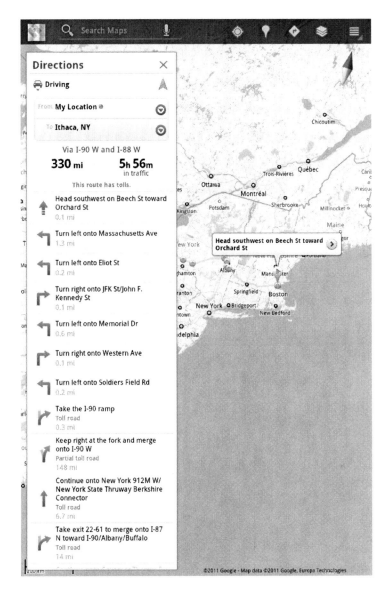

This example uses driving directions, but the other types of directions work much the same way. You can scroll through the entire list of directions. Tap any instruction on the master list of directions (such as "Take Exit 8 for NY-206 towards Bainbridge") and you jump to that map, while still showing your list of directions. You can zoom in and out on the map in the usual ways, and use all the other Google Maps features as well. So as you drive, you can find nearby restaurants, and so on.

Using Layers

Tap the Layers icon to use this very nifty Google Map feature. A *layer* is a different view, or information superimposed over a view. When you tap the Layers icon, you come to a menu that shows you a whole lot of choices, including a satellite view, a view of the terrain, a real-time traffic map, and so on. Your current view has a green checkmark next to it. To switch to any other view, tap it.

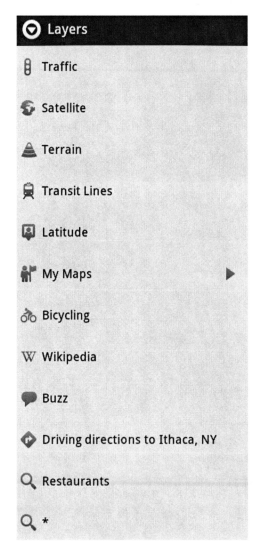

The satellite view is self-explanatory—it's a satellite image of the location. As you zoom in, the photo may at first appear blurry, and it may take a little while for the photo to resolve itself, so be patient. Not only can you zoom in and out of the photo, but you can change perspective as well, by holding one finger stationary while moving the other.

 The layers on Google Maps often change, as Google adds new information and makes deals with other companies to add their layers. So check Layers often to see what new things are in store for you.

The terrain view is reminiscent of a map in a geography textbook. It shows you a representation of an area's elevation, forests, deserts, mountains, and so on.

Traffic

The map can show you how bad the traffic is on highways and major metropolitan thoroughfares. Turn on the Traffic layer, and, where available, the app indicates traffic congestion with the following color coding:

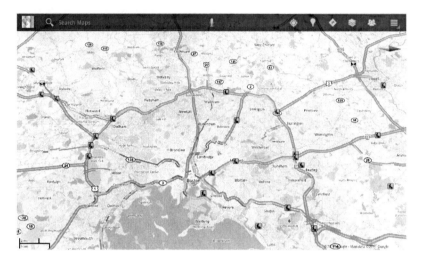

- **Green** means the traffic is flowing very nicely—at least 50 miles per hour.
- **Yellow** indicates slower-moving traffic, between 25 and 50 miles per hour.
- **Red** means a traffic jam; avoid it if you can. It means that traffic is moving at less than 25 miles per hour.

Make sure to look for small orange icons with a symbol of a man at work. They show where there is construction or maintenance going on. Tap any of the symbols, and you get a description of the work.

Buzz and Latitude

The Layers menu has a number of other options: Buzz, Latitude, and, if you've previously used turn-by-turn directions, the last set of directions you requested. Both Buzz and Latitude are Google services. Buzz is a social networking service that lets you post your current location and find out what the "buzz" is near you, and for you to post what you think the "buzz" is. Latitude lets you share your current location with your friends, and to see their locations on your Tab. If you've previously used the Places feature to find businesses, such as restaurants, Layers has entries for them as well. You can also use Layers to get a terrain view, bicycling directions, and so on.

More Layers

When you tap Layers at the top of Google Maps, down at the bottom of the screen, you see a More Layers option. Tap it, and you get even more layers, some of them extremely useful, such as one that shows bike paths on a map, and another that shows transit lines. Keep checking back, because Google keeps adding new layers to Google Maps.

How Your Galaxy Tab Finds Your Location

Google Maps' usefulness really comes into play when it's combined with your Galaxy Tab's ability to find your location. Your Tab finds where you are in two ways:

- **GPS.** Your Tab's built-in GPS chip works just like the one in a Garmin or TomTom, although it's not quite as accurate. (Hey, those devices only do GPS, not video chat or 3D games, so cut your tablet some slack.) GPS works best when you have a good view of the sky. If not, your Tab switches to locating you via Wi-Fi.

- **Wi-Fi positioning.** The Wi-Fi chip on your Tab can do more than just connect you to a Wi-Fi network—it can also help determine your location. It does this by using information about Wi-Fi networks near you—information contained in a large database. Then, using the information about the Wi-Fi locations and your distance from them, it calculates your location. It's not as accurate as GPS, but it still works pretty well.

 Note If you've got a 3G or 4G Galaxy Tab, it can also use the cellular network to provide location information.

Searching Maps

Google Maps makes it easy to search for a business or other location. Given that Google is the premier search site on the Internet, would you expect anything less? To search, type your search term in the search box at the top of the screen. When Google Maps finds what you're looking for, it displays the location and shows a pushpin in it.

You have countless ways to search the maps. Here are some of the most common:

- **Address.** Just type an address, including the state or Zip code. Don't bother with commas, and most of the time you can skip periods as well. You can use common abbreviations. So, if you type *157 w 57 ny ny*, then you do a search for 157 West 57th Street, New York City, New York.

- **Intersection.** Type, for example, *blanchard and concord cambridge ma*, and Google Maps displays the location at the intersection of Blanchard Road and Concord Avenue in Cambridge, Massachusetts.

- **City.** Type, say, *san francisco ca*, and you see that city.

- **Zip code.** Type any Zip code, such as *02138*.

 As you enter search terms, Google Maps displays a list of matching results. You can speed up entering your search by choosing from the right search term when it appears, rather than tapping in the entire address.

- **Point of interest.** Type *central park* or *washington monument*. In many cases, when you search for a point of interest, a pane will appear with information about it on the map.

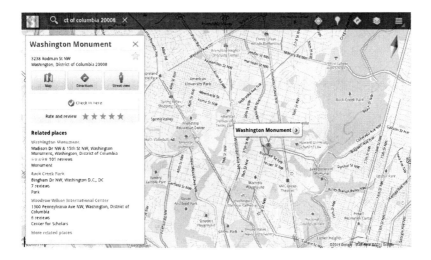

- **Airport code.** If you know the three-letter code, you can type, for example, *sfo* for the San Francisco International Airport, or *bos* for Boston's Logan Airport.

When Google Maps finds the location, it marks it with a pushpin. Tap the pushpin for more information about the location, as explained earlier in this section.

Street View

Here's perhaps the most amazing feature in Google Maps—Street View. It's a full, 360-degree panoramic, photographic view of streets and an entire area—an entire city, if you like. Street View is a great way to plan, for example, a walking tour of downtown Boston. (Make sure to visit the State House and its golden dome on top of Beacon Hill if you head there.)

Street View is available only after you search for an address or a business and select it, or choose a point on the map, and then select it so you can get more information. Tap the Street View button, and you go to Street View, it all of its photographic glory.

 A great way to get to Street View for a city is to search for a point of interest, such as the Empire State Building. Tap to get details about the point of interest, and when you do, tap the More icon, and then select Street View.

Tap here to show Street view.

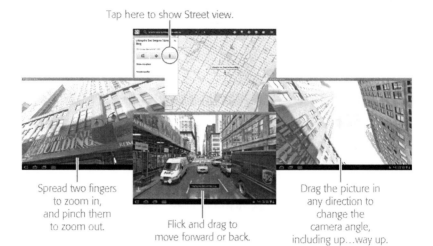

Spread two fingers
to zoom in,
and pinch them
to zoom out.

Flick and drag to
move forward or back.

Drag the picture in
any direction to
change the
camera angle,
including up...way up.

Turn-by-Turn Navigation

The turn-by-turn directions your Galaxy Tab offers are helpful, but your Tab offers something even more powerful—turn-by-turn navigation, just like the GPS gizmos made by Garmin and TomTom.

Tap Navigation from the Apps Menu. You've turned your Tab into a true, full-blown GPS navigator, complete with the usual annoying robot-like female voice. But it does the job. It tracks your location as you drive, and displays it on a map. When you're approaching a turn, it tells you what to do ahead of time. It shows you all the information you need, including distance to your next turn, current location, time to your destination, and more. So forget buying that $300 GPS unit—it's built right into your Tab for free.

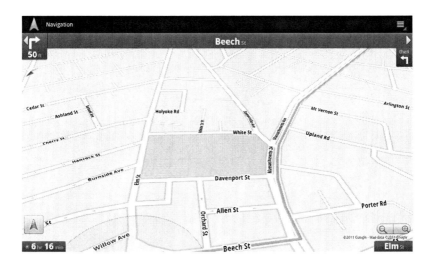

Tip Turn-by-turn navigation works even if you don't have a data connection or a Wi-Fi connection because it uses your Tab's GPS radio.

Turn-by-turn navigation includes lots of other nice features built into it. To get to them all, tap the Menu key while you're in the Navigation app. You can even ask the Navigation map to plot a route that avoids highways and tolls when you drive. Press the Menu key and select Route Info, and then tap the Gear button ⚙. A pop-up asks if you want to avoid either or both.

Part 3

Books, Media, and Games

9 Books and Magazines

Your hardworking Galaxy Tab has a great trick up its virtual sleeve for you—it's a stellar electronic book, magazine, and newspaper reader. With it, you can choose from thousands of books, magazines, and newspapers, and have them all within easy reach whenever you want.

In fact, the Galaxy Tab can even read books formatted for the Kindle or Nook, because you can download Kindle or Nook readers for free from the Android Market. You can even sync your Kindle or Nook books with your Tab. And it's got the excellent Google Books app built right into it as well.

So get ready to curl up with your favorite book, magazine, or newspaper— but first curl up with this chapter.

Using Google Books

You've already got a great eReader built into the Galaxy Tab—Google Books. Tap the Books icon on the Home screen or in the App Menu and get ready to start reading.

If you already use Google Books on the Web, the Nook, or another Android device, you see that your books are right there, just waiting for you to dig in. The information about the books you're reading automatically synchronizes among all your devices. Tap the book you want to read; that's all it takes.

Note Depending on your settings, and whether you've already read an individual book, a book may not be available if you don't have an Internet connection. You can choose to store individual books or all of your books on Google's servers, on your Galaxy Tab, or on both. For details, see page 205.

Finding, Downloading, and Paying for Books

To get new books, you use the books section of the Android Market. Tap the Books button to browse and search for books.

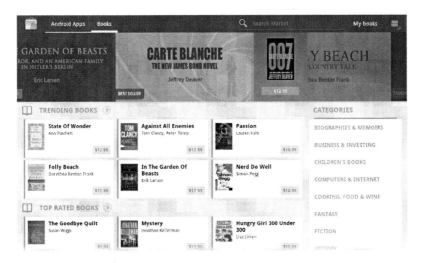

 Tip Google Books has plenty of books available for free, so if you don't feel like buying anything, that's no problem. You can just read the free books.

The Books section is organized just like the rest of the Android Market, with differing categories on the right, featured titles taking up the main part of the screen, and a search box up top. (For details about how to use the Android Market, see page 90.) Tap the "My books" button at upper right to get back to the Books app. The Menu button at upper right offers more information about your overall Android Market use and settings, not just for books.

You can browse by Trending Books, Top-Rated Books, Bestselling Books, or Top Free Books, or by the categories down the right side. And, yes, search (page 93) works here.

When you see a book you're interested in reading, tap it and you see a description, along with reviews and the price. If there are other books by the same author, or books related to the topic, you see links to them on the left side of the screen. Not sure if you want to buy it (or download it, if it's free)? Tap the Free Sample button, and a brief sample excerpt downloads to your Tab. Flick through the pages to read them. (For more about how to read in Google Books, see page 208.)

Want to buy the book? Tap the Menu button, and then select Buy. What happens next varies according to whether you've already signed up for a Google Checkout account, which you need to do in order to pay for the book. (If the book is free, you don't need a Google Checkout account.) If you haven't, then you're sent to a screen to sign up. You have to input the usual information, including credit card information. Once you've done that, you go on to the screen for buying.

Buy

About the book

Make available offline ☐

Help

If you've set up a Google Checkout account, but haven't purchased a book through Google Books before, you first have to agree to the usual gobble-dygook of terms and conditions. Once you do that, you end up on a screen that shows you the name of the book, the price, and which credit card you're using. Tap OK. The book gets downloaded to your Google Books account. You also get an email receipt from Google Checkout.

 Note When you buy a book, it may not show up immediately in Google Books—it may take a little while to be shown as available and to download. So be patient—it'll get there!

If you decide not to preview the free sample of a book before buying, simply tap the Buy button.

Sharing a book

When you're in the Android Market, and you're at the screen with all the book details, you see a Share button  at the top of the screen. That button works just like it does elsewhere on the Galaxy Tab, and lets you share via Gmail, email, and Bluetooth. But when you share, you don't send the book itself. Instead, you send a link to in the Android Market. Whoever gets the link can then go there—in the Android Market on a Galaxy Tab or Android smartphone, or any web browser.

Browsing and Managing Your Books

After you buy books, get free ones, and read samples of others, they all show up when you use the Google Books app. See them all by using the Galaxy Tab's familiar flicking motion to the left or right.

If you've downloaded a sample of a book, the cover of the book shows up in Google Books with the word "Sample" displayed at the bottom.

If you're connected to the Internet, all your books are always available. If a book is in your Google Books account but hasn't been downloaded, then when you tap it to read it, you connect to it online. Google Books downloads the portion of the book you want to read.

If you're not connected to the Internet, only those books that you've downloaded are available for reading. The books that you haven't downloaded show up in your account, but are darkened, to show that you can't read them until you connect.

When you tap one of them to read them, a message pops up telling you that you need to connect to the Internet if you want to read it.

> This book is currently unavailable for offline reading, please check your Internet connection and try again.
>
> OK

You can make sure that you never get this message by making your books available on the Tab. Press your finger on any book, and from the screen that appears, select "Make available offline." A small green pushpin appears underneath the book, showing that it's scheduled for download the next time you connect. Pushpins appear beneath all your other books as well, grayed out. To make any books completely available on your Tab even when you're not connected to the Internet, tap the gray pushpin underneath it, and it turns green, just like the initial book you first decided to download. (You can also get to the screen that lets you make books available offline by tapping the Menu button, and then selecting "Make available offline.")

At the bottom of the screen you see a notice telling you how much free storage space you've got; that helps you decide whether or not to make books available on the Tab. You want to balance the convenience of having books always available versus the space they take up on your Tab.

When you've made your selection, press Done. The next time you connect to the Internet, Tab downloads the book or books you've selected. The Tab tells you the progress of the download as it happens. If you're already connected to the Internet, the download happens immediately. (Once the book is completely downloaded, the download indication beneath it goes away.)

The Descent of Man, Volume 2
Charles Darwin
50% downloaded

Managing your books

Google Books offers a number of ways to manage your book collection. Tap a book that you've bought or that's free and you've added to your collection, and hold your finger there. Here are your choices:

- **About this book.** Brings you to the book description page in the Android Market.
- **Make available offline.** You already know about this.
- **Remove from tablet.** Removes the book from your Tab *and* removes it from your Google Book account.

Press and hold on a book that you haven't bought but from which you've read a sample, and here are your choices:

- **Buy.** Brings you to the screen that lets you buy the book.
- **About this book.** Brings you to the book description page in the Android Market.

> **Note** The Buy and "About this book" options don't work unless you're connected to the Internet.

- **Delete.** This deletes the sample from your Tab.

Ciao Italia in Tuscany
Mary Ann Esposito

Reading Your Books

To read a book, tap it. You can read either in vertical or horizontal orientations. If you read in vertical orientation, then you see a single page. In horizontal, you see two pages. In both instances, you can flick forward and back to the next or previous pages.

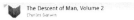
[14] "Catalogue of Acanth. Fishes in the British Museum," by Dr. Gunther, 1861, pp. 138-151.

In the very distinct family of the Cyprinodontidae—inhabitants of the fresh waters of foreign lands—the sexes

Fig. 30.—Xiphophorus Hellerii. Upper figure, male; lower figure, female.

sometimes differ much in various characters. In the male of the *Mollienesia petenensis*,[16]the dorsal fin is greatly developed and is marked with a row of large, round, ocellated, bright-colored spots; while the same fin in the female is smaller, of a different shape, and marked only with irregularly curved brown spots. In the male, the basal margin of the anal fin is also a little produced and dark colored. In the male of an allied form, the *Xiphophorus Hellerii* (Fig. 80), the inferior margin of the caudal fin is developed into a long filament, which, as I hear from Dr. Gunther, is striped with bright colors. This filament does not contain any muscles, and apparently cannot be of any direct use to the fish. As in the case of the Callionymus, the males while young resemble the adult females in color and structure. Sexual differences such as these may be strictly compared with those which are so frequent with gallinaceous birds.[17]

ed in the males.

Fig. 29.—Callionymus lyra. Upper figure, male; lower figure, female.
N.B.—The lower figure is more reduced than the upper.

out the genus Callionymus,[14] the male is generally much more brightly spotted than the female, and in several species not only the dorsal but the anal fin is much elongat-

The male of the *Cottus scorpius*, or sea-scorpion, is slenderer and smaller than the female. There is also a great difference in color between them. It is difficult, as Mr. Lloyd[15] remarks, "for any one who has not seen this fish during the spawning season, when its hues are brightest, to conceive the admixture of brilliant colors with which it, in other respects so ill-favored, is at that time adorned." Both sexes of the *Labrus mixtus*, although very different in color, are beautiful: the male being orange with bright blue stripes, and the female bright red with some black spots In the back.

[13] "Nature," July, 1873. p. 264.

[14] "Catalogue of Acanth. Fishes in the British Museum," by Dr. Gunther. 1861, pp. 138-151.

In the very distinct family of the Cyprinodontidae—in-

To see the table of contents, tap the Table of Contents button near the top right of the screen ▦ . The table of contents drops down. Tap any chapter to jump to it.

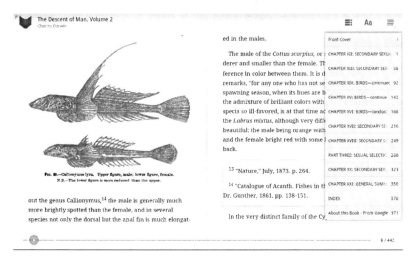

Tap the Setting button Aa and four sets of controls for four different settings appear at the bottom of the screen:

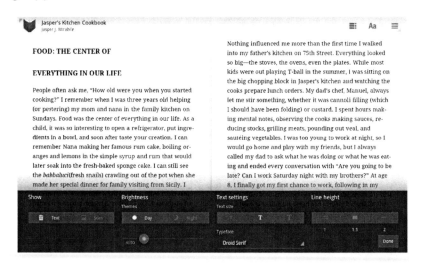

- **Show.** Lets you select your view of the book. Depending on the book, you may or may not have a choice of what to show. On many books, you get a choice between Text and Scan. In Text mode, the text of the book takes center stage—if there are photos or pictures, they often don't interrupt the flow of the text, and are placed on their own pages. In Scan mode, you see the book as it was printed—an actual scanned image of the book.

FOOD: THE CENTER OF

EVERYTHING IN OUR LIFE

People often ask me, "How old were you when you started cooking?" I remember when I was three years old helping (or pestering) my mom and nana in the family kitchen on Sundays. Food was the center of everything in our life. As a child, it was so interesting to open a refrigerator, put ingredients in a bowl, and soon after taste your creation. I can remember Nana making her famous rum cake, boiling oranges and lemons in the simple syrup and rum that would later soak into the fresh-baked sponge cake. I can still see the *babbaluci*(fresh snails) crawling out of the pot when she made her special dinner for family visiting from Sicily. I watched with excitement when my mom filled 150 cream puffs for a holiday dessert or rolled 75 to 100 meatballs for our Sunday dinners.

Nothing influenced me more than the first time I walked into my father's kitchen on 75th Street. Everything looked so big—the stoves, the ovens, even the plates. While most kids were out playing T-ball in the summer, I was sitting on the big chopping block in Jasper's kitchen and watching the cooks prepare lunch orders. My dad's chef, Manuel, always let me stir something, whether it was cannoli filling (which I should have been folding) or custard. I spent hours making mental notes, observing the cooks making sauces, reducing stocks, grilling meats, pounding out veal, and sautéing vegetables. I was too young to work at night, so I would go home and play with my friends, but I always called my dad to ask what he was doing or what he was eating and ended every conversation with "Are you going to be late? Can I work Saturday night with my brothers?" At age 8, I finally got my first chance to work, following in my three older brothers' footsteps by cutting the bread. My first real job was to slice the bread and prepare baskets for the bus help to take to the guests' tables. That was too easy, and I lasted about a month. I wanted to work the salad station.

 To make the Settings, Table of Contents, and other buttons vanish from the top of your screen, tap the screen. Tap it again to bring them back.

- **Brightness.** Lets you select how bright the screen should be. Select either Day or Night to have the Galaxy Tab control it automatically, or if you prefer, move the slider to adjust the brightness yourself.

- **Text Settings.** Changes the text size and typeface.

- **Line height.** Adjusts the height of each line of text. The lower the height, the more lines fit on the page, but the more cramped it appears.

When you're reading a book, look at the bottom of the page. The circle shows your relative position in the book—how far from the front and back you are. The small triangle shows you the previous place you were in the book. On the far right side you see your current page, and the total number of pages.

 118 / 416

Hold your finger on the circle, and you see the chapter and page numbers. Drag the circle to a new location in the book, and you go there.

> **Note** At this writing, several important features were missing from Google Books on Android. You can't bookmark a page, annotate a page, or search through a book. By the time you read this, though, they may be available, so nose around.

Google Books on the Web and Other Android Devices

One of Google Books' niftier features is that you can use it on the Web, your Galaxy Tab, or any other Android device, such as a Motorola Droid X smartphone. Information about all your books is kept in sync—buy a book on your Tab, and it's also available on the Web, for example. So no matter which computer or device you use, you see your latest bookshelf.

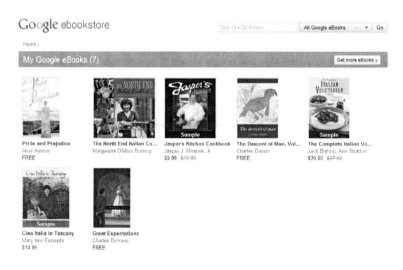

Google Books even syncs the last place in a book you've read. So if you read a book on the Web, for example, when you then read that same book on your Tab, your Tab tells you that there's a new reading position, and asks if you want to use that on the Tab.

> A newer reading position is available in chapter "CHAPTER XXVI", page 154. Would you like to go to this position?
>
> OK   Cancel

Using the Kindle App

If you're a Kindle owner, or if you just like the idea of buying Amazon's Kindle books, you're in luck. Your Galaxy Tab is agnostic when it comes to reading books—you can use the Kindle app as well as Google Books to buy and read books.

 Note This chapter doesn't cover the finer details of the Kindle and its Android app. To learn more, check out *Kindle: The Mini Missing Manual*. (You have to read it as an ebook, but you can do that on the Tab's Kindle app.)

To use the Kindle app, download it from the Android Market. You need an Amazon account in order to use it; if you don't already have one, you can sign up through the app.

Launch the app, and after you log in, you see your Kindle books waiting for you; like Google Books, it automatically syncs with your Kindle account, so if you have books on the Kindle, you can read them on your Tab as well.

To read a book, tap it. As with the Google Books app, you can read in either vertical or horizontal mode, and flick forward or back. Tap the screen, and a bar appears at the bottom of the screen. Drag it forward or backward to a new location.

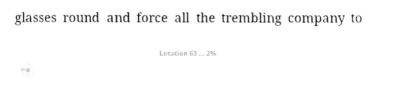

When you tap the screen, navigation and other features appear at the top of the screen. You find these options:

- **Kindle button.** Brings you to the Kindle's home screen, which shows you your entire book collection.
- **Brightness and background color.** Tap to open a screen where you can change the background to black, sepia, or white.

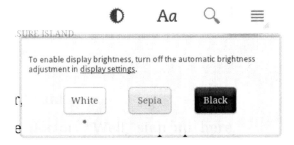

- **Text size.** Lets you change the size of text and the color of the background.

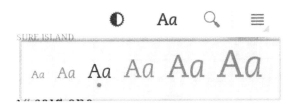

- **Search.** Lets you search through the book for text.

- **Bookmark.** Lets you bookmark the current page so you can quickly jump back to it. Simply tap the ribbon and it turns blue. To remove the bookmark, tap it again and it turns gray.

- **Menu.** Tap for other Kindle options. The Go To option lets you jump to the table of contents, the beginning of the book, or a particular page. "View My Notes & Marks" lets you see all of your bookmarks and any notes that you've made. "Sync to Furthest Page Read" is for when you read Kindle books on multiple devices. It syncs the location of the furthest you've read in a book among all of your devices. Other options let you remove bookmarks, share the progress of your reading with others, or shop for more Kindle books.

Finding and Buying Books on the Kindle App

You find a book on your Kindle app much like you do on Google Books. From the Kindle App's main page, tap the Menu key and then select Kindle Store. You come to a page that lets you browse by categories such as *New York Times* Best Sellers, New & Noteworthy, and so on. You also see recommendations based on your Amazon buying habits. You can do a search as well.

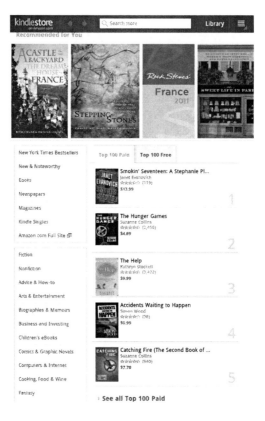

Tap any book to get more information, read reviews, download a sample, or buy it. You pay through your normal Amazon account.

> **Note** If you have a Nook reader or are a fan of the Nook reader, despair not. There's also an Android app for that, so download it from the Android Market for free.

More Kindle Options

From the Kindle's main screen, tap the Menu key, and you come to other options, like changing the sorting order of your Kindle books, and removing items from your Kindle account.

Magazines and Newspapers

Your Galaxy Tab is superb for reading magazines and newspapers, not just books. Whether you want to keep up with fast-breaking news, spend time with a long, leisurely feature article, or browse the latest magazine photos, it's easy.

One way to do so is to simply head to the newspaper or magazine website on the Tab's browser. When you want to read a publication only occasionally, that works fine, and this section shows you how to do it.

But if you're a regular follower of a publication, its Android app is usually a better way to go. Then there's the Tab's own newsreader called Pulse, which lets you essentially create your own publication by mashing up content from multiple magazines and web-sites.

To see whether your favorite magazine or newspaper has an Android app, head to the Android Market (page 90). Search specifically for a tablet

version of the newspaper or magazine app, because if there is one, it will have more features than the typical Android smartphone version and an interface created for the Tab's bigger screen.

Perhaps the best magazine or newspaper app is *USA Today*'s tablet app. Download it, and you can browse the latest news on your Tab's big, beautiful screen. And you can even see the newspaper's signature infographics, complete with surveys.

The *New York Times* also has an Android app, although it's pretty bare bones—pretty much a simple listing of the most recent stories. Tap any to read the story itself, along with graphics and multimedia content.

The New York Times

𝔗 Top News

Afghans Build Security, and Hope to Avoid Infiltrators

12:15 AM ET | Officials concede that with more than 8,000 army and police recruits enlisting each month, the task of screening is monumental.

Two-Day Strike in Greece Ahead of Austerity Vote

11:16 AM ET | Greeks went on a general strike Tuesday, a day before a vote on unpopular austerity measures that are deemed critical to unlocking international financial support.

New Drugs Fight Prostate Cancer, but at High Cost

10:44 PM ET | The drugs, mainly for men with late-stage prostate cancer, can extend lives for additional months, but some cost more than $90,000 for a course of treatment.

THE CHAMPIONS

A Congressman's Pet Project; a Railroad's Boon

12:15 AM ET | Representative John L. Mica has been the 61-mile SunRail line's biggest supporter since he first proposed it in 1992.

Judge Explains 150-Year Sentence for Madoff

9:39 AM ET | The sentencing of Bernard L. Madoff required balancing the law against the public anger his fraud had inspired.

U.S. Endorses France's Lagarde as New I.M.F. Chief

10:00 AM ET | The French finance minister Christine Lagarde was expected to be named Tuesday, with the American endorsement all but sealing her victory.

THE CAUCUS

Bachmann Poses Challenge for Male Rivals

8:38 AM ET | Michele Bachmann's entry into the presidential race will be another test of gender's impact on American politics.

Teacher Grades: Pass or Be Fired

12:13 AM ET | A job evaluation system that places significant emphasis on classroom observations is disliked by unionized teachers but has become a model for many educators.

MOVIE REVIEW | 'TRANSFORMERS: DARK OF THE MOON'

They're at It Again, and Chicago Takes the Hit

11:04 AM ET | "Transformers: Dark of the Moon" is among Michael Bay's best movies and by far the best 3-D sequel ever made about gigantic toys from outer space.

DEALBOOK

On Obama, Wall St. Shows a Reluctance to Commit

8:09 AM ET | Despite Barack Obama's comments about "fat cats," a number of bankers continue to back the president — although some do it quietly.

Tokyo Electric Power Defeats Shareholders' Efforts to Exit Nuclear Business

9:35 AM ET | Despite the hostility of a rowdy crowd, the operator of the stricken Fukushima Daiichi nuclear plant beat a motion that would have forced the company to abandon its nuclear program.

French Company Says It Will File Anticompetitive Suit Against Google, Seeking Damages

8:21 AM ET | A French Internet company, 1plusV, says Google blocked its Web sites and robbed it of advertising revenue.

THE LEDE BLOG

Hague Prosecutor Calls for Libya to Arrest Qaddafi

11:13 AM ET | The chief prosecutor of the International Criminal Court in The Hague called on Col. Muammar el-Qaddafi's inner circle to arrest him.

CITY ROOM

Last Day of School, and They Do Take Attendance

8:57 AM ET | How do you motivate students to attend the last few days of school when there is really no academic reason for them to be there? Tricks, lures and clever scheduling.

ideajam | Watch Now | brought to you by the innovators at (intel) 8

MOVIE REVIEW | TRANSFORMERS: DARK OF THE MOON'
They're at It Again, and Chicago Takes the Hit

A scene from "Transformers: Dark of the Moon," the third film in the series.

By A. O. SCOTT
Published: June 29, 2011

There are filmmakers whose work is characterized by thrift, efficiency and devotion to the subtleties of cinematic expression. And then there is Michael Bay, whose films are symphonies of excess and redundancy, taking place in a universe full of fire and metal and purged of nuance. I'm not judging, just describing, and since today's theme is bluntness, I might as well come out and say that "Transformers: Dark of the Moon" is among Mr. Bay's best movies and by far the best 3-D sequel ever made about gigantic toys from outer space.

I apologize if this sounds like faint praise, but let me provide some perspective. The second of Mr. Bay's "Transformers" movies, "Revenge of the Fallen," released in 2009, struck me as not only the worst movie of that year — measured in raw box office dollars, it was certainly among the most popular — but also as irrefutable evidence that our once proud civilization was in a state of precipitous decline. Perhaps my own enjoyment of "Dark of the Moon" is further evidence. I can't decide if this movie is so spectacularly, breathtakingly dumb as to induce stupidity in anyone who watches, or so brutally brilliant that it disarms all reason. What's the difference?

But this is not about me: it's about the war between Autobots and Decepticons, rival tribes of extraterrestrial fighting machines — literally! — capable of assuming the shape of motor vehicles. Though a computer-enhanced actor briefly appears playing President Obama, no Transformer is on hand to thank him for rescuing the auto industry.

Speaking of which: in the series's latest bit of tongue-in-cheek revisionist history, it is disclosed that John F. Kennedy fast-tracked the moon landing not in order to beat the Soviet Union in the space race, but rather to secure a site where a giant Autobot vessel had crash-landed after a big war on Cybertron. ("Transformers" scholars will recall that the Hoover Dam was built for similar purposes.) The actual Buzz Aldrin shows up to confirm that the giant leap for mankind of July 20, 1969, was actually a small incident in the endless Autobot-Decepticon war, which will, in our own time, lay waste to much of the city of Chicago.

Plot summary is unnecessary: the script, by Ehren Kruger (who joined the franchise with "Revenge" and here proves himself to be a crucial asset), is its own Wikipedia. Everything will be explained, as the cameras swirl and jump and the music (by Steve Jablonsky) rumbles and blasts. "Drop the bridge!" someone will say, referring to one of the drawbridges that span the Chicago River. A few seconds later, you will see the bridge dropping and, just in case you are uncertain of what is going on (maybe you were texting your friend, who sneaked into "Bad Teacher" with hopes of hearing Cameron Diaz swear), someone else will say "The bridge is dropping!"

So you don't have to pay terribly close attention if you want to grasp the basic political and military issues. The Autobots like freedom, the Decepticons do not, and mankind — or at least American mankind, which

 idea**Jam**

Using Pulse

You have another way to read newspapers and magazines, and it uses all of the Galaxy Tab's considerable features and big screen real estate. With it, you can grab articles from any newspaper or magazine, browse the latest updates from social networking sites such as Facebook, and create your own private mashup of news and updates from all over the world. It's one of those apps that you need to try to get a full understanding of how re-markable it is. It's built for Honeycomb tablets, so it's truly spectacular on the Tab.

Using Pulse, you grab articles and information from all over the Web, and display them in a big tablet-friendly format with lots of photos and graphics. You customize exactly what kinds of stories and publications you want to show.

Tap any story to read it, and then to share it with others. To share the story, tap the Facebook or Twitter link you see. Then log into your account to share the story. Tap the icon next to the Twitter link to share the story via email.

Pulse is already setup to grab a variety of news from around the Web, but it's easy to change that to your own selection. On its navigation bar at the top of the app, tap PAGE3, PAGE4, or PAGE5, and you come to a screen that lets you add an entire category already prepopulated with news sources chosen for you by Pulse, or lets you choose your own news sources.

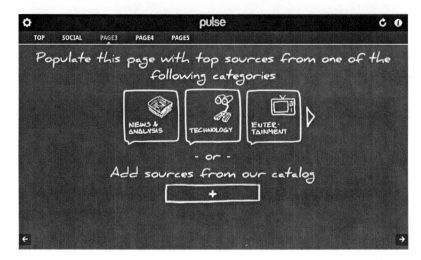

Tap a category—News, for example—and you get articles from a prese-lected list, such as *The Atlantic*, *Salon*, the *Huffington Post*, and others.

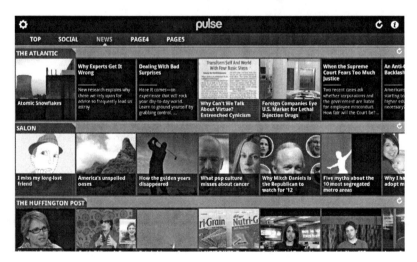

You can instead choose to add sources from the Pulse catalog. When you do that, a list of sources appears. Tap any to add them to your Pulse feed.

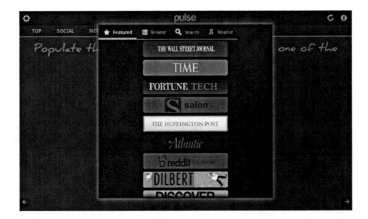

When the list of sources appears, don't settle for what you see in front of you—there are plenty more. At the top of the screen, you see icons for browsing through all of Pulse's sources, searching through them, or using Google Reader.

Tap Browse, and you see the entire list of sources from Pulse, by category. Tap any category to see all the sources in that category—and there are plenty of them. When you come to the list, tap the + button next to any to add it to Pulse.

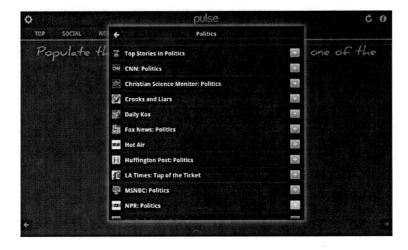

Once you're done, you've got your own customized news feed.

Want to check out Facebook updates and information from other social networking sites? Tap the Social button, and you see information from social networking sites. Log into Facebook, and you see updates from friends.

Edit your pulse feeds

You'll most likely want to change your Pulse feeds constantly as you come across new sites and get tired of old ones. Tap the Settings icon in the upper-left portion of the screen and you come to a list of your feeds, by page. Tap the X on any feed to delete it. Tap the + button to add new feeds.

10 Music

Your Galaxy Tab does a great job of playing and managing music, so much so that you may no longer feel the need to carry around another music player. It includes an excellent built-in music player and manager, and a 3.5-mm headset stereo jack that you can connect to headphones or external speakers.

This chapter gives you all the details about playing and managing music on your Tab, including transferring music files and other files to it.

Transferring Files from Your PC and Mac to Your Galaxy Tab

Your Galaxy Tab is not an island—it's built to work with your computer as well. If you've got a music collection on your PC, for example, you can copy that collection to your Tab and listen to music there. You can also transfer pictures and videos between your Tab and your PC or Mac. In fact, you can transfer any file between your Tab and your computer.

You don't need to be a techie to transfer files; it's generally easy to do. How you do it varies slightly according to whether you've got a PC or a Mac.

Transferring Files from Your PC

To start off, connect your Tab to your PC with your Tab's USB data cable. Connect the micro USB plug into your Tab, and the normal-sized USB plug into your computer's USB port.

Depending on your computer configuration, a number of things may happen at this point. Your computer may automatically recognize your Galaxy Tab as a storage device. If it doesn't, then it may need to install a driver, which it most likely does automatically. After it installs a driver, it pops up a notice in the System Tray telling you it's done so.

From now on, when you connect your Tab, an AutoPlay screen may appear on your PC (as it always does when you connect a USB device to your PC). If it does, select "Open device to view files," and Windows Explorer should open. You can then use Windows Explorer to transfer files between your PC and your Tab. If not, launch Windows Explorer. Your Tab now shows up as a removable disk, just like any USB drive.

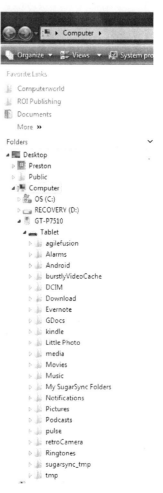

 Before unplugging your Tab from your PC, right-click the Safely Remove Hardware icon in your Windows notification area and select Safely Remove Hardware. Then unplug the USB cord.

You can now use your Tab as if it were any USB flash device—copying files to and from it, creating folders, and so on. That's fine in theory, but in practice, what folders should you transfer files to? Several important folders contain information you might want to transfer from your Tab to your PC, or vice versa.

 Your Tab may not show up in your computer with the name "Galaxy Tab." It may instead have a name such as "GT-P7510." But no matter what it's called, it's still your Galaxy Tab.

You see a lot more folders, but these are the important ones:

- **Downloads.** If you've downloaded content to your Tab from the Internet, such as pictures or web pages, you see it in here.

- **DCIM/camera.** Here's where the Tab stores all the photos you've taken. Drag photos from this folder to your PC to copy them, or drag photos here from your PC to put them into the Tab's Gallery. See page 245 for more information about the Gallery.

- **Music.** The Tab stores music here, although it might also store music in other places. If you download music files using the Amazon music app that's built into the Tab, for example, you find an Amazonmp3 folder where your music is stored.

 Note: If you have DRM-protected music or media on your PC, then when you transfer that music to your Galaxy Tab, the Tab can't play it. DRM stands for *digital rights management*, and it limits the distribution of music files that have been paid for, making it difficult for them to be played on devices other than the one the music was purchased on.

- **Pictures.** Drag photos here, and they also show up in your Gallery. Create subfolders if you want them to show up in their own separate albums—for example, Thanksgiving 2011—and then drag the photos into those subfolders.

- **Movies.** Here's where to drag movies and videos.

Up to Speed

What 3pg Means to Me

There's some tech-talk you need to know before transferring videos from your Tab to your PC. When you record videos on your Tab, they're recorded in a format called .3pg. Depending on the versions of Windows and Windows Media Player you have, your PC may not be able to play those videos. If you have Windows 7 and Windows Media Player 12 or above, then you're set. But if you have Windows Vista, Windows XP, or any version of Windows other than Windows 7, then you're out of luck, since Windows Media Player 12 or above doesn't run on those operating systems.

However, if you're willing to try being a geek for a while, then you can transfer the .3pg files to your PC, and then use a file conversion program to convert the .3pg files to a format that older versions of Windows Media Player can handle, such as .wmv. Go to *www.download.com* or *www.pcworld.com/downloads/downloads.html*, and search for *3pg* or *media converter*.

Transferring Files from Your Mac

As with a PC, first connect your Galaxy Tab to your Mac using the USB cable. But unlike with the PC, after you connect, nothing happens—your Mac doesn't recognize the Tab. It needs special software to do that. Go to *www.android.com/filetransfer* and download the Android File Transfer tool. It works only with Mac OS X 10.5 or later. Once you do that, use the tool to transfer files, in the same way as in Windows. The tool looks and works much like Finder.

Playing Windows Media Files

If you've got a collection of files in Microsoft's Windows Media Audio (.wma) and Windows Media Video (.wmv), you'll be pleased with what you're about to hear: Your Tab's Music app plays .wma files, and its Gallery plays .wmv files. The Android operating system normally doesn't play those file types, but Samsung did a little bit of magic (adding what's called a codec) to let your Tab play them. Some smartphones, such as the Droid, Droid 2, and Droid X play these music files, while other smartphones, and the Xoom tablet, do not.

You can also use various conversion tools to convert .wma to .mp3 and .wmv video files to .mp4 files that can be played on the Tab. Go to *www.download.com* or *www.pcworld.com/downloads/downloads.html*, and search for terms such as "media converter."

Playing Music

Before you play music, of course, you first need to get it onto your Tab. The best way to do that is to transfer music from your PC or Mac to your Tab, as described in the first part of this chapter. You can also buy or download music via apps, such as the Amazon MP3 app available from the Market. (At this writing, rumor has it that Google is working on a music service as well.)

Using the Music App

You play and manage your music using the Tab's Music app. Tap the Music app on your Home Screen to launch it.

You come to a screen with a 3D interface that lets you scroll through your entire music collection by flicking—the "New and recent" view. But there are plenty of other views as well. (When you switch from "New and recent" to another view, the interface changes from 3D to 2D.) Tap the triangle next to the "New and recent" button at the upper left, and you see these other choices:

- **New and recent.** Shows the newest music in your collection, and the music you've played most recently.

- **Albums.** Lists all the CDs (albums) in your music collection. If a thumbnail picture of the album is available, you see it next to the album listing. Each album lists its name and its singer, composer, band, or orchestra, and the number of cuts in the album. Tap the album to see a list of all the songs in the album. To play any song, tap it.

- **Artists.** Shows every singer, composer, and band in your collection, and the number of songs or albums you have from that particular artist.

  Tap the artist's name, and you see a list of all of her albums, including the album name, and how many songs are included from that album, even if that's only one song. Tap an album's name, and you see a list of all the songs it contains. To play any song, tap it.

- **Songs.** Displays an alphabetical list of every song in your music collection. It shows the song name and artist. Tap a song to play it.

- **Playlists.** Here's where you find all your playlists—groups of songs that you've put together in a specific order for a specific reason. You might have several party playlists, a playlist of songs you like to listen to while you work, another for working out, and so on.

  To see the contents of a playlist, tap the playlist. Tap any song to play it from that point until the end of the playlist. To play the entire playlist, hold your finger on the playlist, and then tap Play.

- **Genres.** Displays your music by genre, such as Classical, Jazz, Hip-Hop/Rap, and so on.

Playing Music

Tap a song to play it, and a screen loaded with information and controls appears.

Among other controls, you find the familiar Pause, Play, Previous, and Next ones at the bottom of the screen.

Also at the bottom of the screen is a slider that shows you the progress of the song. It includes the total length of the song, and how much of it you've already played. Move the slider to go to a specific location in the song.

The Shuffle button ![shuffle] is also useful. The music player normally plays the songs in your playlist or album in order, from first to last. Tap the Shuffle button to have the songs in your current album or playlist play in a random order—you'll never know what's coming next.

If you can't get enough of the current album or playlist, tap the Loop button ![loop], and it plays endlessly from beginning to end, from beginning to end, from beginning to...you get the idea. When you tap it, the Loop button turns green plays the album or playlist in a loop. Tap it again, and it plays the current song continuously. The Loop button displays the number 1 ![loop1] to show you that you're in this mode. Tap the button again to turn looping off.

The left side of the screen contains the Song, Artist, and Album buttons and information. It tells you the name of the song, artist, and album, but those buttons do more as well. Tap the Song button to add the current song to a playlist. Tap the Artist button to see all the music you have from the artist. Tap the Album button to return to the Album view.

Album View

Tap an album, and you see a listing of all of its songs. Tap the first song, and it plays, followed by every other song in the album, in turn.

As the music plays, you see a small animated indicator next to the song being played , showing the song's loudness. At the bottom of the screen you see the usual music controls for play, pause, and so on. It's called the Now Playing Bar, and if a song is playing, it shows up everywhere you go, even if you're in another album.

> **Tip** To turn off the Now Playing Bar, tap the Menu button, and then select "Hide now playing bar." To turn it back on again, tap the Menu button and select "Show now playing bar."

Want to shuffle the album? You guessed it: tap the Shuffle button.

Creating Playlists

Wherever you are, you have an easy way to add music to a playlist or create a new playlist. When you're playing an album, tap the triangle to the right of a song, and a menu appears that lets you play a song or add it to a playlist. When you're playing a single song, tap the Menu button, and then select Add to playlist. You can then add it to an existing playlist or create a new one and add it to the list.

To play a playlist, go to the Playlist view of the Music app (page 230) and then tap the playlist you want to play.

Using Your Galaxy Tab While Playing Music

Because the Galaxy Tab is built for multitasking, you can play music even when you're doing something else with your Tab. Open the Music app, start the music, and then feel free to use other apps and features. The music keeps playing. While music is playing, a small icon of a pair of headphones appears in the Notification Panel. Tap it, and you get a small version of the usual set of controls for playing music.

Even when your Tab is locked, the music keeps playing (if you were playing music before it locked). You have to unlock the Tab to use music controls, though.

Using the Google Cloud Music Player

You can update the Galaxy Tab's built-in music player to the Google Cloud Music player, a remarkable piece of software that lets you play music that isn't on your Tab and instead lives in the *cloud*—a bunch of big Google computers that store your music and stream it to your Tab.

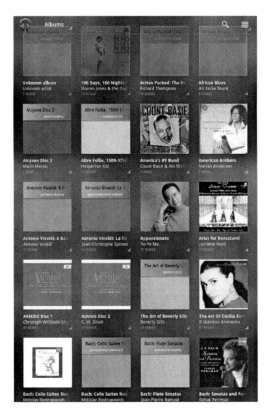

To upgrade to the Google Cloud player, head to the Android Market (page 90). Once you've done so, you'll not only be able to play music on your Tab, but also any music that you upload to the cloud—potentially thousands more songs than your tablet can hold. The Cloud Music Player looks and works much like the built-in Music player, but it has extra features for playing music from the cloud. For details, see page 230.

Using the Samsung Music Player

If you're looking for a quick way to play music, without frills or many extra features, you'll want to give Samsung's Music Player a try. To run it, tap the up arrow in the bottom middle of the Galaxy Tab screen; this displays the half-a-dozen built-in Samsung apps. Then tap Music Player.

 Tip If the Music Player doesn't show music when you launch it, tap the small list icon at the top right of the screen, next to the X. You'll then see a list of your music.

It's simple, straightforward, and self-explanatory. It runs as a widget, listing all the music on your Galaxy Tab. Tap a song to play it. The song will be highlighted in blue and you'll see a visual indication of the loudness of the music. At the bottom of the widget are the usual controls for playing, pausing, and navigating through music.

Tap the rightward-facing triangle at the top of the screen and you'll switch views—you'll see a picture of the album playing. The rightward-facing triangle turns to a list icon. Tap the list icon to see a list of your music.

Tip When you run the Music Player widget-sized, it always appears on your screen, playing your music, even when you're running another app. To make the widget go away, tap the X on the upper-right of the screen. The widget vanishes, but the music still plays. Down in the Notifications area, you'll see an icon of a music note. Tap it and the music note is replaced by a small set of controls for playing the current song. To close the player completely, tap the X.

If you'd like to run the player full-screen and get access to some extra features, tap the upward-facing arrow on the upper left of the screen. The player goes full screen, and you've got extra features, including shuffle, more ways to navigate through the song and your music collection, and so on.

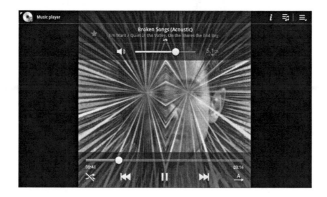

Tap the Menu button on the upper right of the screen for extra options, such as creating a playlist and changing the order of your music. To switch between the full-screen album view and full-screen list view, tap the icon to the left of the Menu button.

To get more information about the current track, including a biography (if one is available) of the current artist and his discography, tap the small Information button.

For an even more complete list of all of your music, and to navigate through it by album, artist, genre, composer, and so on, tap the icon of a CD on the upper left of the screen.

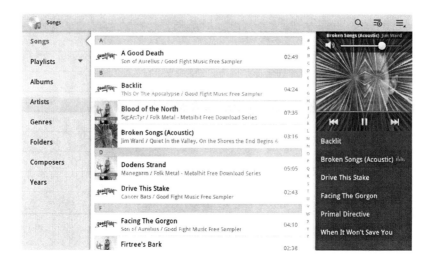

Using the Music Hub

There's another way to play and manage music on your Tab—use the built-in Music Hub app. Get to it from the Apps tray.

There's a big difference between the Music Hub and the Music Player. The Music Hub is designed for purchasing and playing music. You can't, for example, use it to play music that you've dragged into your Tab, or music from the cloud. Instead, it's a hub for buying music, and then playing and managing music you buy. It's easy to use, so if you want to buy music, head over. Keep in mind, though, that if your interests stray far from popular and pop, you may not find much that interests you.

11 Camera, Photos, and Video

Your Galaxy Tab is great at many things, and its multimedia capabilities are among the best of them. It's got a big, beautiful 10.1-inch high-definition screen to show off pictures and videos, and two built-in cameras: a 5-megapixel camera and a 2-megapixel webcam. This chapter gives you all the details about taking and viewing photos and videos with your Tab.

Opening the Gallery

You have five ways to get photos or videos into your Galaxy Tab:

- Transferring them from your PC or Mac (see page 227 for details).
- Taking a photo using the Tab's built-in camera.
- Downloading them from the Web.
- Getting them by email.
- Using Google's Picasa photo-sharing service on the Web.

 Note You don't need to do anything to make photos, pictures, and videos show up in the Gallery. The Galaxy Tab automatically finds and displays them, wherever they are.

No matter how you get them, though, you view them in the same way, by using the Gallery app. Here's how to use it:

1. In the App Menu, tap the Gallery icon.

   The Gallery screen appears. You see all of the "albums" on your Tab. Each album shows photos, pictures, and videos organized by folder—for example, Family, Tahiti (you should be so lucky!), and so on. Underneath each album is its name and how many photos are in it.

Tip When you hold your Galaxy Tab at an angle, you see that the album display is 3D—thumbnails appear behind the primary thumbnail for each album. Tilt and move the Tab, and those 3D thumbnails move their direction.

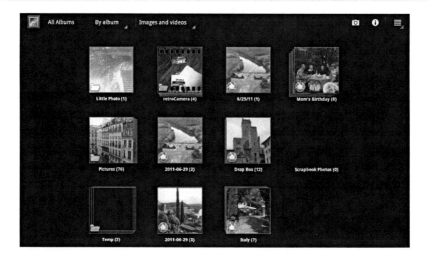

2. Tap an album.

   The screen fills with thumbnails of the photos in the album. If you hold the Tab horizontally, then you see 18 thumbnails and portions of three others. If you hold it vertically, then you see 24 thumbnails and small portions of six others.

Note Some albums have thumbnails underneath them that indicate their origin. For example, if you use Google's Picasa online photo site and sync to it, any albums synced from Picasa have a small Picasa symbol underneath them.

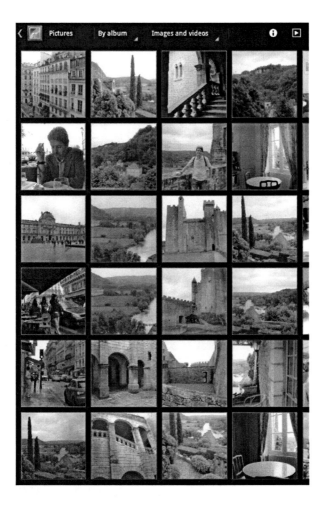

3. Tap the photo you want to view.

 Your videos also appear in the Gallery app, and you view and work with them in exactly as you do with photos.

The photo displays on the Galaxy Tab's big, beautiful screen. Now you can see why you wanted the Tab—the big screen is spectacular for viewing photos. On the upper left of the screen, you see the file name of the photo. Down at the bottom of the screen is a filmstrip that shows all of the pictures in your current album; tap any to view that picture. And across the upper right are icons for performing a variety of actions, such as launching a slideshow and sharing the photo. (For more details about how to use these buttons, see page 252.) After a moment, the buttons and filmstrip vanish.

Depending on the photo's length-to-width ratio, and whether you're holding the Tab horizontally or vertically, it may not fill the entire screen. If it doesn't, you see black space along the sides or at the top and bottom.

Tip To make the buttons and film strip appear again after they vanish, tap the photo.

What Do Those Album Icons in the Gallery Mean?

If you're in the main Gallery, notice a number of icons in the lower-left corner of each of your albums. Here's what they mean:

- **A folder icon**  means that the album is in a folder in your Galaxy Tab's storage.

- **A camera icon** shows the album of photos you've taken with the Tab's camera. Not that you really need to know, but the photo lives in the Tab DCIM/camera folder, because that's where your Tab stores the photos you take.

- **A Picasa icon** means that the album is in Google's photo-sharing site. Your Tab is set to automatically sync photos with your Tab. For more details about Picasa, see page 257.

Browsing an Album

When you browse an album, you find several controls along the top:

- **Album name** 2009-06-28 Venice displays the name of the album.

- **By album** By album lets you change whether you want to browse by album name, time of photos, location of photos, or tags that have been applied to photos. Tap it to reveal the options and make your choice.

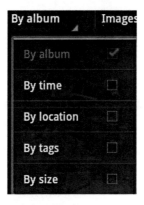

- **Images and videos** Images and videos lets you change whether to display both images and video, only images, or only video. Tap it to reveal the options and make your choice.

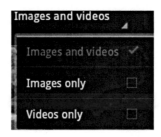

- **Information** displays a panel that shows a variety of information about whatever picture is highlighted, including whether there are any tags, the time and date it was taken, where it was taken (if that information is available), resolution, file size, camera maker, when it was last modified…there's far more than you need here, including details such as the aperture, exposure time, and whether a flash was used.

> **Note** A *tag* is a keyword that you can attach to a photo's file information to make it easy to find later. The tag isn't visible in the photo itself. You can add any tag you want, such as Family, Food, and so on. Some cameras automatically add tags to photos, including the date and time they were taken. The Tab can also add *geotag* information—the location where the photo was taken.

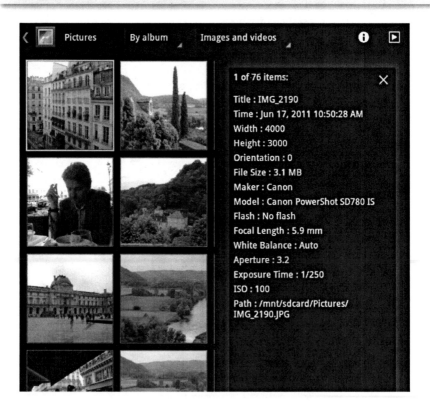

Pictures | By album | Images and videos

1 of 76 items:

Title : IMG_2190
Time : Jun 17, 2011 10:50:28 AM
Width : 4000
Height : 3000
Orientation : 0
File Size : 3.1 MB
Maker : Canon
Model : Canon PowerShot SD780 IS
Flash : No flash
Focal Length : 5.9 mm
White Balance : Auto
Aperture : 3.2
Exposure Time : 1/250
ISO : 100
Path : /mnt/sdcard/Pictures/
IMG_2190.JPG

- **Slideshow** plays a slideshow of all the photos in the current album.

Viewing Pictures

Now that you've got photos on your screen, the fun begins—viewing them in different ways, and flicking through them:

- **Zooming** means magnifying a photo, and you've got the power to do that at your fingertips—literally. Double-tap any part of the photo, and you zoom in on that area; double-tap again, and you zoom out. You can also use the thumb-and-forefinger spread technique (page 59) to zoom in more precise increments. Once you've zoomed in this way, you can zoom back out by using the two-finger pinch technique or the double-tap technique.

- **Panning** means moving the photo around the Tab's screen after you've zoomed in, so you can see different areas. Use your finger to drag the photo around.

> **Note** Zooming and panning still work when you hold the Tab horizontally—simply use the same techniques as when the Tab is vertical.

- **Rotating** means turning your Tab 90 degrees so it's sideways. When you do so, the photo rotates and fills the screen in the new orientation. This technique is especially useful when you have a horizontal photo that looks small when your Tab is in its normal vertical position. Rotate the Tab, and like magic, the picture rotates and fills the screen properly. If you're holding the Tab horizontally and viewing a vertical picture, simply rotate the Tab 90 degrees, and your photo rotates as well.

- **Flicking** (page 32) advances you to the next or previous photo in your list. Flick from right to left to view the next photo, and from left to right to view the previous one.

 If you flick the photo when you're zoomed in, you don't move to the next photo. Instead, you just pan it. Zoom out if you want to use the flick technique to move to the next photo.

Photo Info, Slideshows, and More

Tap a photo, and a toolbar of icons appears across the top:

- **Tap the Slideshow button** , and a slideshow of all the photos in that album starts to play, beginning with the current photo.
- **Tap the Share button** , and you can share the photo via Google's Picasa photo-sharing service (see page 257 for details), Bluetooth, Gmail, or Email, or in any other way that the software on your Tab allows.
- **Tap the Delete button** to delete the photo.
- **Tap the Menu button** to get details about the photo, rotate it right or left, crop it, or use it as your wallpaper or as a photo for a contact.

Working with Multiple Photos

In the previous section, you learned about ways to work with individual photos. But what if you want to work with multiple photos at once—share them or delete them, let's say?

When you're viewing photos in an album, press and hold your finger on the first photo you want to work with in a group. It turns green. Then press and hold your finger on the next, then the next, and so on, until you've selected all that you want to work with. They're all green.

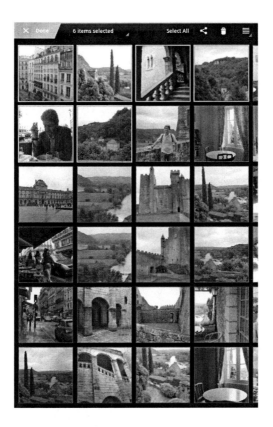

At the top of the screen, you get a message telling you how many you've chosen. If you want to select all the photos in the album, tap Select All. Now that you've got your photos selected, tap the appropriate button on the top of the screen for taking an action. You can share them or delete them in the same way you can individual photos. Tap the Menu key, and you can rotate them left or right. After you complete your action, the photos are deselected.

If you want to call the whole thing off, tap the X button.

 The options you have for working with multiple photos vary according to whether you've taken the photos on the Galaxy Tab, or whether you've copied the photos to the Tab from your computer or online. The option for deleting a group of photos won't appear when you select a group of photos that have been copied to the Galaxy Tab, but it will appear when you select a group of photos that you've taken on the Tab.

Handy Options in the Gallery

Notice that if you're at the top of the Gallery—that is, viewing all of the albums in it—there's a toolbar across the top with familiar buttons.

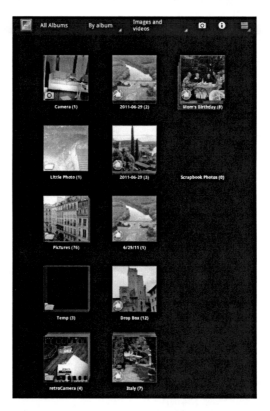

You already know what just about all of those buttons can do, except two:

- **Camera button** . Yes, you guessed right. Tap it to launch the camera app. See page 265 for more details.

- **Menu button** ▤. Tap this and a new option appears—Make available offline. Tap it, and then press Done.

As this book went to press, Google's photo-sharing service was called Picasa. But rumors were flying that it would be renamed Google Photo. So if you find a service called Google Photo rather than Picasa, don't be confused—it's the same thing with a different name.

Sharing Photos with Picasa

You have many ways to share photos with others, especially on the Web. If you're interested in sharing photos from your Tab with others via a web-based photo-sharing service, your best bet is Picasa from Google, since you can upload photos to it directly from your Tab with a simple tap or two.

 This chapter won't cover all of Picasa's features on the Web. To learn more about those, head to *www.picasa.com*.

Right out of the box, your Tab is set to share photos using your Picasa account—in fact, it's set to sync with your Picasa account as well (page 263). So if you have a Picasa account, the albums and photos you have there will automatically show up in the Tab's Gallery. When you view albums in the Gallery, any that are from Picasa will show the Picasa icon in their lower-left corners ▢.

Your Tab is set to share and sync photos with the Picasa account connected to the Tab's primary Gmail address. So you might want to log into that Picasa account on the Web, and make sure that you're sharing photos using the account you think you are. And you also might want to log into it and make sure that the account settings are exactly what you want.

Head to *www.picasaweb.google.com* with a computer or your Tab, and then sign in with the email address and password of the Google account that's your primary Google account for your Tab. Again, though, you don't need to take this step if you don't want to. Your Tab is already set to work with the Picasa account connected to your Tab's primary Gmail account.

 If you go to *www.picasa.com* with your PC, then you're asked to download Picasa software, but you don't need to do that. That's only if you want to download and use the Picasa photo-editing software on your PC. Photo sharing via Picasa on the Web doesn't require that software. Look for the Picasa Web Albums link, and click that to get to Picasa on the Web. If you go to *www.picasa.com* with your Tab, then you may be asked to download Linux software. Again, you don't need to do this. Look for the Picasa Web Albums link, and click that to get to Picasa on the Web.

Now go to the Gallery on your Tab. From here you can upload your photos to Picasa. You can either upload a single photo or multiple photos. Here's how to upload multiple photos:

1. Open an album, and then select the photos you want to share by pressing and holding your finger on each until it turns green.

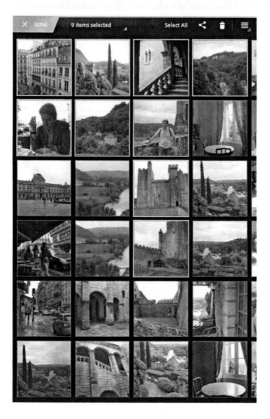

2. Tap the Share button ![share], and, from the screen that appears, select Picasa.

3. On the screen that appears, fill in the form. Type a caption for the photo or photos. (If you select multiple photos, they all share the same caption.)

4. Select the Picasa album to which you want to upload the photos by tapping the small triangle next to the album name (by default, it's Drop Box).

   If you want to add a new album and upload to that, tap the + sign, type in the new album name, and select whether you want the album to be public or unlisted—that is, visible only to you and those you designate.

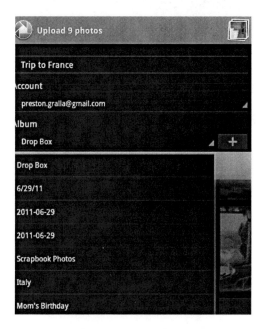

5. Tap the Upload button, or tap Cancel if you decide not to upload.

A notice on your screen tells you that the photos are being uploaded. The Notification Panel also tells you that they're being uploaded.

6. If you want to see the progress of the files being uploaded, tap the notification.

Thumbnails of all files you're uploading appear, along with information about each—whether it has successfully uploaded, whether it's waiting to be uploaded, and whether it's in the progress of being uploaded. If it's in progress, then you see what percentage of the photo has already been uploaded.

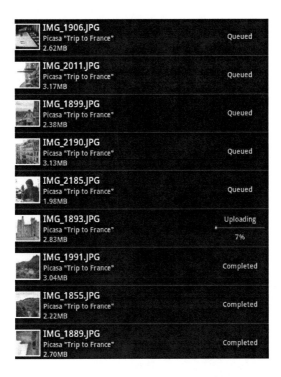

IMG_1906.JPG Picasa "Trip to France" 2.62MB	Queued
IMG_2011.JPG Picasa "Trip to France" 3.17MB	Queued
IMG_1899.JPG Picasa "Trip to France" 2.38MB	Queued
IMG_2190.JPG Picasa "Trip to France" 3.13MB	Queued
IMG_2185.JPG Picasa "Trip to France" 1.98MB	Queued
IMG_1893.JPG Picasa "Trip to France" 2.83MB	Uploading 7%
IMG_1991.JPG Picasa "Trip to France" 3.04MB	Completed
IMG_1855.JPG Picasa "Trip to France" 2.22MB	Completed
IMG_1889.JPG Picasa "Trip to France" 2.70MB	Completed

The Tab notifies you when the upload is complete.

7. Head to Picasa on the Web with either your PC or Galaxy Tab.

There your photos are, in all their Tab-taken glory! You can now use them and share them like you can any other Picasa photos.

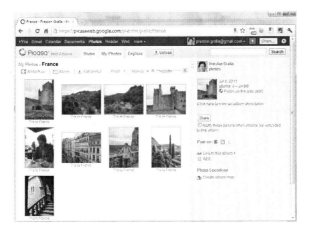

Using Picasa on the Web with Your Galaxy Tab

When you visit *www.picasaweb.google.com* with your Galaxy Tab, you see and use the Picasa site, just like you see it and use it on a computer.

Google has also built a site specifically designed for mobile phones, and if you'd like, you can head there on your Tab as well. Go to *www.picasaweb .com/m* using your Tab's browser. But it's a very bare-bones site, stripped down for smartphones, and not particularly suitable for your Tab's large screen.

Turning Off Picasa Sync

Out of the box, your Galaxy Tab syncs albums from Picasa to your Tab by downloading them, and then syncing any changes.

 Note Although the Tab downloads and syncs albums from Picasa, it doesn't automatically upload albums and photos from your Tab to Picasa. Instead, you have to manually upload photos, as described in this section.

You can, however, tell your Tab not to download and sync Picasa albums—for example, to save storage space on your Tab. To do it, from the Home screen, tap the Notifications Panel, and then tap Settings→Accounts and Sync. In the Manage Accounts section, tap your Google account. Uncheck the box next to Picasa to stop the syncing. Any Picasa albums already on your Tab remain there, but no new Picasa ones will be added.

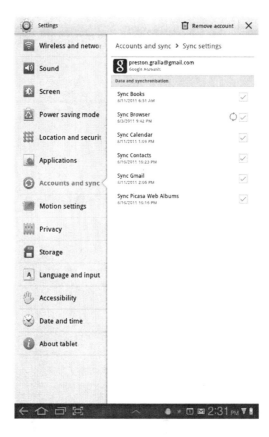

Videos in the Gallery

The way you view and work with videos in the Gallery is essentially identical to the way you work with photos, with just a few minor differences:

- When you tap a video, it opens with a right-facing triangle—the Play button. Tap the triangle to play the video. When the video plays, a circle moves along a progress bar to show where you are in the video. Drag the circle forward or back to move forward or back in the video. Tap the Pause button to pause the video; tap the Play button to start playing it again.

Taking Still Photos

Your Galaxy Tab has a 5-megapixel camera for taking photos, and it's a snap to use. To launch the camera, tap the Camera app in the Apps Menu, or launch it directly from the Gallery (see page 245).

Frame your shot on the screen. You can use the camera either in the vertical or horizontal orientation. Take the photo by tapping the shutter button on the screen. You hear the familiar snap sound of a photo being taken. After the photo is taken, it's saved to your Tab's storage. A thumbnail appears in the lower-left portion of the screen. Tap the thumbnail, and you go to the picture in the Gallery.

The Camera app bristles with controls. Here's what they do:

- **Return** 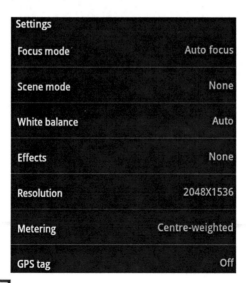 sends you to where you were before you launched the camera. If you launched the camera from the Gallery, you return there, and if you launched it from the App Menu, you return there.

- **Camera settings** ⚙ lets you set a variety of camera settings, such as whether to store geographic information using your GPS, the exposure to use, picture resolution, whether to autofocus, whether to add effects, and others.

Settings	
Focus mode	Auto focus
Scene mode	None
White balance	Auto
Effects	None
Resolution	2048X1536
Metering	Centre-weighted
GPS tag	Off

- **Exposure** lets you change the exposure settings by moving a slider.

- **Timer**  lets you set a timer so that you can take a photo of yourself. You can choose no timer, or else 2, 5, or 10 seconds.

- **Shooting mode**  lets you select a *shooting mode*, essentially a group of already created settings ideal for certain types of photos, like a single shot, a portrait (what it calls a "smile shot"), a panorama, and an action shot.

- **Switch cameras** switches between front- and rear-facing cameras.

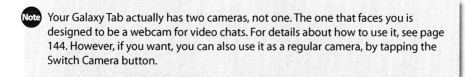

Note Your Galaxy Tab actually has two cameras, not one. The one that faces you is designed to be a webcam for video chats. For details about how to use it, see page 144. However, if you want, you can also use it as a regular camera, by tapping the Switch Camera button.

- **Flash mode** lets you turn the flash on or off, or let the camera decide whether to use it.

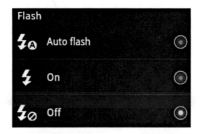

Flash

⚡ᴀ Auto flash ◉

⚡ On ◉

⚡⊘ Off ◉

- **Switch video/photo** switches between using your camera to capture photos or video.
- **Battery indicator** 🔲 shows whether your Tab is plugged in to a power source.
- **Camera button** ⚪ lets you tap to take a photo.

Note To learn how to transfer photos between your Tab and your computer, turn to page 227.

Taking Video

Recording video is much the same as taking a still photo. Put the Tab into Camera mode, tap the screen, and then switch to Camcorder mode. To start recording, tap the red button (it's where the Camera button used to be). The red button turns into a gray square. To stop recording, press it again.

The Tab has a few minor differences in the camera controls for taking video and photos:

- **Settings button**  offers different settings for video than for photos. In video, Settings only lets you change the video resolution and use effects, such as grayscale, sepia, and negative.

- **White balance** replaces the Timer button in photo settings, and lets you change the white balance, depending on the light where you're shooting—daylight, cloudy conditions, incandescent lighting, and fluorescent lighting.

In addition, the button you tap to take a video is a red button, rather than a shutter, as in the camera. And when you record, you see the elapsed time of your video.

What the Flash?

When viewed on the Web, YouTube requires a technology called Flash to play videos. The Galaxy Tab can use Flash, but when it was released, Flash support wasn't yet built in. (Some other tablets, notably the iPad, ban Flash altogether.) So if you have an early Tab and you haven't updated it, you may not have Flash yet. YouTube uses a different format for videos designed for the YouTube app, and it's built into the Tab, so it doesn't stop you from playing YouTube videos.

But on its website, YouTube does use Flash. So if you head to *www.youtube.com*, open a video, tap its Play button, and the video won't play, it probably means you don't have Flash. To get Flash, make sure your Tab's operating system is up to date, as described on page 392. Then go to the Market (page 64) and download Flash.

YouTube

What fun is video if you can't share it? You can always send video files to your friends via email or text message…or share them with the world by uploading them to YouTube. Keep your Galaxy Tab handy, and who knows, your cute laughing baby or sleepy kitten could be the next viral video sensation.

To visit YouTube and watch and share videos, launch the YouTube app in the Apps Menu. You come to a gallery full of YouTube videos, a mix of most popular videos, videos from your YouTube subscriptions, and videos recommended to you based on the past videos you've viewed.

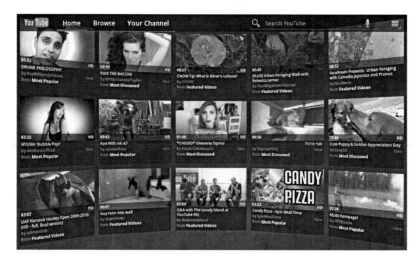

To change your YouTube mobile settings, like the quality of video display, tap the Menu key, and then select Settings. To sign into (or out of) your YouTube account, tap the Menu key and select the appropriate option.

Search YouTube in the usual way, using the search box at the top of the screen.

Playing a Video

To play a video, tap it. The video begins playing automatically. You can play in either the vertical or horizontal orientation.

When you play the video, the usual video controls appear at the bottom of the screen for pause and play, and then vanish.

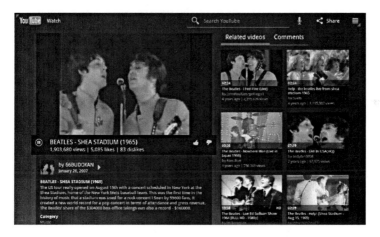

To make video controls appear, tap the video, and they appear not just at the bottom of the video, but on the video as well. You also see a familiar progress bar across the bottom that lets you move forward or back. To the left of the screen there's often an HQ (high quality) button. Tap it to reload the video at a higher quality.

To control the volume, don't use YouTube controls. Instead, use the Tab's volume sliders.

To make the video play full-screen, tap the Full-Screen button  to the left of the video. Once it's playing full-screen, tap the Shrink button ⊠ to return to the normal view.

After a few seconds, the controls disappear. To make them come back, touch the screen.

While you're watching (or pausing) any video, you can do more with it. Tap the Share button to share it with others via Bluetooth, email, or Gmail. Tap the Menu button, and you can perform a variety of tasks, like copying the video's URL, saving it to your Favorites, and flagging it for inappropriate content.

 When you flag a video as being inappropriate, YouTube reviews the video to see whether it violates the company's guidelines for pornography, drug abuse, gratuitous violence, predatory behavior, and so on.

At the bottom of the video are the familiar YouTube features, including giving the video a thumbs-up or thumbs-down, and getting more information about it. To the right of the video are related videos.

Finding Videos

With the countless videos available on YouTube, you can easily find one you want to play. You can either search or browse. To search, merely type in your search term. To browse, tap the Browse button at the top of the screen. You can then browse through YouTube by category, and also see the top-rated or newest videos.

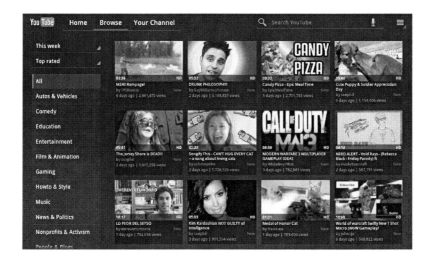

Media Hub

If you want to rent movies and TV shows on your Galaxy Tab, there's a simple way to do it—use the Media Hub. From the Apps Menu, tap Media Hub, and you're ready to go.

You'll likely have to register first. After that, you'll be able to browse and search for movies TV shows. Choose what you want, pay your fee, and enjoy watching.

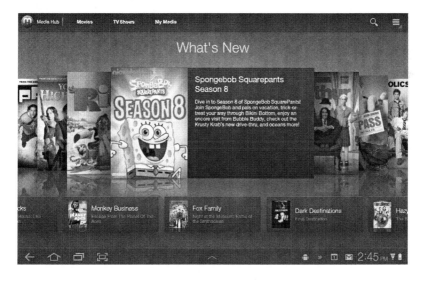

Part 4
Getting Productive

12 Gmail and Email

You want email? You've got email. Your Galaxy Tab does a great job of handling whatever email task you throw at it. Want to send and receive attachments like pictures; Word, Excel, and PowerPoint files; and PDFs? Your Tab can do that. How about working with just about any email service out there? It can do that, too. You can also manage your mail, sync your mail, and plenty more, right on your Tab. It's a great way to have your email always at hand.

This chapter shows you how to get the most out of email on your Tab.

Understanding Email on Your Tablet

Your Galaxy Tab runs on Google's Android operating system, so it comes as no surprise that its main built-in email app is for Gmail. You don't have to use Gmail if you don't want to, though; you can use your current email service instead. Or you can use both.

Gmail on the Tab works a bit differently from other email services, so this chapter covers both methods.

Setting Up Gmail

Android is built from the ground up to integrate with Google services—search, Google Maps, Gmail, Picasa, and plenty more. If you already have a Gmail account, then when you set up your Tab, you tie into that account. If you don't have a Gmail account, you first need to set one up.

 Note When you first bring your Galaxy Tab home, you may already be set up to use Gmail. Sometimes sales staff at retail stores or service providers set up your Gmail account right in the store for you.

When you use the Gmail app on your Tab, it synchronizes with your web-based Gmail. So when you delete an email on the Tab, for example, it deletes it on the web-based Gmail; when you create and send an email on your Tab, it shows up in your Sent folder on the Web; and so on.

Signing up for a Gmail account is free and takes only a few minutes. You can create it on the Web or on the Tab. To do it on the Web, head to *www .gmail.com*. Fill in the usual information, such as first and last name, login name, and password. The login name you choose becomes your email address. If you use the login name ***petey.bigtoes***, then your email address is *petey.bigtoes@gmail.com*. So make your login name something pleasant and easy to remember.

 Note When you create a Gmail account, you're actually setting up an account for all of Google's services, not just Gmail. You use the same account to access Google Calendar and other services. In other words, if you have a Google Calendar account, then you already have a Gmail account. Use that information when setting up Gmail on your Tab.

Now that you have a Gmail account, you're ready to set up Gmail on your Tab. When you set up your Gmail account, you're also setting up your Calendar account and importing your Gmail contacts into your Tab. From the Home screen, tap the Gmail icon. After a brief welcome screen, Gmail asks if you have a Google account. If you haven't already set one up, tap "Create Account," and then fill in the information required.

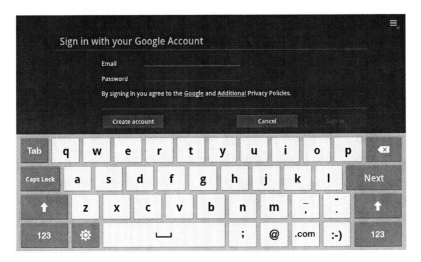

 Note When creating a Gmail account, make sure to leave the box next to "Automatically configure account" turned on. That way, the Tab does all the heavy lifting of properly configuring your new account.

If you already have a Gmail account, tap Sign In. Enter your Gmail address and the other basic information. If you have a Google Contacts list, the Tab automatically starts downloading it in the background; it also syncs your mail.

Tip If you have multiple Gmail accounts, then you can have the Galaxy Tab handle more than one. To set up a second account, when you're in Gmail, tap the Menu button at the top of the screen and then, at the top of the next screen, tap "Add account." From the screen that appears, tap "Create account" to create a new Gmail account, or else type an existing Gmail account's email and password, and then tap "Sign in."

Reading Mail in Gmail

Once you've got your Gmail account set up, it's time to start reading mail. Launch the Gmail app by tapping it on the Home screen or App Menu. Gmail works slightly differently depending on whether you hold your Tab vertically or horizontally—and to make things more confusing, what you see when you launch Gmail varies depending on the last things you've done. Basically, whatever you were doing in Gmail the last time you used it is what you see when you next launch it—for example, browsing through mail in a particular location.

 Note While most email programs use folders to let you organize your email, Google uses labels in its web-based email, and that's what you use on the Tab.

When you launch Gmail on your Tab for the first time, on the left-hand side, you see a list of every Gmail *label* (the term Gmail uses for a folder). The Inbox label is highlighted, and on the right side, you see a list of your most recent email in that label. So far, the horizontal view and vertical view are the same.

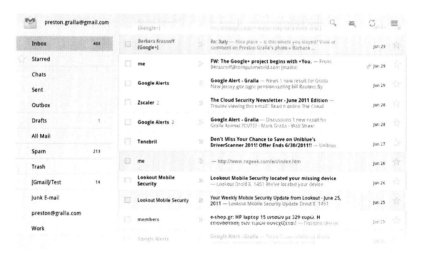

Now tap one of the email messages to read it. Here's where things get different, depending on whether you're holding your Tab vertically or horizontally. Hold your Tab horizontally, and in the left pane you see a list of all the mail with the same label as the email you just tapped. In the right pane, you see the email message.

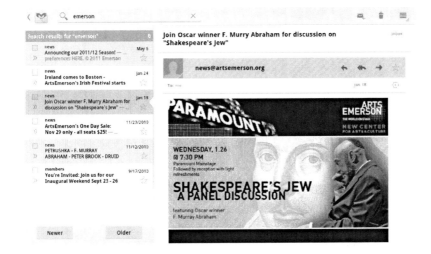

In the left pane, mail you haven't read is boldfaced and has a white background; the rest of your mail is in a normal font and has a gray background. At top left is your email address, and just above the message you're reading is the label you're viewing, and the total number of unread emails in that label.

The right pane shows the message. You can scroll up, down, and sideways in the message using the normal Tab gestures of dragging and flicking.

 Note The Tab regularly checks your Gmail account for new mail, and if it finds any, it sends a notification via the Notification Panel. Tap the notification to launch Gmail. If you want Gmail to check for mail right now, tap the Refresh button ↻ at the top of most Gmail pages.

When you're viewing mail in a list like this, each piece of mail in the list at left shows the following:

- The sender.
- The subject line.
- The date it was sent; or, if it was sent today, the time it was sent.

Now say that you hold the Galaxy Tab vertically. Tap the message you want to read, and things look different.

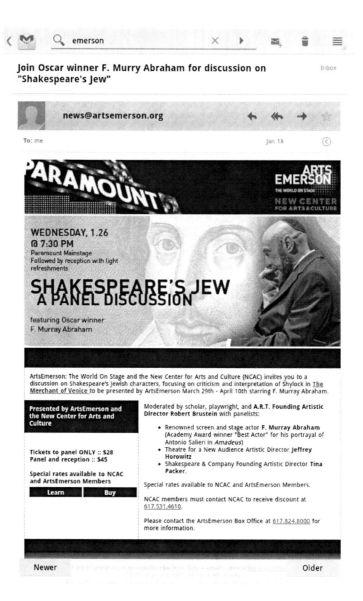

Now you see only the message itself; the left-hand pane and its list disappears. You navigate through the email message using the usual Tab gestures.

Notice the Gmail icon in the upper-left corner. That's not just for branding; it actually serves a very useful navigation function—think of it as walking you back up the navigation ladder. So, for example, say you're holding the Tab vertically and you're reading a message. You see only the message at that point, with no left pane. Tap the Gmail icon, and you go back to the label's list view. Tap it again, and you go to the view that shows all your labels. The same type of navigation works when holding the Tab horizontally. When you're viewing a list of all email in a label, tap the icon and you get to the view showing all your labels.

Ready for a fancy Galaxy Tab trick? If you're holding the Tab vertically and viewing an email, turn it horizontally. You go to the horizontal two-paned view, with the list of emails in your current label in the left pane, and the email message at right.

So, which view is best? That depends on what you're doing. For browsing and scrolling through many emails, the horizontal view is best. You can scan the list, tap a message, and read it in the right pane. Tap another message, and it shows up in the pane instead. But if you're reading a long email message, then the vertical view is best; when you're in that view, the message gets more screen real estate.

 When you leave Gmail, the next time you open it, it opens to the last task you were doing—for example, browsing through your Inbox.

When you read a message, no matter which view you're in, all the links in the email message are live—tap them, and you go to the web page to which they're linked, using the Tab's web browser. Tap an email address, and a new email message opens to that address. Tap a YouTube video, and the video plays, and so on.

In fact, in many instances, the text in the email message doesn't even need to be a link for the Tab to take some kind of action on it. If you tap a street address, for example, the Tab shows you that location in Google Maps.

 Gmail, Google Calendar, and your Gmail contacts are all setup to sync between your Tab and your various Google accounts on the Web. This all happens automatically, in the background, without your having to take any action. You can turn syncing off, or choose to sync manually, though. For details, see page 379.

Handling Graphics in Gmail

You get two basic kinds of graphics in Gmail. Some are embedded in the content of the message itself—for example, a company logo. Other times, the sender attaches an image to a message—like a family member sending you Thanksgiving photos.

If the graphics are embedded in the content of the message, you see a button titled Show Pictures. In some cases, you don't really need to see the graphics (who cares what a company's logo looks like, really?). In that case, do nothing. However, in other cases, the graphic is an integral part of the message, like a graph or a map. If that happens, tap Show Pictures. You see all the graphics on full display, right in the message.

If someone has attached a graphic, you see a small thumbnail of the graphic displayed in the email message. Tap Show Pictures and you see the graphic itself, right in the email. To view the graphic in the Gallery and make use of all of the Gallery's considerable features, tap View. (To learn more about the Gallery, see page 245.)

To save the picture to your Tab, tap Save, and it gets downloaded to the Gallery.

Attachments in Gmail

Gmail lets you preview and download a variety of attachments, including graphics in the .jpg, .png, and .gif formats; and Microsoft Office files, such as Word, Excel, and PowerPoint files, among others. Some file attachments, though, you can't preview or download.

If you get an attachment that you can preview, then you see a paper clip icon near the top of the mail. The attachment's name and a View and a Save button also appear next to the paper clip icon. Tap the View button, and the attachment opens. If it's a Word, Excel, or PowerPoint file, it opens in an app called QuickOffice that's built into the Galaxy Tab.

Tip Tap the Save button next to an attachment, and it gets saved to your Tab. However, you may have a tough time finding it; sometimes the attachment seems to vanish. Fear not—it exists. It's probably in the */mnt/sdcard/Download* folder. How to get to that folder to see it? You need a file manager app. A very good free one is Astro, available in the Android Market. For more details about Astro, see page 115.

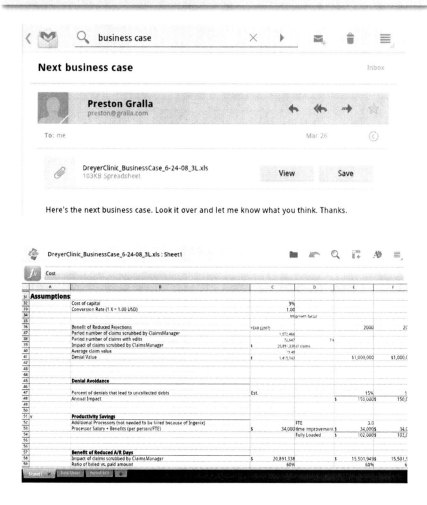

Add the Sender to Your Contacts

If you're reading an email message from someone and want to add her to your Contacts list, tap the picture or graphic to the left of her name. A screen appears that lets you add the contact to your Contacts list.

Add contact

Add "<news@artsemerson.org>" to contacts?

OK   Cancel

If the person is already in your Contacts list, then when you tap the name, a list of icons appears that lets you respond to her in a number of ways, including by email, chat, video chat, and so on.

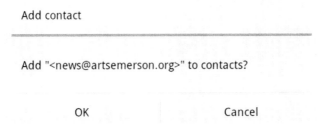

More Message Tricks

Want a streamlined view of your email message so you can read it at glance, and do away with the various buttons used for replying to and forwarding mail? It's easy to do. Just tap the colored bar at the top of the email. The buttons disappear…and so does the body of email message. The message gets put right into the bar itself (or at least as much as will fit there) for a stripped-down look at the email. Tap the message again, and the normal view returns.

Now would you like to see even more details about the mail? Tap "Show details," and you see more information, including the date and recipient (that means you, and any others who were copied on the email). Tap "Hide details" and the details vanish.

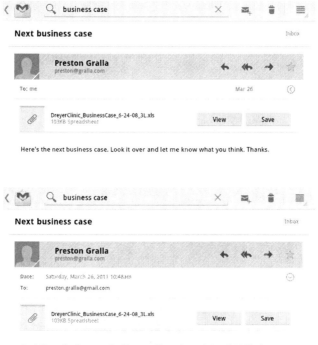

Replying and Forwarding in Gmail

Near the top of the screen in Gmail, next to the sender's name, you find a small toolbar of icons for replying to and forwarding mail:

- ← Replies to the message's sender only. A new email window opens, addressed to the sender, with the original email text quoted in it. If there's an attachment in the original email, it isn't included.

- ↞ If the email was sent to multiple people, this replies to the sender of the message, *and* to all the recipients in a new email window, with the original message quoted in it. You can always add new recipients or delete existing ones. If there's an attachment in the original email, it isn't included.

- ➥ This forwards the message. It opens a new email window with a blank To: field that you can fill in. The message includes the entire email you opened, including any attachments.

- ☆ Marks the message as being important by turning the star gold. From now on, a gold star appears next to the message in the Inbox or any other label you view it in. If the message already displays a star, tap it to remove it. You can also go to the Star label and see only starred email.

 Tip You can also star or unstar mail in the Inbox or any other label. To add a star to an email message, tap the star icon. To take away a star, tap any gold star, and it turns gray.

Understanding Gmail's Organization

Gmail has its own terminology and worldview when it comes to handling email, so you have some new terms and ideas to get used to. Here are the most common Gmail concepts:

- **Labels.** Think of these as email folders. Your regular email program has a folder called Inbox, for example, and lets you create other folders, such as Family, Work, and so on. Gmail calls these email containers *labels*.

  That said, there's a slight underlying difference between the way you work with Gmail's labels and how you work with your email program's folders. In your typical email program, you might move mail between folders by dragging. Not so in Gmail. In Gmail, you affix a label to an email message. When you do that, that email automatically appears when you sort for that label.

  Labels actually give you more flexibility than folders, since you can attach multiple labels to a single email message to have it show up in multiple labels. For example, if you get an email from your brother about advice for your upcoming trip to France, you can add the labels Family and France to the email. That message then shows up in both your Family label and your France label.

The Tab's Gmail app is designed to work in concert with Gmail on the Web. So you can't do everything in the Gmail app that you can do on the Web. The Tab's Gmail app can't create labels, for example, so to create new ones, you must visit your Gmail account on the Web, using either the Tab's browser or a computer.

- **Overall mail organization.** Because Gmail uses labels rather than folders, you may find mail in more than one location. Also, unlike some email software, Gmail gives you the option of viewing all mail in one single area titled All Mail, including both mail you've sent and received.

  Chats appear in Gmail on both the web client and on the Tab.

 If you use Google Chat, either on a computer or on your Galaxy Tab, then the conversations you have appear in your Gmail All Mail label. They also show up in the Chats label. If you use the Google Buzz social networking service, then that information shows up in All Mail as well.

- **Archive.** In some instances, you get mail that you want to keep around but don't want showing up in your Inbox, because your Inbox would otherwise get too cluttered. So Gmail lets you *archive* messages. Archiving a message doesn't delete it, but it removes it from your Inbox. You can still find the message listed in your All Mail label. You can also find it by searching.

Managing Incoming Mail in Gmail

Once you've read a Gmail message, it's time to decide what to do with it. Navigation buttons at the top of the email help:

- **Archive.** Tap this button to archive the message. It vanishes from your Inbox, but still appears in All Mail.

- **Delete.** Sends your email to the Gmail Trash. The mail is available in the Trash for 30 days, so you can view it there if needed—but after 30 days it gets deleted forever. When you delete mail, you see a notification at the top of your Inbox, telling you how much mail you've deleted, and letting you undo the deletion—in other words, take the message out of the Trash.

- **Menu.** ≡ Tap this button, and you get several more options.

That's just the beginning, though. Tap the Menu key, and you have these options:

- **Mark unread.** When new mail comes into your Inbox, its background is highlighted in white, and its text is bold. After you read it, the background turns gray, which marks it as being read. This feature lets you easily see which messages you haven't yet read. If you want to keep the current email message looking like a new one (because you want to make sure you read it again later, for example), then tap this button.

Mark unread

Report spam

Mute

Refresh

Settings

Help

Feedback?

- **Change labels.** Even if you haven't applied a label to a piece of mail in your Inbox, it already has a label pre-applied to it—Inbox. Tap this button to change the label by adding more labels to the message, or taking away existing labels, such as the Inbox label. If you take away the Inbox label, then the message appears in All Mail, but not your Inbox. When you tap the button, a screen appears with your labels on it. The labels for the mail you're reading have green checkmarks next to them. Add checkmarks for all the labels you want to add, and remove checks for labels you want to remove.

Labels

☑ Inbox

☐ [Gmail]/Test

☐ Junk E-mail

☐ preston@gralla.com

☐ Work

OK   Cancel

Mail stays in your Inbox until you take away the Inbox label. So if you want to keep your Inbox clean, remove the Inbox label from incoming email regularly. It's a good idea to add other labels to your messages, though, so you can easily find them later.

- **Report spam.** Tap the Report Spam button, and a note goes to Google saying you believe the email is spam. Google uses that information to determine which mail should be considered spam and automatically rerouted into people's Spam labels.

 When you get a message that Gmail considers spam, it isn't automatically deleted. Instead, it shows up in your Spam label. It doesn't appear in All Mail, or anywhere else in Gmail. It also doesn't appear when you search through your email.

- **Mute.** Tap, and the email and all conversations related to it bypass your Inbox and are automatically archived. When you mute a piece of mail, you're not just archiving that one piece of mail, but the entire "conversation" of which it's a part. Let's say, for example, you subscribe to a mailing list, and there is a long, ongoing series of back-and-forth emails about a topic in which you have no interest. (Justin Bieber, anyone?) You're tired of seeing mails in that conversation pop up in your Inbox. Tap the Mute button, and you don't see it in your Inbox anymore. However, it still appears in All Mail.

- **Refresh.** Need to find out if you've gotten email this very instant? Tap Refresh and Gmail checks for you.

- **Help.** As it says, tap here to get help with Gmail.

- **Feedback?** Want to let Google know what you think about Gmail on your Galaxy Tab? Select this, and your browser opens to a page with a survey and feedback form.

You find two more navigation buttons at the bottom of the email—Newer and Older. Tap Newer to open the next piece of email, and tap Older to open the previous email.

If you're holding your Galaxy Tab horizontally, then the Newer and Older buttons aren't at the bottom of the email itself. Instead, they're in the left-hand pane, which lists all of your email.

Managing Multiple Email Messages

You can also handle groups of messages rather than individual ones. In your Inbox, each piece of incoming mail has a box to its left. Tap that box to select the message; a green checkmark appears next to it. To select multiple messages, just turn on their checkboxes.

When you select the messages, a menu bar appears at the top of the screen that tells you how many messages you've selected, and gives you options to apply to all of the selected mail. You can change their labels, mark them all unread, star them, archive them, or delete them. Tap the Menu button, and you can report them as spam and mute them. Tap Done, and the mail gets deselected.

Changing Sync Settings

To change whether you want to sync the mail in Gmail on your Tab with your Gmail account on the Web, from the Home screen, tap the Notifications Panel, then tap Settings→Accounts and Sync. From here you can change whether to sync the mail on your Tab with your email account.

Writing Messages in Gmail

When you want to create a new Gmail message while you are in Gmail, tap the Compose button ⬛. A new, blank message form opens, and the keyboard appears so you can start typing.

 If you want a larger keyboard and you're in vertical mode, turn your Tab 90 degrees.

Write your message this way:

- **Type the recipient's address in the To field.** As you type, Gmail looks through your Contacts list, as well as people you've sent email to in the past, and displays any matches. (Gmail matches the first few letters of first names as well as last names as you type.) If you find a match, tap it instead of typing the rest of the address. You can add as many addresses as you want.

- **Send copies to other recipients.** Tap + Add Cc/Bcc, and two new lines appear beneath the To field—Cc and Bcc.

  Anyone whose email address you put in the Cc and Bcc boxes gets a copy of the email message. The difference is that while everyone can see all of the Cc recipients, the Bcc copy is sent in private. None of the other recipients can see the email addresses you enter in the Bcc field.

 Note The term *carbon copy* comes from those long-gone days in the last century when people typed mail, documents, and memos on an ancient device called a typewriter. To make multiple copies, they added a sheet of carbon paper and another sheet of typing paper. The force of the keys striking the paper would imprint ink on the second sheet using the ink in the carbon paper.

- **Type the topic of the message into the Subject field.** A clear, concise subject line is a good thing for both you and your recipient, so you can immediately see what the message is about when you scan your Inbox.

- **Type your message into the Compose Mail box.** Type as you would in any other text field. You can also use copy and paste (page 39).

- **Add an attachment.** To add an attachment, tap Attach ✐ . You go to the Gallery to attach a photo. When you attach a file, a paper clip icon appears beneath the subject line, and you see the file name and size. Tap the X button if you want to remove the attachment. You can keep adding attachments, if you want.

- **Tap Send, Save Draft, or the Discard button.** Tap Send, and the message gets sent immediately. Save Draft saves the message to your Draft label, where you can later review it, edit it, and send it. Discard gets rid of the message for good.

Adding a Signature

The Gmail app can automatically add a signature—your contact information, for example—to the bottom of every outgoing message. To create a signature of your own, press the Menu button, and then select Settings. Then tap the name of your Gmail account—it's your Gmail address. If multiple accounts show up, tap the one to which you want to add a signature. From the screen that appears, tap Signature. Type in your signature, tap OK, and the signature is appended to the bottom of all messages you send.

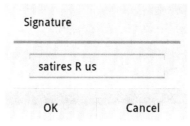

Signature

satires R us

OK   Cancel

 Note The signature is appended to the bottom of outgoing Gmail, but not your other email accounts. You need to set up signatures separately for each email account and each Gmail account.

Working with Labels and Search

Labels are an excellent way to organize your email in Gmail, because they're far more flexible than folders. A single message can appear in as many or as few labels as you want.

To see all of your labels, no matter where you are in Gmail, repeatedly tap the Gmail icon at the upper-left corner of the message, and you come to a listing of all your labels. Tap any label to see all the messages in that label.

Gmail automatically creates these labels for you:

Inbox	381

- **Inbox** contains all your incoming messages.

- **Starred** shows all the messages you've starred (page 289).

- **Chats** contains the contents of all chats done via Google Talk.

- **Sent** lists all the messages you've sent.

- **Outbox** shows mail you've created and asked Gmail to send, but that has not yet been sent.

- **Drafts** contains mail you've created but not completed.

- **All Mail** contains all mail and chats, except for Spam and Trash. It also includes mail that you've archived (page 290).

- **Spam** contains all mail marked as spam, either by you or by Google.

Inbox   381

☆ Starred

Chats

Sent

Outbox

Drafts   22

All Mail

Spam   342

Trash

[Gmail]/T...   14

Junk E-mail

preston@...

Work

Tip You can remove mail from Spam by going into the Spam label, reading a message, and then tapping "Remove label" from the bottom of the screen.

- **Trash** contains mail you've deleted but that hasn't been removed from the trash yet because it's not more than 30 days old.

 Tip If you use Gmail's Priority Inbox on the Web, then you also see a label here called Important that shows all the messages that Gmail has flagged as being important to you. For details about how Priority Inbox works, and to set it up on the Web, go to *http://mail.google.com/mail/help/priority-inbox.html.*

If you've created any labels other than these using Gmail on the Web, then you see them here as well. Remember, you can't create new labels in Gmail on the Tab. To create a new label, visit Gmail on the Web using your Tab's browser or a computer.

Searching Gmail

Google makes what many consider the best search engine on the planet, so it's no surprise that it builds Google Search into Gmail on the Tab. Searching is straightforward, as you would expect.

To search, tap Search at the bottom of the screen when you're in Gmail. As you type, Gmail displays previous searches you've done that match those letters and narrows the search as you type. If you see a search term you want to use, tap it. If not, type the entire search term, and then tap Search.

business case	⬉
better days	⬉
emerson	⬉
jay	⬉
turkey	⬉
burgundy	⬉

After you enter your search terms, you see a display of all matching email. Gmail searches through the To:, From:, and Subject: fields, as well as the text of the messages themselves. It even searches through the names of file attachments. In the upper-left corner, you see the search term you entered.

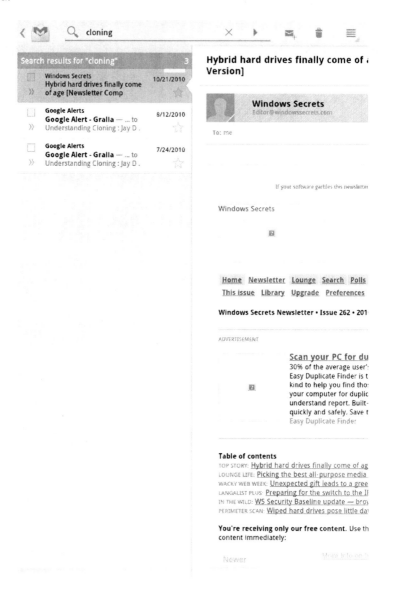

Advanced Gmail Searching

Gmail lets you do some pretty fancy searching—after all, Google is the search king. So you can search by To:, From:, Subject:, specific labels, and a lot more. Say you want to search for all email with the word "Halloween" in the subject line. Type the following in the search box:

```
Subject:Halloween
```

You can search other Gmail fields, as shown on the following list (head to *http://tinyurl.com/gmail-search* for a more complete list):

- **From:** Searches for mail from a specific sender.
- **To:** Searches mail for a specific recipient.
- **Subject:** Searches the subject line.
- **In: <label>** Searches in a specific label.

You can combine these search terms with one another, and with a search of the text of the message. So to search for all email in your Work label with the word "budget" in it, you'd do this search:

```
In:Work Budget
```

Gmail Settings

Don't like the way that Gmail works on your Galaxy Tab? No problem—just change it. Tap the Menu button, and then select Settings. You can change a number of global email settings—that is, settings that affect every one of your Gmail accounts—or you can change other settings on each Gmail account individually, if you have more than one.

Tap General Preferences to change global settings. Everything here is simple and straightforward—whether Gmail should ask you for confirmation before deleting, archiving, and sending messages, for example. Just tap the option you want to turn on, and a green checkmark appears next to it. Tap it again, and the checkbox turns off.

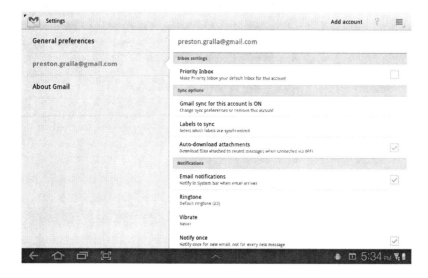

To change settings for an individual Gmail account, tap the account, and you come to another full screen of settings. Again, the settings you can change here are straightforward, such as whether to sync mail between your Tab and Gmail on the Web, whether to sync labels with Gmail on the Web, whether to automatically download attachments, whether to receive notifications, and if so what ringtone to use, and so on. And, as explained on page 295, here's where you can create a signature for your Gmail account as well.

Add a Gmail Widget

If you want to check your email regularly, you don't even need to run the Gmail app. Instead, add a Gmail widget to one of your Home screens. Adding a widget is an easy way to use Gmail on your Tab, because that way, you can see information about your incoming mail in Gmail, without having to use the app itself. Just glance at the widget and you see the latest mail. You can also create a new message from it.

To add the Gmail widget to your Home screen or any panel, first go to the panel where you want to add the widget. Then tap the + button, and on the bottom half of the screen tap Widgets. Scroll through the widgets until you come to the Gmail widget. Tap it, and it flies into the panel.

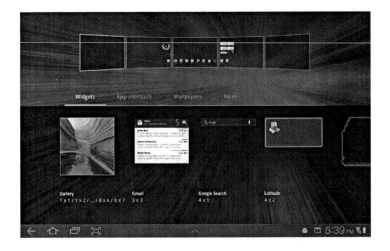

Now head to that screen, and you see the widget. Its displays how many unread messages you've got in your Inbox, and shows information about the latest mail (sender, subject line, date and time). You can scroll through your email by dragging or flicking. Tap any email, and you're sent to the full-blown Gmail app, with the message open in it. Tap the Create Mail icon 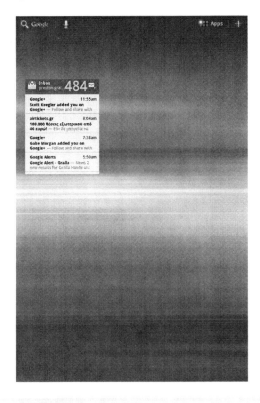 to launch the normal screen you use to create a Gmail message. Tap the Gmail icon to go to the full-blown Gmail app.

Setting Up Email Accounts

You're not confined to using Gmail on the Tab—you can use your other email accounts as well. You can easily add email accounts to your Tab. First, from the Home screen, tap the Notification Panel, and then choose Settings→Accounts and Sync. Tap Add Account at the top of the page. You see a list of the various kinds of accounts you can add, including a general email account, a Google account, a social networking account, and a corporate email account, among others.

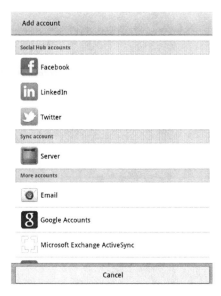

Tap Email and fill in the first page of information, including your email address and password. If you want this to be your default email address for the Tab—in other words, whenever you send an email, you want to use this account—check the box next to "Send email from this account by default." Tap next. You must specify what type of email account this is—POP3, IMAP, or Exchange. You use Exchange only if it's a corporate account, and if that's the case, then you need some more information from the IT pros where you work. (See page 334 for details.)

If you're techie enough to know whether your account is POP3 or IMAP, make your choice. If you're not, check with your mail provider. (In most cases, it's a POP3 account.) And in either case, you can refer to the next section, which explains the ins, outs, ups, and downs of POP3 and IMAP accounts.

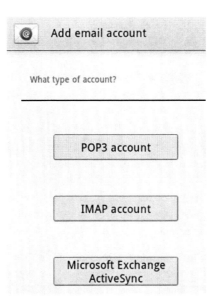

When you've made your choice, you go to several more screens. These screens are filled with details that only techies can love (and truth be told, even they don't really love these details that much). However, generally, leave these screens exactly as you see them. Usually, they work as is. Tap Next at each screen until you get confirmation that your account is setup.

And if it's not set up correctly? In that case, get in touch with your mail provider. You need nitty-gritty details such as your server name, port number, and so on. Get all that information, head back here, and armed with it all, you can set it up. You may even want to start setting up the account when you call your mail provider, and have the screens open on your Tab, so that techs can walk you through the process.

 Here's a quick and easy way to get all the techie details to set up your email account if you're having problems—go to your computer's email software, and get the information from there. Where you find the information varies from software to software. If you've got Outlook 2010, when you're in Outlook, click the File tab at the top of the screen, select Account Settings, and from the screen that appears, double-click the account you're trying to set up on your Tab. You see all the server settings that you need.

POP3 and IMAP Accounts

As a general rule, your email account uses one of two technologies:

- With a **POP3 (Post Office Protocol)** account, the POP server delivers email to your Inbox. From then on, the messages live on your Galaxy Tab—or your home computer, or whichever machine you use to check email. You can't download another copy of that email, because POP servers let you download a message only once. So if you use your account on both a computer and your Tab, you must be careful to set up the account properly, as described in the box on the next page, so you don't accidentally delete email. Despite this caveat, POP accounts remain the most popular type of email accounts, and are generally the easiest to set up and use.

- With an **IMAP (Internet Message Access Protocol)** account, the server doesn't send you the mail and force you to store it on your computer or Tab. Instead, it keeps all your mail on the server, so you can access the same mail from your Tab and your computer—or even from multiple devices. The IMAP server always remembers what you've done with your mail—what messages you've read and sent, your folder organization, and so on. So if you read mail, send mail, and reorganize your folders on your Tab, when you then check your mail on a computer, you see all those changes, and vice versa.

  That's the good news. The bad news is that if you don't remember to regularly clean out your mail, your mailbox can overflow if your account doesn't have enough storage to hold it all. If your IMAP account gets full, then when people send you email, their messages bounce back to them.

 Note With the exception of a Gmail account, you can add only email accounts that you've previously set up to your Galaxy Tab. If you get a new email account at work or home, get it all set up before you try to add it to your Tab.

Reading Mail

On the Galaxy Tab, reading email on a non-Gmail account is much like reading Gmail. In the Apps Menu, tap Email to launch the Email app, and it immediately downloads any waiting mail. As with Gmail, the Email app displays the subject line, time and date of delivery, and the sender of each message. It also displays the first line or so of the message.

Note If you've organized your mail into folders on your computer, that organization isn't reflected on the Galaxy Tab. You can't see or use the folders from your computer's email software.

 Gralla

Inbox	2	**Hybrid Cars & SUVs**	Jul 9
		Go Green With a Fuel Efficient Hybrid! — Go Green With a Fuel Efficient Hybrid! Click here. Find deals on you...	
		rsantalesa@optonline.net	11:35am
		Re: [Ipg-link] Prominent lawyer in the news (was: little more oomph ... please ?) — None of the below. S...	

Load more messages

Workaround Workshop

Keeping Your POP Mailboxes in Sync

The difference between POP and IMAP accounts is that POP email lives only on whatever machine you download it to. With IMAP, a copy automatically remains on the server so you can download it again on another device. Say you read incoming email on your Galaxy Tab, delete some of it, keep some of it, and write some new messages. Later that day, you go to your desktop computer and log into the same email account. You don't see those incoming messages you read on your Tab, nor the ones you sent from it.

When you're using both your Tab and home computer to work with the same POP account, how do you keep them in sync? By making your POP account act more like an IMAP account, so it leaves a copy of all messages on the server when you download them to your home computer. That way, you can delete messages on the Tab, and still see them in your Inbox at home.

In Outlook 2010, choose File→Account Settings, double-click the account name, and then select More Settings→Advanced. Turn on "Leave a copy of each message on the server." Also turn on "Delete messages from server after they are deleted from this computer," so that you don't fill up the server space allocated to your account.

To get to these settings in earlier versions of Outlook, choose Tools→E-mail Accounts→E-Mail→View or Change Email Accounts→your account name→Change→More Settings→Advanced.

In Entourage, choose Tools→Accounts. Double-click the account name, and then click Options.

In almost all ways, reading mail in the Email app is just like reading email in Gmail, with only very minor differences. To read a message, tap it. If the message has images, then they aren't displayed off the bat; to see them, tap Show Pictures. Rather than using a paper clip to show there's an attachment, it uses the word "Attachment." Tap it to preview the attachment in a thumbnail, and then tap either View or Save, depending on what you want to do with the attachment.

When you're viewing a message, notice one different icon at the top of the email—a folder icon 🖉. Tap it, and if you have an IMAP account you see the folders created on the server. However, with a POP3 account, you don't see other folders here aside from Trash.

Another difference is that when you're viewing a message and tap "Show details," a box pops up with details about the email, rather than displaying them right in the email itself.

Message Details

Subject:	Surf's up!
From:	Preston Gralla <preston.gralla@gmail.com>
Date:	12:17pm, Jul 8, 2011
To:	Preston Gralla <preston@gralla.com>

Close

Handling Attachments and Pictures in Email

More and more email messages contain pictures. Sometimes, the picture is in the content of the message itself, such as a company logo. Other times, the picture is an attachment, like a family photo. Email handles the two types of graphics differently.

If the graphics are embedded in the content of the message, you see a button labeled Show Pictures. If you're not curious to see the graphics—most of the time they're logos and ads, anyway—do nothing. However, if the graphic is an important part of the message, then tap Show Pictures. You see all the graphics on full display, right in the message.

Attached files or pictures display differently than they do in Gmail. Rather than using a paper clip to show there's an attachment, you see the word "Attachment." Tap that word, and what you see differs according to the kind of attachment you've received. If it's a picture, then you see a small thumbnail. Tap either View or Save, depending on what you want to do with the picture.

Surf's up!

Preston Gralla
preston.gralla@gmail.com

To: Preston Gralla   12:17pm, Jul 8   Show details

Message   Attachment 1

big gabe surfing.jpg   17KB   View   Save

If the attachment isn't an image, when you tap Attachment, you see the name of the file. You can then view it or save it. If it's a Word, Excel, or Power-Point file, then the preview opens in an app called QuickOffice that's built into the Tab.

Adding the Sender to Your Contacts

If you get a message from someone and would like to add him to your Contacts list, open the email, and then tap the sender's name. You can then add the contact. And as with Gmail, if you already have the contact, when you tap, it, a small toolbar appears with icons that represent the various ways you can get in touch with the person.

Managing, Creating, and Sending Mail

You manage and send email in the same way as you do in Gmail. So head back to those sections in this chapter (see pages 290 and 293) for details.

Account Settings

As with Gmail, if you want to change the way your email account works, you can do it. Tap the Menu button, and then select Account Settings. As with Gmail, some settings affect all of your non-Gmail accounts, and others affect only individual accounts.

The Email Preferences screen affects all accounts. You see only two settings here—one that shows what screen appears when you delete a message, and another that determines the size of the text in email.

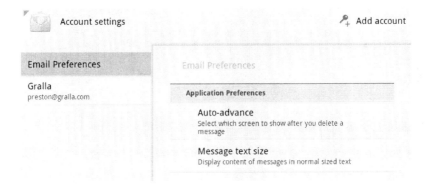

Tap an individual account to change settings for just that one account. The settings here are self-explanatory—things such as how often to check for new mail, whether to receive notifications, adding a signature, and so on.

Email Preferences

Gralla
preston@gralla.com

Gralla

General settings

Account name
Gralla

Your name
Preston

Signature
Append text to messages you send

Inbox check frequency
Every 15 minutes

Default account
Send email from this account by default ☑

Notification settings

Email notifications
Notify in System bar when email arrives ☑

Select ringtone

Vibrate
Also vibrate when email arrives

Server settings

Incoming settings
Username, password, and other incoming server settings

Outgoing settings
Username, password, and other outgoing server settings

Remove account

Remove account

Changing Sync Settings

One important thing is missing from the account settings—whether to sync mail. To get to those settings, from the Home screen, tap the Notification Panel, tap it again to expand it, and then tap Settings. Then choose Accounts & Sync. From here you can change whether to sync the mail on your Tab with your email account.

Add an Email Widget

As with Gmail, you can add an Email widget to your Home screen, so that you can see incoming email, scroll through it, and create new mail, all from the widget.

Create it the same way you do a Gmail widget. First go to the panel where you want to add the widget. Then tap the + button, and on the bottom half of the screen, tap Widgets. Scroll through the widgets until you come to the Email widget. Tap it, and it flies into the panel.

Now head to that screen, and you see the widget. It displays how many unread messages you've got in your Inbox, and shows information about the latest mail (sender, subject line, date and time). You can scroll through your email by dragging or flicking. Tap any email, and you go to the full-blown Email app, with the message open in it. Tap the Create Mail icon  to launch the normal screen you use to create an email message.

There is one slight difference between the Email and Gmail widgets: When you tap the email icon on the upper-left corner of the Email widget, rather than sending you to your email program, it changes the view of mail it shows, from your Inbox, to your unread messages, to your starred messages, and then back again, as you tap.

Using Web-Based Mail Programs

Gmail is a web-based mail program, but the Galaxy Tab includes a special app that lets you use it without having to visit the Web. But there are other web-based mail programs out there, such as Yahoo and Windows Live Hotmail. In some instances, these web-based mail programs have apps you can download from the Android Market. But not in all cases.

Still, you can use just about any web-based email service on the Tab, and most likely very easily. Visit the site with your web browser, and you should be able to use the email site just as if you were using it on a computer. In some cases, when you visit the site, you're automatically routed to a site specifically built for Tabs or smartphones, so all the features are formatted nicely for your Tab.

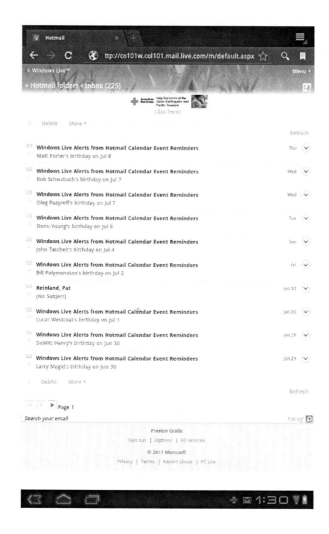

Tip In some cases, the downloadable app may not be built by the company that owns the web-based email service, but instead by a third party. It's generally better to find an app built by the original developer.

13 Calendar

O f all the ways you can use your Galaxy Tab to keep track of your life, the calendar may be the most important. Need to remember the meeting this afternoon, the dinner date tonight, the tennis game tomorrow morning? Forget paper-based calendars—your Tab puts them to shame.

Better still, your Tab's calendar is actually Google's Calendar, so whether you're looking at your calendar on your Tab or on your PC, you see the exact same thing, because the Tab syncs with Google Calendar. So no matter where you are, you know where you need to be today, tomorrow, and beyond.

Using the Calendar

To run the calendar, tap the calendar icon in the Apps Menu. The calendar immediately loads. You're looking at events imported from Google Calendar, so if you're already using Google Calendar, then you see your appointments instantly. If you've never used Google Calendar, you see a blank calendar.

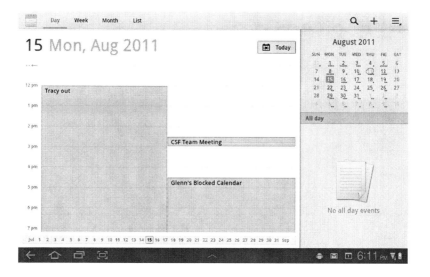

Tip You can place a Calendar widget to display your calendar on any of the Galaxy Tab's Home pages. The widget can perform common tasks such as creating, editing, and viewing tasks. And you can click the widget to go to the full-blown Calendar. For details, see page 330.

Your Google Calendar and the Tab's calendar automatically sync wirelessly, so you should see the most up-to-date calendar information on the Tab's calendar. Syncing means that not only does your Tab calendar grab the latest information from your Google Calendar on the Web, but when you make any changes to your calendar on the Tab, Google Calendar gets updated with that information as well.

If you have more than one calendar (page 328), you can see information from all calendars in one unified view.

Tip When you first set up your Galaxy Tab, you either chose to set it up with an existing Google account, or you created a new one. If you set it up with an existing account, then your Tab calendar automatically syncs with your existing Google Calendar and displays all its events. If you created a new account, you started with a blank Google Calendar.

Navigating the Calendar

You navigate the calendar by tapping buttons across the top of the screen. Most are self-explanatory (such as Day, Week, Month, and Search). Tap the Today button 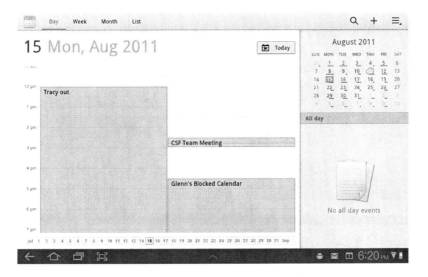 to get to the current day, as explained in the next section. Tap the Add button + to add a new event. The Calendar button doesn't appear to do anything when tapped; it's just letting you know you're in the Calendar app—as if you couldn't tell that by looking at the calendar itself! But if you're creating an event, that icon changes slightly and shows a small triangle at upper left. Tap that, and you return from the event-creation page to the main calendar.

Calendar Views

You have five different ways to look at your calendar. You get to them by tapping the appropriate navigation buttons across the top of the calendar:

- **Day.** Tap here to see the calendar for the day you've highlighted, arranged by hour. Flick up and down to go through all hours of the day. Swipe your finger to the left or right to see the next day's calendar, or the previous day's calendar.

- **Week.** Here you get a weekly view. Swipe left or right to see the next week or previous week, and flick up and down to see later or earlier in the day.

Tip The calendar works in both vertical and horizontal orientations. The vertical orientation is most useful for the day view, and the horizontal orientation for the week and month views.

- **Month.** This view shows you the entire current month. Colored vertical bars indicate appointments and events, and show you their duration. Flick up and down to see the next or previous month. In the month view, your calendar looks very busy—or at least it does if you're a busy person. The monthly calendar cannot show all the events for each day. If there are any more events for a day than it can display, it will tell you how many other events you have that day, apart from the ones displayed.

2   3 more
| Glenn Busy
| Preston busy
| dentist

- **Today.** This choice can be confusing, because what it shows depends on what you're viewing when you choose it. If you're in Day view, it shows you the view of the current day. If you're in Week view, it shows you the entire current week, and highlights the current day. And if you're in the Month view, it shows the current month and highlights the current day.

- **List.** This shows all the events in your calendar in a list format.

 When you run the Galaxy Tab calendar, you're not actually looking at Google Calendar on the Web. Instead, the Galaxy Tab calendar syncs with Google Calendar on the Web, but holds the information in the Tab itself. So if you're not connected to the Internet and you've previously updated Google Calendar on the Web but not yet synced it to the Tab's calendar, then the Tab's calendar doesn't have any information you added since the last sync. And if you're not connected and create or edit an event, that information doesn't show up on Google Calendar until you connect to the Internet and sync.

Adding Events to the Calendar

You have several different ways to create an appointment (which Calendar calls an *event*):

- Tap the Add button ✛. You can do this in any view.

- In Day, Week, or Month view, hold your finger on the time you want to make an appointment. When you hold your finger on a day in the Month view, you'll add an all-day appointment.

When you create an event by holding your finger on the Day, Week, or Month view, a small box appears that shows you the date and time of the event you want to add. Type in details of the event into the box, and tap done. You'll create the event. In the Day and Week view, the event will be scheduled for an hour. In the Month view, it will be scheduled for all day.

That's fine if you don't need to add details to the event, such as where it's being held, whether it repeats, if you need to invite people, and so on. To do all that, instead tap the Add button, and you arrive at a screen that has every bit of detail you can imagine—and most likely, a lot you can't imagine—about the event you want to create. At the bottom of your screen, the keyboard appears.

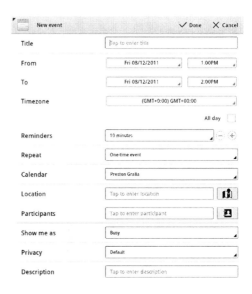

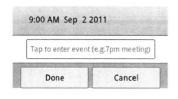

Here's what you need to fill in:

- **Title.** Type in the name of the event here. Are you having lunch with Auntie Em? Drinks with Rick Blaine? Playing tennis with Rafael Nadal? Here's where to name it.

 A small triangle to the right of a calendar entry shows if there's more than one option available for that entry—for example, choice of a time zone, whether an event will repeat, and many others. Don't try tapping the triangle to display the available choices, because it won't display them. Instead, tap right on the entry itself; that brings up all your choices.

- **From, To.** Tap these fields to choose the starting and ending days and times of the event. In either the From or To fields, tap the date, and a screen appears that lets you choose the date. The same holds true when you tap the time.

 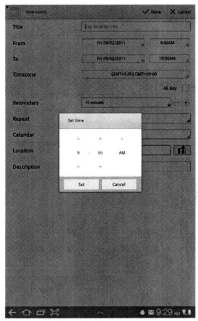

- **Timezone.** This one's simple; tap it to select the time zone. If you're using your current time zone, no need to tap.

- **All day.** If the event lasts all day, forget setting the start and end times. Instead, tap this checkmark, and the calendar automatically schedules the entire day for the event. When you select "All day," though, the event appears at the top of the calendar for that day, and isn't shown on each hour of the calendar for that day.

- **Reminders.** After you create the event, the Tab can flash reminders before the event, telling you that it's about to happen. You can choose at what increment of time to send the reminder, anywhere from 1 minute to 1 week. Or you can tell it not to flash reminders. You can also customize the reminder—for example, to remind you 7 minutes before the event.

 Tip You can set more than one reminder for an appointment. For details, see page 324.

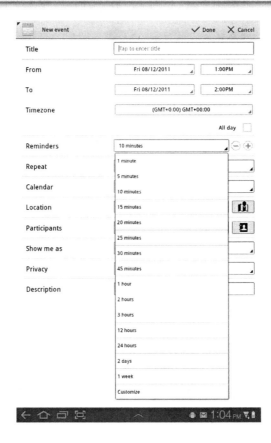

When you set a reminder time, you get a notification in the Notification Panel before the appointment. Tap it, and you see a list of all of your upcoming events, including the one for which you received the notification. For each, you see the time and date, place, and name of the event.

You can then Snooze the reminder so it disappears until another interval of time passes (the interval that you've set), and then pops up again. Or you can dismiss it, which means it will vanish forever, never to be heard from again.

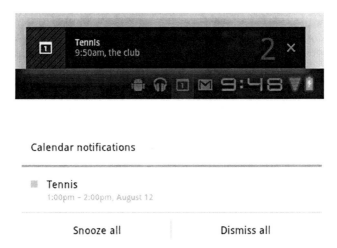

 The alert also pops up when you visit your Google Calendar on the Web.

- **Repeat.** Will this be a one-time event, or one that repeats? If it repeats, the Tab gives you a lot of flexibility about how to choose that. You can tell an event to repeat every day at the same time, once a week at that time and day of the week, monthly, or even yearly on that date.

 When you choose to repeat an event on a monthly basis, you can't have it repeat on a certain date of the month (the 15th, for example). Instead, you get the choice of having the event repeat on the same day of the week of the month—for example, the first Wednesday of the month, or the third Tuesday of the month.

- **Calendar.** If you have more than one Google Calendar, select the calendar where you want the appointment to appear by tapping here, and then selecting the calendar. The event appears only on that calendar. If you have only one calendar, ignore this menu.

 One of your calendars will be titled My Calendar. That's not your Google Calendar; it's your personal calendar that the Galaxy Tab creates for you. That calendar doesn't allow you to invite people to appointments, and so doesn't include the Show Me As, Privacy, or Participants entries. Choose a different calendar than My Calendar if you are going to invite people to the event you're scheduling.

- **Location.** Type in the place where the event will be held. You can also tap the Google Maps icon, and search for a location, which will then be input into this box.

- **Participants.** If other people are involved, type their email addresses here, separated by commas.

You can also choose to select people from your Contact list. Tap the Contact list icon, and then search through the contact list for people you want to include. Put checkboxes next to those you want to include, and then tap Done. They'll all be added to the list.

Each person you select will then show up on a separate line beneath the input box. To eliminate any of the participants, tap the - key next to their names. A line will appear through their names. Tap + to add them again.

If the participants are on a group calendar with you, you will be able to check their schedule by tapping the Participants Schedule button.

When you've done all that—and don't worry, it goes a lot faster than it sounds—tap the Done button. Your event now shows up on your calendar.

 Tip For more information about using a group calendar and how to set all its options, head to your Google Calendar on the Web: *www.google.com/calendar*.

- **Show me as.** Even though you've set an event, you can still show yourself as available on your calendar if someone else wants to schedule you—for example, you may plan to go to your health club to exercise, but if something important comes up, you'll forgo it. So make your choice between Busy or Available here.

- **Privacy.** Sometimes, you want others to see an event you put on your calendar ("Board meeting"), and other times you don't want them to see it ("Dog grooming"). This option lets you make the event private, so only you can see it; or public, so others in the group calendar can see it.

- **Description.** What will you be doing? Having lunch? Meeting with your accountant? Skydiving? Tap in a description. If you're inviting other people, keep in mind that the invitation will be sent to them, so make the description clear (and keep it clean).

Getting Notifications About Who Has Accepted

If the appointment you created requires someone else—a dinner invitation, say—he gets an email, and either accepts the invitation or not. Either way, you get a notification emailed to you, with links for responding to the person who accepted if you wish, responding to multiple people, or replying. Tap the appropriate key, type your text, and your email gets sent.

 Note If you cancel an event, the person gets an email notification that the event was cancelled.

Editing, Rescheduling, and Deleting Events

To look at one of your appointments, tap it. You see a summary of the appointment, including the date and time, place, attendees, and any reminders. Tap "Send via" if you want to send information about the appointment via email or Bluetooth. Tap the Delete button to Delete it. If it's an invitation to you, tap Yes to confirm your attendance.

To edit something you've scheduled or added, or to see the full details concerning the invitation, tap Edit. You're now at the familiar screen you used to create the event. You can edit everything about the event—name, location, place, duration, and so on. When you're done, tap Done.

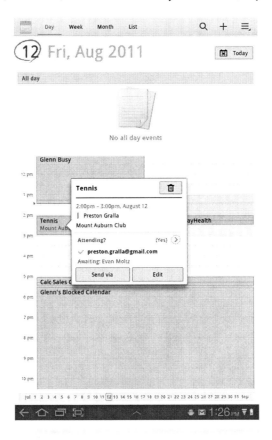

Adding multiple reminders

Are you the kind of person who needs to be reminded multiple times about an appointment? The Tab can do that for you, by reminding you, say, a day ahead of time, and then an hour ahead of time, and then 15 minutes ahead of time.

From the appointment page, tap the + button next to Reminders. You can keep adding reminders by tapping the + button.

Accepting an Invitation

If you're a social kind of guy or gal, you'll not only invite other people to events, but you'll sometimes get invited as well. If they use Google Calendar or the Galaxy Tab calendar, they can use them to invite you to events.

You get the invitation by email, and it contains all the important information about the event, including the time, who scheduled it, who else is attending, and so on. Tap "More details" to get still more information. When you do so, you can choose to get more details via either your web browser or the calendar itself. In practice, both options have the same result—they launch your browser and take you to a Google Calendar page showing more details about the event.

Down at the bottom of the screen, you can say whether you're going—Yes, No, or for those constitutionally unable to commit to anything (you know who you are), Maybe. Tap your response, and you go to a Google Calendar page confirming your choice. There you can write an additional note or change your response. The person creating the event gets notified of your status via email.

You can accept invitations sent via email not only on the Tab's email, but also via your normal email service. So, for example, if you're a Gmail user, you can accept the invitation on Gmail either on the Web or on your Tab.

Searching the Calendar

Trying to remember when you scheduled a tennis game next month? Need to find out the name of the Vice President of Frummery you met sometime in the last 6 months? You don't need to spend hours hunting through your calendar. Just do a search. After all, this calendar is from Google—the king of search.

To search, tap the Search button, type in your search terms, and your calendar does the rest. It displays all matching results from all of your calendars. Tap any to see details. To widen the time period it searches, tap the appropriate text ("Touch to view events before December 2, 2011," for example).

Geolocation and the Calendar

Here's one of the many reasons the Tab's calendar beats a paper-based one hands down—geolocation. When you create an event, send an invitation to an event, or receive an invitation to an event (as long as an address is provided, or a business or landmark such as a restaurant, park, health club, and so on), the Tab turns it into a live link that, when clicked, shows its location in Google Maps.

So when folks get your event invitation, they can see exactly where to go on Google Maps. And you can use all of Google Maps' capabilities, including getting directions, getting additional information about the business or area, and more. On the event invitation, tap the location link to see the location in Google Maps. Tap the location on the map for a list of options. (For more details about using Google Maps on the Tab, see page 179.)

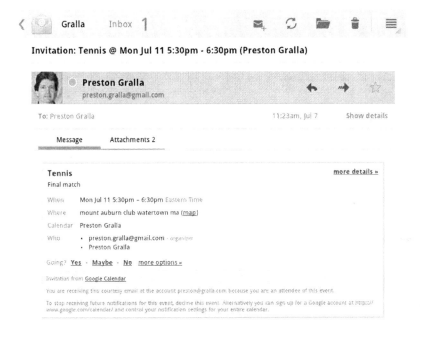

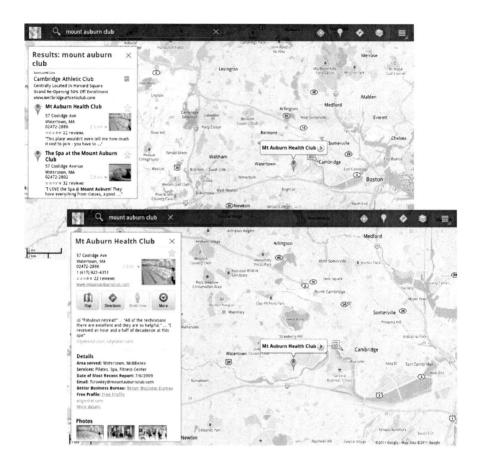

Working with Multiple Calendars

Got more than one Google Calendar? If so, then you've got more than one Galaxy Tab calendar, because the Tab's calendar mirrors and syncs with Google Calendars. If you have more than one calendar, when you create a new event, you see a triangle at the far side of the Calendar line. Tap the box next to it, and you see all your Google Calendars. Tap the calendar where you want the event to appear.

You can't change which calendar automatically appears in the Calendar area when you create a new event—it's the same one every time. So even if you choose a different calendar to create an event, the next time you create a new event, that first calendar automatically shows up. The same holds true for Google Calendar on the Web. Whichever calendar you created first is the calendar that automatically appears.

Your calendars are color-coded, so as you look at your schedule, you can see at a glance which calendar events are on. The color appears just to the left of the event itself. So that you know which color corresponds to which calendar, you see a listing of your calendars with the corresponding colors.

If you like, you can turn off the display of one or more of your calendars. You'll learn how to do that in the next section.

Setting the Calendar Options

If you're the kind of person who likes fiddling with settings, you're in luck—you can change a variety of settings in the Tab's calendar. Tap the Menu button at the top right of the screen, and then tap Settings.

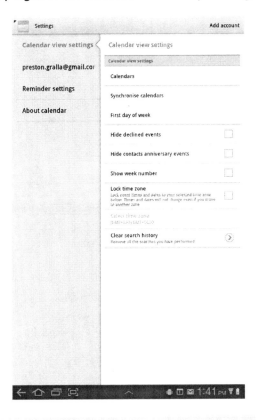

Everything is fairly self-explanatory—you can choose to hide events that you've declined, set the day that you want the week to start on, set your home time zone, choose a ringtone for calendar notifications, and so on. If you want to add a new calendar, tap About Calendar→Add account, and then fill in the information. You have a choice of adding a Google Calendar, a corporate calendar, or a Samsung account. If you're adding a corporate calendar, you need information from your IT staff—see page 337. To change which calendars show up, tap the name of your Gmail calendar (it will be your Gmail address, just below the Calendar view settings). You'll see a list of all of your calendars. Those with green checks next to them will appear; those without checks won't. Put checks next to those you want to appear, and take away checks from those you don't want to appear.

Creating and Using a Calendar Widget

Here's a quick way to see your calendar and create events, without having to launch the Calendar app itself. Use a Calendar widget, and you can interact with your calendar right on your Home screen.

Go to the panel where you want the widget to appear. Tap the + button and from the screen that appears on the bottom half of the Tab, tap Widgets. You see a list of all of your available widgets, including the calendar. Tap the Calendar widget and it will fly to the panel.

Head to that Home screen and you see the widget, which lists all of your day's events. You can see more than just today, though; flick through and you see every day for a week. Each event is color-coded.

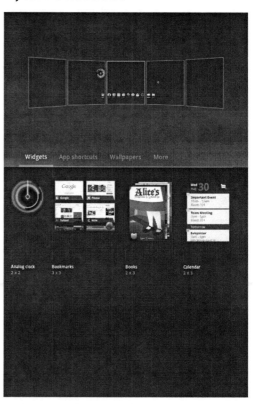

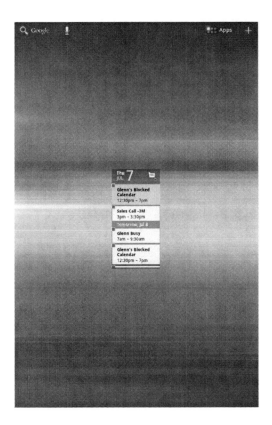

Tap any event, and you head to the listing of the event in your full-blown calendar. Tap the little calendar with a + sign 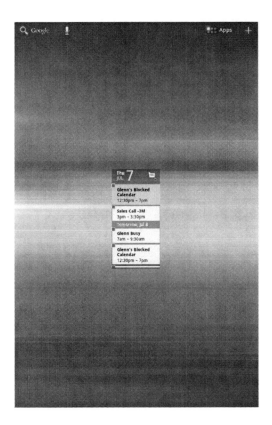 and you head to the normal page you use when creating a new calendar event.

Google Calendar on the Web

The web-based version of Google Calendar lets you set many of the options for your calendar that you can't set on the Galaxy Tab. So in your computer's browser, head over to *www.google.com/calendar* to set those options. When you visit *www.google.com/calendar* in your Tab's browser, you arrive at the normal web-based version of Google Calendar, just as if you were visiting it on a computer. If you have problems using the calendar, tap the link under "Mobile version" and you come to a version specifically designed for smartphones and tablets. You can create new events, but you don't have as many options as you have on your computer. The mobile version is somewhat stripped down.

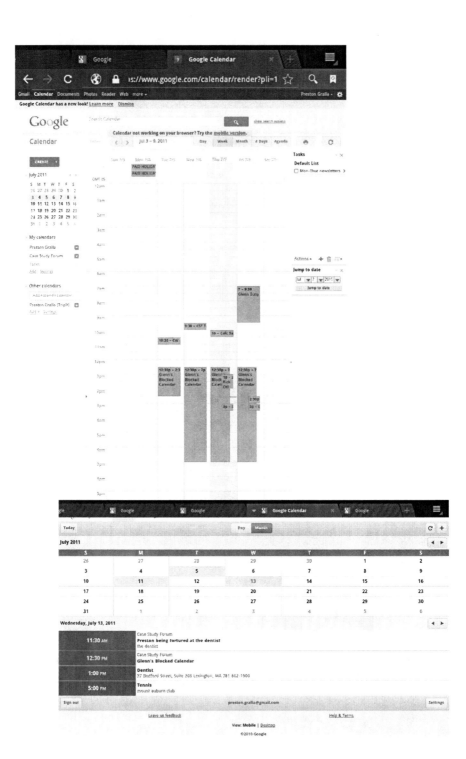

What Happened to Google Tasks?

If you're already a Google Calendar or Gmail user, you may have come across Google Tasks, a very simple and useful way to keep track of all your to-dos. When you use Google Calendar on the Web, your task list appears at the right side of the screen. But the Tasks feature is nowhere to be found on either the Galaxy Tab calendar, or on the Google Calendar version designed to be viewed on the Web with your Tab browser.

Ah, but that doesn't mean you can't get to it on the Tab. You can. It's just that Google has put it somewhere you didn't expect. Go to *http://gmail .com/tasks*. You find Google Tasks there, in all its glory.

Synchronizing Your Calendar with Outlook

When you set up your Galaxy Tab calendar, you either hooked it to an existing Google Calendar or you had to create a new one. But not everyone in the world uses Google Calendar. Plenty of people use other calendars—notably, the one built into Outlook.

There's no direct way to synchronize your Tab Calendar with Outlook, but that doesn't mean you have to manually keep two sets of calendars in sync, by adding and deleting appointments in both places.

Luckily, there's a workaround. It's a bit kludgy, but it works. First, synchronize Outlook with Google Calendar on your PC. That way, Google Calendar and Outlook will stay in sync. Then, sync your Tab with Google Calendar. You're essentially using Google Calendar as a go-between—it shuttles information between Outlook and your Tab.

One way to do this calendar two-step is to download the free Google Calendar Sync (*www.google.com/support/calendar/bin/answer.py?hl=en&answer =89955*) and use that to synchronize.

An even better bet, if you're willing to pay a little bit of money, is Companion-Link for Google (*www.companionlink.com*). Not only does it sync your calendar, but it also syncs your Outlook contacts with your Gmail contacts, which means you can keep your contacts in sync between your Tab and Outlook. You can try it free for 14 days. If you decide it's worth paying for, it'll cost you $39.95.

 Note Neither of these pieces of software work for syncing Google Calendar with Macs and iCal. However, Google has posted instructions for syncing iCal with Google Calendar at *http://bit.ly/a2ifOE*.

Corporate Calendar and Microsoft Exchange

The Galaxy Tab works with a timesaving, if long-winded, piece of technology called Microsoft Exchange ActiveSync. Simply put, if you use an Outlook calendar at work, then you can view that calendar right on your Tab—that is, if the IT gods where you work make it so. You can't set up Exchange on your own.

If you're lucky enough that your IT gods deem it to be a good thing, then you can see your work calendar on your Tab alongside your other calendars. It automatically shows up there, with its own color code, just like any other calendar.

Once the IT gods have set up Exchange, it's time for you to go to work. First, ask them what information you need. Expect tech-talk, but you need it.

Next, when you're in the calendar, tap the Menu button at the top right of the screen, and then select Settings→About Calendar→Add account. Select Microsoft Exchange ActiveSync. Type in your corporate email address and password, then tap Next. Now the techie stuff comes in. Type in the information for each screen exactly as you've been told. If you can't do it, don't despair. Take your Tab over to a tech and ask for help. Don't feel bad about asking—that's what they're paid the big bucks for!

14 Getting Work Done with Your Galaxy Tab

Your Galaxy Tab may not wear a pinstriped suit and a rep tie, but that doesn't mean it can't be a good corporate citizen. In fact, it can easily hook into enterprise-wide resources like your corporate email account and calendar.

A big reason is your Tab's ability to work with Microsoft Exchange Active-Sync servers. These systems are the backbone of many corporations, and they can automatically and wirelessly keep tablets and smartphones updated with email, calendar information, and contacts. So when you're hundreds or thousands of miles away from the office, you can still be in touch as if you were there in person.

Setting Up Your Galaxy Tab with Your Company Account

First, let the IT department know that you'd like to use your Galaxy Tab to work with the company's network and computers. They can set up the network to let your Tab connect. Then all you have to do is add the company account to your Tab, which works much the same way as adding a new email account.

To get started, tap Settings in the Apps Menu, or else from the Home screen, tap the Notification Panel and tap Settings. Tap Accounts and Sync; at the top of the Accounts and Sync screen, tap "Add account," and then tap Microsoft Exchange ActiveSync from the screen that appears.

On the first screen, type in your corporate email address and password and tap Next.

On the next screen, enter all the information that your IT folks supplied you—the domain name and user name, password, email address, server, and so on.

 Make sure to enter the information in exactly the same way as the IT staff gave it to you, including maintaining capitalization. If you make even a single mistake, you may not be able to connect.

Ask the IT department exactly what you should use as your user name. If no one's around, here are some things you can try:

- The first part of your work email address. For example, if your email address is *goodguy@bighonkingcompany.com*, your user name may be *goodguy.*

- The first part of your work email address, plus the company's *Windows domain*. For example, *honkingserver\goodguy*. If this looks familiar, it may be what you use to log into the company network at work.

When you're done, tap Next, and you're set up and ready to go. If you run into any problems, check with the IT staff.

As with your Gmail account, you can choose whether to have your Galaxy Tab sync your mail, calendar, and contacts. Your new corporate account will show up in the Manage Accounts section of the Accounts & Sync screen. Tap it, and you can turn each of those on or off. You may now use your corporate account the same way you use your other accounts for email, contacts, and your calendar.

Virtual Private Networking (VPN)

A virtual private network (VPN) is a kind of virtual tunnel that lets authorized people into the network, while blocking everyone else. If your company has a VPN, you need to connect to it to do things like check your email while you're away from the office. Check with the IT staff. If your company has a VPN, and if you're permitted to use it, they'll give you the information that lets your Tab connect to the corporate network over the VPN. They'll also set up an account for you.

Here's what you need to set up your Tab to access the VPN:

- **The type of technology it uses.** Your Tab can work with pretty much any kind of VPN technology out there. Ask whether yours uses PPTP (Point-to-Point Tunneling Protocol), L2TP (Layer 2 Tunneling Protocol), L2TP/IPSec PSK (pre-shared, key-based Layer 2 Tunneling Protocol over the IP Security Protocol), or L2TP/IPSec CRT (certificate-based Layer 2 Tunneling Protocol over the IP Security Protocol). (You don't have to memorize these terms. There's no quiz later.)

- **Address of the VPN server.** The Internet address of the server to which you need to connect, such as *vpn.bigsecurehoncho.com*.

- **Name of the VPN server.** The name isn't always necessary, but check, just in case.

- **Account name and password.** The IT folks can supply you with this.

- **Secret.** When it comes to VPNs, there are secrets within secrets. If you use a L2TP connection, then you need a password called a Shared Secret in addition to your own password in order to connect.

- **Other special keys.** Depending on which VPN protocol you use, you may require additional keys, which are essentially passwords. Again, the IT folks know this.

- **DNS search domains.** These servers essentially do the magic of letting you browse the Internet and do searches.

Once you've got all that, you're ready to set up the VPN. Tap Settings in the Apps Menu, or else from the Home screen, tap the Notification panel and tap Settings. Then choose Wireless and networks→VPN Settings→Add VPN. A screen appears asking you which of the VPN protocols you'll use for the VPN. Choose the one your IT folks told you to use.

After that, you come to a screen that asks for all the information you've gotten from your IT folks. When you've entered all that, press the Menu key, and then tap Save. Your VPN connection and its settings are saved.

From now on, when you want to connect to the VPN, go back to the VPN settings screen. Tap the VPN to which you want to connect. You may need to enter a user name and password or passwords (these are the ones you've been given by the IT folks). When you do that, tap Connect, and you make the connection. The Notification Panel shows you that you've got a

VPN connection and displays a notification if you've been disconnected, so that you can make the connection again. At any point, to disconnect, open the Notifications Panel, touch the notification for the VPN, and touch it again to disconnect.

Using Google Docs

An increasing number of companies and government agencies use Google Docs for creating and sharing documents, including word processing files, spreadsheets, presentations, and more. Google Docs works much like Microsoft Office, but the software and all the documents live on the Web, where you can share them with others. The basic service is free for individuals, although companies of all sizes can pay for the useful corporate features.

With the Tab's browser, you can view all the documents you have access to on Google Docs. To use Google Docs on your Tab, launch your browser and visit Google Docs on the Web at *http://docs.google.com*. (If that doesn't get you to the right location, check with your IT department.)

 If your Google Docs account is associated with an account other than the main one on your Galaxy Tab, then you may have to sign in. Otherwise, you're probably automatically signed in when you visit Google Docs.

You come to a page that shows you all the documents you have access to in Google Docs. You can choose to see them all in a list or view only the ones that you created (Owned by Me) or those that you have starred.

To view any document, tap it. The document opens in a built-in Google document viewer. You can navigate to different pages by tapping the arrows at the top, or zoom in and zoom out using the buttons at the upper left.

 If you have PDF files in Google Docs, you can read those as well.

Creating and Editing Google Docs Documents

There are, in fact, two ways to create and edit documents in your Google Docs account, by using Google's free Google Docs app, or another free app called Gdocs. You can search for both in the Android Market (for details about finding and installing apps, see Chapter 4).

Google Docs

When you install and run the app, it takes you to Google Docs on the Web. You'll see all of your documents, categorized for easy access. From here you can browse, search, and then open and edit documents, or create new documents. To search through your documents, tap the Search button on the upper right. To create a new document, tap the Create New Document button, to the left of the Search button, then follow the simple directions.

Tap the Menu button at the bottom of the screen for changing your Google Docs settings, switching to another Google Docs account, sending feedback, and getting help.

To browse your documents, tap any category, and you'll see that Google Docs app mirrors the way that Google Docs looks on the Web. To change the sort order of documents, tap the Menu button at the bottom of the screen and choose Sort by. As with Google Docs on the Web, tap any file to view it.

When you open a file, you can edit it—tap the Edit button on the upper right of the screen. The file opens for editing. Double tap anywhere you want to edit text, add text, and so on.

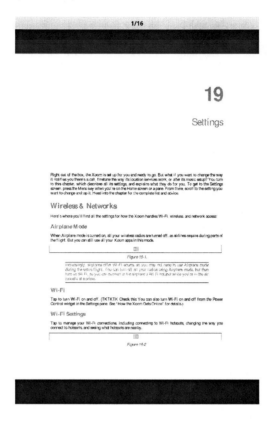

Gdocs

Gdocs isn't a particularly pretty solution, but it does get the job done, especially if you're in a pinch and need to do some quick-and-dirty editing. (And it's free, so stop complaining.) Download it, enter your Google Docs account information, and you can then browse through the documents on Google Docs, although it's tougher to do than via the browser, since you can't see a clean, categorized list.

When you find a document you want to edit, tap it, and it gets download-ed to your Tab. After the document is downloaded, press the Menu key, tap Folders, and then tap "Local documents." You see a list of all the docu-ments you've downloaded. Edit it (keep in mind that the editing tools are fairly rudimentary). When you're done, save the file. You can then sync it so that it uploads to your Google Docs account.

You can also create new documents, and upload them to your Google Docs account. Tap the App Menu key on the bottom left of the keyboard, to the left of the Tab's normal navigation buttons, and then choose Add Docu-ment. When you've created the document, tap the Menu button again, and then select Save.

Microsoft Office

The gold standard for creating and editing documents is Microsoft Office, and although your Galaxy Tab can't rival a computer when it comes to edit-ing, you can create, edit, and view Microsoft Office documents using the QuickOffice app that comes on the Tab. It's basic and bare-bones, but it gets the job done.

 Tip QuickOffice may not show up as an app in your App Menu, but it's still there, ready to do its work. If you get sent an email with an Office document attachment and open it, QuickOffice springs into action and opens the file when you tell it to. And if you've downloaded an Office document as well, then when you open the docu-ment, QuickOffice opens.

If you're willing to spend a little money, get Documents to Go from the Android Market. There are two versions: a free version, which lets you view word processing documents and spreadsheets, and a full version, which lets you edit word processing documents and spreadsheets, do basic edit-ing of presentations, and view PDF files. The full version costs $14.99.

Again, though, don't expect Documents to Go to do everything you can do on a computer. Still, it's nice to be able to edit documents when you absolutely need to.

Part 5
Advanced Topics

15 Controlling Your Galaxy Tab with Your Voice

Tired of tap-tap-tapping away on your Galaxy Tab? Would you prefer instead to talk to it and have it obey your commands? Just say it, and it's done. Want to send an email, search the Internet, get directions to a city or street address, listen to music, and more? Rather than having your fingers do the walking, have your voice do the talking, and you can do all that and more.

You do all this using an app built into your Galaxy Tab called Voice Actions. It's simple and straightforward, as you'll see in this chapter. So save some wear and tear on your fingers and get talking.

Using the Magic of Voice Actions

Possibly the most amazing part of your Galaxy Tab's amazing Voice Actions feature is this: The only thing you really need to know about it is how to talk. Your voice is its command.

Launch it in one of two ways:

- Tap the Voice icon 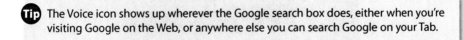 to the right of the Google search box.
- Run the Voice Search app from the Apps Menu.

> **Tip** The Voice icon shows up wherever the Google search box does, either when you're visiting Google on the Web, or anywhere else you can search Google on your Tab.

Another amazing thing about the Voice Actions feature is that it seamlessly uses two different speech technologies to do what you tell it to: voice recognition and speech-to-text. With voice recognition, it recognizes the action you want to take, and then accomplishes the action: "Send email" or "Navigate to," for example.

 Note Many Android smartphones include an app that's similar to Voice Actions, called Voice Commands. Voice Commands is more limited than Voice Actions, and it's not available on the Tab.

With speech-to-text, Voice Actions translates your words into written text and, for example, embeds that text in an email message. Say you tell your Tab: "Send email to Ernest Hemingway. Consider using 'young woman and the sea' as title because demographics are better." Your Tab finds Ernest Hemingway's contact information and then sends him the email "Consider using young woman and the sea as title because demographics are better." If you say a term ("Ernest Hemingway") instead of a command ("send text"), your Tab launches a Google search for that term.

 Note Voice Actions work only if you're connected to the Internet, either via 3G or 4G, or by Wi-Fi.

Whichever way you launch Voice Actions, a screen appears with a picture of a microphone and the words "Speak now." Tell your Tab what you want it to do, and it displays a "Working" screen to show you that it's deciphering what you said. Remember, if you're sending an email message, you can dictate the message itself.

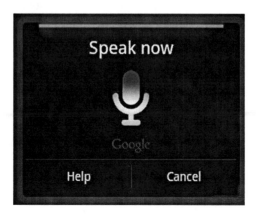

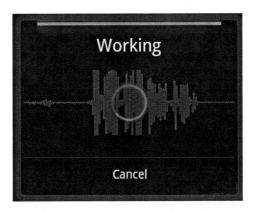

Next, the Tab does what you tell it—for example, composes an email. If you tell it to compose an email, it doesn't immediately send it. Instead, it shows you the message, so you can send it, edit it, or cancel it.

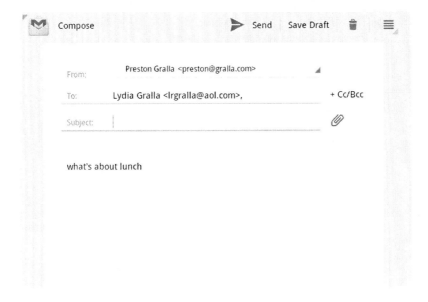

What You Can Do with Voice Actions

Here are the commands you can issue with Voice Actions, along with how to use them:

- **Send email to [recipient] [subject] [message].** Composes an email message to the recipient with the subject and message that you dictate.

- **Navigate to [address/city/business name].** Launches your Galaxy Tab's Navigation app to guide you with turn-by-turn directions to an address, city, or even a specific business.

 In addition to looking through your contacts, the Tab also searches contacts in social networking services such as Facebook that you've installed on your Tab.

- **Map of [address] [city].** Launches Google Maps and opens it to the address or city you named.

- **Directions to [address] [city].** Launches Google Maps and shows directions for how to get to the address or city you name. If the Tab knows your location, it uses that as the starting point. If it doesn't know your location, you must type it when Google Maps launches.

- **Listen to [artist/song/album].** Don't expect this to launch the Music app and play music—that's not what it does. Instead, it works in concert with a radio app, similar to Pandora, which you can download from the Market. When you speak the instruction, it plays the radio station that you've already created for the artist, song, or album. If you haven't created one, then it creates it for you. If you have multiple apps that can play music, the Tab asks which you want to use to complete the action. Once you choose an app, you get a notice asking whether you want to visit a web page with more information about the app or just launch it right away. Tap OK to launch the app.

 If you always want to use the same app for listening to music, when the screen appears asking you which app to use, tap "Use by default for this action," and then tap the app you want to use.

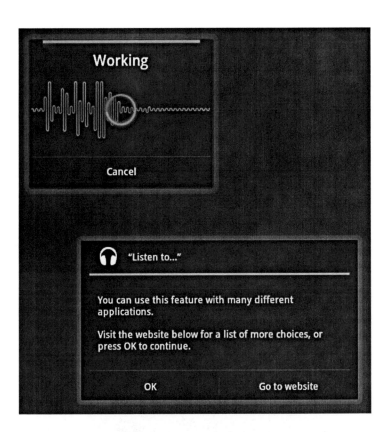

Working

Cancel

🎧 "Listen to..."

You can use this feature with many different applications.

Visit the website below for a list of more choices, or press OK to continue.

| OK | Go to website |

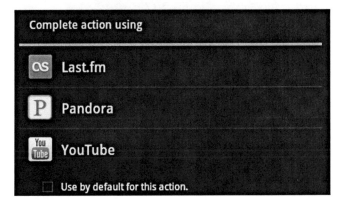

Complete action using

Last.fm

Pandora

YouTube

☐ Use by default for this action.

- **Go to [website].** Launches your browser and goes to the website you dictated. Often, rather than going straight to the website, it displays a list of sites or searches that matches what you dictated. Tap the one you want to visit.

- **[Search term].** Simply say your search term, and the Tab searches the Web using Google.

- **[Contact name].** Say the name of a contact you want to open, and then simply say your search term, and the Tab opens your contact.

Using Voice Actions

When you give a command using Voice Actions, your Tab may do one of several different things, depending on what you're asking it to do and whether it understands what you're saying clearly. Say, for example, you're asking it for directions to Cornell University. If it understands you clearly, it pops up a message that reads "Directions to Cornell University." If it's what you want your Tab to do, either tap Go, or else wait a moment, and the Tab does your bidding and shows you the directions. If it's not what you want your Tab to do, tap Cancel, and speak again.

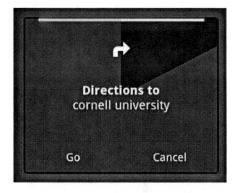

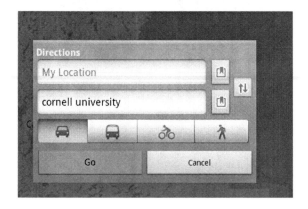

There may be times when the Tab is more or less baffled by what you want it to do. In that case, it gives you a variety of options from which to choose. If you're doing an Internet search, for example, and it can't understand the words you want it to search for, then it pops up a list of the most likely matches.

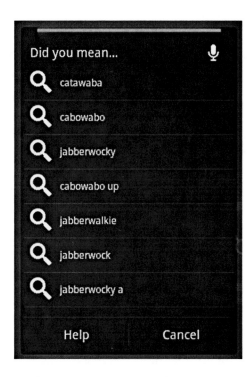

In other instances, it may ask what action you want to take. In each instance, just tap what you want it to do. If what you want to do isn't listed, tap Cancel and talk again.

Sending Email with Voice Actions

If you don't use Voice Actions properly when you're sending an email, then it's more trouble than it's worth. So take these steps to make sending email with Voice Actions faster than a speeding bullet:

- **Speak slowly and distinctly.** Think of Voice Actions as a foreigner with a reasonable grasp of English, but still learning. Speak slowly and distinctly, pronouncing each word carefully. But don't speak too slowly and take long pauses between words—if you do, Voice Actions thinks you're done and then composes the message before you've finished dictating it.

- **Speak the words "subject" and "message" in order to fill in those email fields.** After you say the name of the person to whom you want to send an email, say the word "subject" and then say the subject of the email. Then say the word "message" and dictate the message you want sent. If you don't do that, then your Tab becomes confused. It may interpret what you want to be the subject line as several email addresses, for example, and put in addresses you don't want.

Voice Actions does a very good job of converting your speech into text when you dictate an email. But it's not perfect. So you might be leery of using Voice Actions to dictate a message, worrying that when you dictate, "I love you, too," the message sent will read, "I move YouTube."

 Note Voice Actions, like most other apps on your Galaxy Tab, was made by Google.

Not to worry. Before you send a text message or email, you get a chance to edit the text. Your Tab displays your message first, giving you the opportunity to edit, send, or cancel. Edit it as you would any other email—the address, subject, Cc, Bcc, text of the body, and so on.

How Voice Actions Is Different on a Galaxy Tab Than on a Phone

Google first built Voice Actions for an earlier version of Android that runs on smartphones, and Voice Actions still works on smartphones. But your Galaxy Tab is missing a number of Voice Actions features for the simple reason that it's a tablet, not a phone.

So, for example, you can't say to your Tab, "Call Livingston Seagull," and have your Tab look up Livingston Seagull in your Contacts list and then make a call, because your Tab's not a phone. Similarly, you can't tell your Tab "Send text to Pablo Casals," and have your Tab send a text message to Pablo Casals—again, because your Galaxy Tab's not a phone. (Given that Pablo Casals is no longer among the living, of course, even issuing that command on a smartphone might not give you the results you're hoping for.)

When you use a Voice Action that your Tab can't perform, you get an error message telling you that it simply can't do what you're telling it to do.

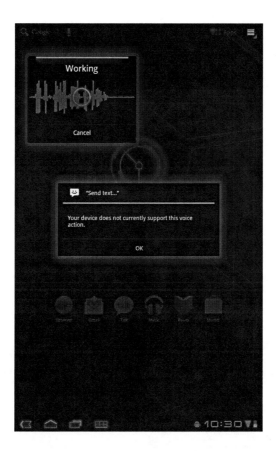

Blocking Offensive Words

If you're worried that Voice Actions may display, use, or search for offensive words, you're in luck—out of the box, it doesn't do that. If someone speaks an offensive word using Voice Actions, your Tab doesn't recognize it. Say an offensive word—in order to perform a Google search on it, for example—and your Tab searches instead for the first letter of the word followed by asterisks, like this: f***. It then shows you Google results for just the first letter.

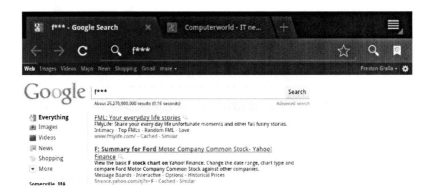

If, for some reason, you feel the need to have Voice Actions take actions when you speak offensive words, you can do that, though—after all, it's a free country. To do it, from the Home screen, tap the Notification Panel and select Settings→Language and Input→Voice Recognition Settings, and then turn off the "Block offensive words" checkbox.

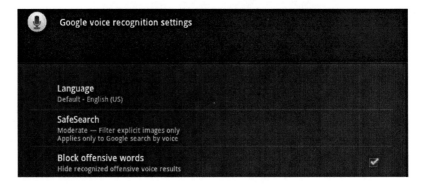

Note When you turn off the "Block offensive words" checkbox, that affects not only Voice Actions, but also voice input—for example, when you are creating an email and choose to dictate your words rather than typing them.

Sending a Voice Recording

Pssst! Want to know a secret Voice Actions feature? You can use it to record a message and then send it to anyone via email. You won't find this documented anywhere by Google, but it works.

First, launch Voice Actions as you normally would. Then say "Note to self" and speak the message you want to record. Voice Actions records your voice, composes an email to yourself, and attaches the recording to the email. It also types in the text of your message.

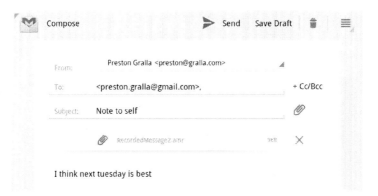

Most likely, you don't really want to send this message to yourself. So edit who you're sending the message to—add a different recipient, for example, and delete your own email address. You can also delete or edit the text of the message. Send it as you would any other message, and it goes on its merry way, with your voice recording attached.

Here's the kicker, though: Depending on the computer or device of the recipient of the message, she may or may not be able to listen to it. The recording uses the .amr file extension, and so whoever receives it must have a computer or software that can play that format. Android devices, such as your Galaxy Tab or an Android phone, can play it, naturally. Macs can play it using QuickTime. Windows computers may not be able to play it, because Windows Media Player doesn't handle the .amr extension. But some add-ins can do the trick. For example, QuickTime for the PC can play the extension.

Changing Your Language

Are you fluent in a language other than English, and would like to use that for Voice Actions and voice search? It's easy to do. To do it, from the Home screen, tap the Notification Panel and select Settings→Language and input→Voice recognition settings→Language. Turn on the Personalized Recognition checkbox. Select the language you want to use, and then speak away.

16 Settings

Right out of the box, your Galaxy Tab is set up for you and ready to go. But what if you want to change the way its location services work, or alter its music setup or privacy features? This chapter describes all of the Galaxy Tab's settings, and explains what they do for you. To get to the Settings screen, from the Home screen, tap the Notifications Panel to open it, tap it again to expand it, and then tap the Settings button Settings.

Wireless and Networks

Here's where you find all the settings for how the Tab handles Wi-Fi, wireless, and network access:

Flight Mode

When Flight mode is turned on, all your wireless radios are turned off, as airlines require during parts of the flight. But you can still use all your Tab apps in this mode. You can also turn Flight mode on and off from the expanded Notifications Panel.

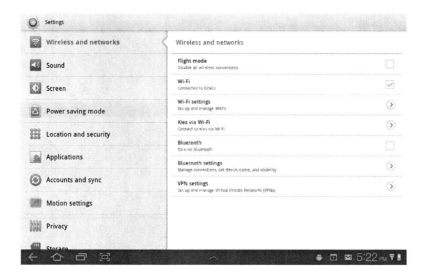

 Note Increasingly, airplanes offer Wi-Fi access, so you may not need to use Flight mode during the entire flight. You can turn off all your radios using Flight mode, but then turn on Wi-Fi, so you can connect to the airplane's Wi-Fi hotspot while you're in the air (usually at a price).

Wi-Fi

Tap to turn Wi-Fi on and off. You can also turn Wi-Fi on and off from the expanded Notifications Panel.

Wi-Fi Settings

Tap to manage your Wi-Fi connections, including connecting to Wi-Fi hotspots, changing the way you connect to hotspots, and seeing what hotspots are nearby:

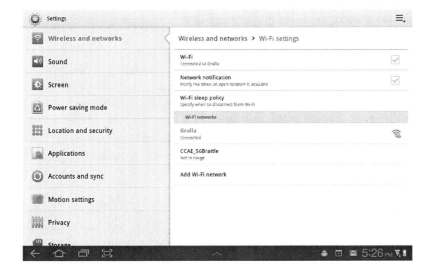

- **Wi-Fi.** Turns Wi-Fi on and off.

- **Network notification.** If you don't want the Galaxy Tab to display a notification when an open Wi-Fi network is nearby, uncheck this box. Otherwise, leave it turned on.

- **Wi-Fi sleep policy.** Lets you set when you should automatically disconnect from a Wi-Fi network. Tap it, and you get a choice of whether your Tab disconnects when the screen turns off, never disconnects when you plug in, or never disconnects.

Underneath these settings, you see "Wi-Fi networks," which lists all nearby Wi-Fi networks, and any other networks to which you have connected. Tap any to connect to it. If you want to add a Wi-Fi network that's not nearby or that is not broadcasting its name (SSID), tap "Add Wi-Fi network," and fill in details about the network name and its type of security. (See page 51 for details.)

 When you're on the Wi-Fi settings screen, tap the Menu button at the top of the screen, tap Advanced, and you come to a screen full of options that only a techie can love, and that lets you set advanced options such as specifying your Wi-Fi frequency band.

- **Mobile Networks.** If you have a 3G or 4G connection, this section is where you control your settings. Select "Activate device" if you haven't yet activated it, and turn on the "Data enabled" checkbox to give your Tab data access over a mobile network. If you leave an area that's covered by your network, then maybe you can still connect your Tab to a cellphone network. When you roam, if you're outside your company's network, you can instead connect to another carrier, and use that carrier instead of your own. Depending on your plan, you may be charged for roaming. Tap "Data roaming" if you want your Tab to access data services when you roam.

Bluetooth

Tap to turn Bluetooth on and off.

Bluetooth Settings

Tap to access all your Bluetooth settings:

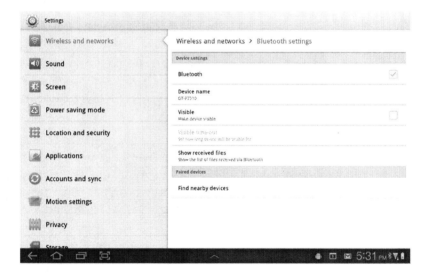

- **Bluetooth.** Turns Bluetooth on and off.
- **Device name.** Displays the name of your Galaxy Tab. To rename it, tap it and from the screen that appears, type a new name, and then tap OK.
- **Visible.** Tap if you want your Tab to be *discoverable* by other Bluetooth devices. In other words, they can see it and connect to it, if you let them.

- **Visible timeout.** When you make your Tab discoverable, it only stays discoverable for a specific amount of time. If another device doesn't discover it within that time, the Tab shuts off as a safety precaution. Tap here to change how long it takes to shut off if it isn't discovered. Your choices are two minutes, five minutes, an hour, or never.

- **Show received files.** If you've connected your Tab to another Bluetooth device and gotten files from it, then tapping this shows you the files you've received.

- **Find nearby devices.** Tap this, and the Tab looks for any Bluetooth devices within range and then lists them. You see devices listed there that are either nearby or that you've paired with in the past. Note that there's a difference between pairing and connecting. When you pair, you simply give two Bluetooth devices the capability to communicate. But they can't communicate with each other until you connect them. To pair, tap the device the Tab found. The device receives a notification that you want to pair, and someone needs to OK that pairing. You then tap OK on your end, after you receive a notification that the device is willing to be paired. At that point, they're paired but not connected—you're told they're paired and you see a wrench icon and a small Bluetooth icon. Tap the name of the paired device to connect to the device; tap it again to disconnect. Tap the wrench icon  and you come to a screen that lets you unpair, rename the device to which you've paired, and connect to the device to use its connection to the Internet.

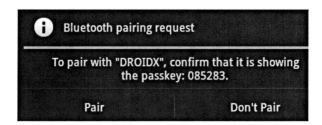

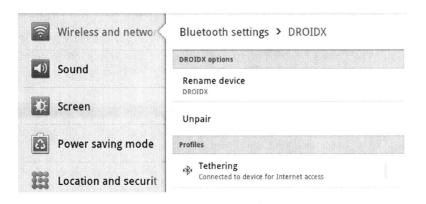

	Wireless and networ
	Sound
	Screen
	Power saving mode
	Location and securit

Bluetooth settings > DROIDX

DROIDX options

Rename device
DROIDX

Unpair

Profiles

Tethering
Connected to device for Internet access

 Note If you choose only to disconnect from the other Bluetooth device, you close the connection, but the pairing remains. In other words, the initial work you did to make sure the devices can pair remains, Tab remembers all the details about the other device, and you can quickly connect to it again. If you unpair from it as well as disconnect from it, you have to walk through the steps of pairing all over again.

VPN Settings

Here's where you can set up a virtual private network (VPN) connection with your workplace or, if you've already set it up, change any settings, such as its URL, password, means of authentication, and so on. You need to get information from your company's IT gurus to make the connection, so check with them for details. See page 339 for more information about setting up a VPN on your Tab.

Sound

Here's where to go to change just about everything about the way that your Galaxy Tab handles sounds, such as playing music, and even the display. Tap Sound to get to these options:

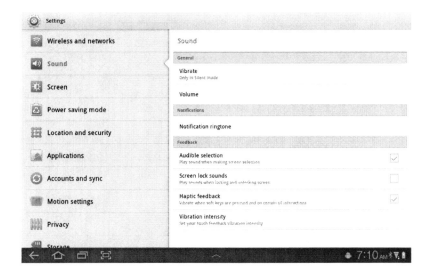

- **Vibrate.** Tap to choose when your Tab vibrates when you receive notifications—always, never, only in Silent mode, and only when not in Silent mode.

- **Volume.** Tap to set the overall volume and also for notifications and alarms. A slider appears that lets you set the volume for each individually. The top button sets the notification volume, the one below it sets the volume for media and music, the one below that sets the alarm volume, and the bottom sets the volume for systems sounds, such as when you turn on the Galaxy Tab. The Tab plays the new volume level when you move the slider, so if you're not satisfied with what you hear, change it again until you reach the level you want.

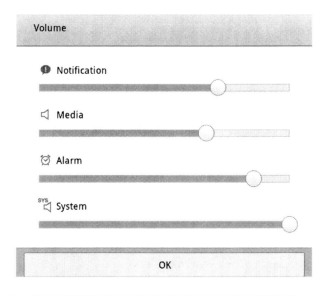

To set the overall sound volume for your Tab, you can also use the physical volume buttons, usually located along one of its sides or the top.

- **Notification ringtone.** Sets the ringtone you hear when you receive notifications, such as when new email has arrived. Tap it, and you come to a list of all of your available ringtones. Flick through the list, tap the one you want, and then tap OK. When you tap a new one, you hear the sound, so you can decide whether you want to keep it or choose a different one.

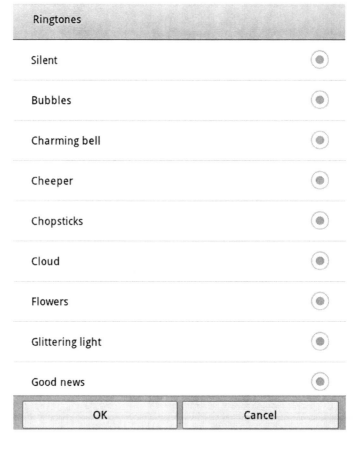

- **Audible selection.** Tap if you'd like a sound to play when you make a selection on the Galaxy Tab's screen. This can get noisy, so choose it with care.

- **Screen lock sounds.** Tap, and the Tab makes a sound every time your screen locks, and when you unlock it.

- **Haptic feedback.** Controls whether the Tab vibrates when you tap keys on the keyboard, or during certain other interactions. It works no matter how you've set the general Vibrate settings.

- **Vibration intensity.** This lets you set how powerfully the Galaxy Tab should vibrate.

Screen

Change your display options here. Tap to get to these options:

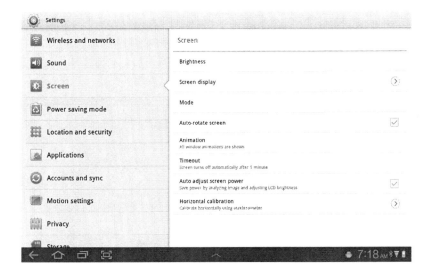

- **Brightness.** Normally, the Galaxy Tab chooses a screen brightness appropriate for that level of lighting—less light in the dark, and more in sunlight, for example. If you'd prefer to set it at a specific brightness level, and have it stay at that level until you change it, tap this option. From the screen that appears, uncheck the box next to "Automatic brightness." A slider appears that lets you manually set the brightness level.

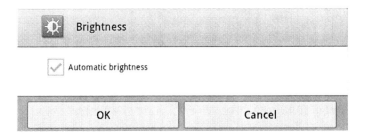

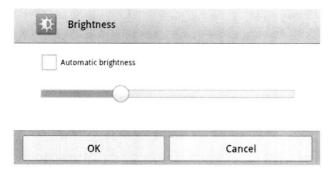

- **Screen display.** Tap to choose what wallpaper to use for your screen, and what wallpaper to use when the screen is locked.

- **Mode.** This lets you change the vividness and other attributes of your screen's color. Tap it and you get a choice of Dynamic (colors are richer), Standard (the default mode), and Movie (as the name says, best for watching movies).

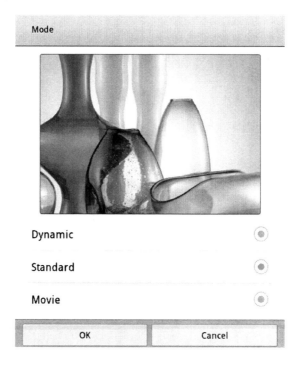

- **Auto-rotate screen.** Make sure this checkbox is turned on if you want your Tab to automatically rotate the screen whenever you change the Tab's orientation—from horizontal to vertical, for example.

- **Animation.** At times, your Tab uses animated effects between screens. Out of the box, it shows all animations. Tap this option, and you can turn off all animations, show just some of them, or show all animations.

- **Timeout.** In order to save battery life, the Tab's screen goes blank after 1 minute. You can change that to as low as 15 seconds, or as many as 30 minutes. Tap this option, and then choose the interval you want.

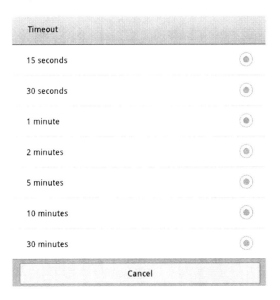

- **Auto-adjust screen power.** The Tab gets better battery life when this option is turned on (which is how it comes out of the box). When turned on, this feature analyzes the image you're viewing onscreen and automatically adjusts the LCD brightness to save battery power.

- **Horizontal calibration.** Your screen can respond to motion, so tap here to calibrate it to respond more effectively to motion. When you tap it, a screen appears telling you to put the Tab on a flat surface. Do that, tap Calibrate, and wait a few seconds while the Tab calibrates itself.

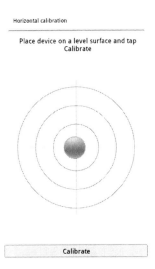

Power Saving Mode

Here's where to go if you're looking to go as long as possible on a battery charge. Here are your options:

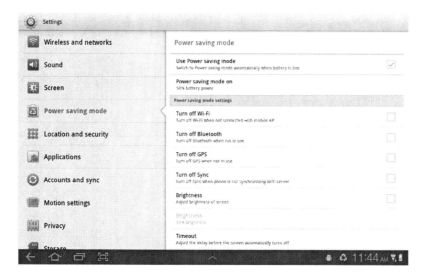

- **Use Power Saving Mode.** Tap the checkbox and a green check appears; power saving mode is turned on. Tap it again to make the check go away; power saving mode is turned off.

- **Power saving mode on.** Tap it to select at what percent of power left in your battery power saving mode should kick in. Your choices are 10%, 30%, 50%, and 70%. Out of the box, it's set to 50%.

- **Power saving mode settings.** These settings, for Wi-Fi, GPS, Bluetooth, Sync, Brightness, and Timeout, are all self-explanatory. For example, check the boxes next to Turn off Wi-Fi, Turn off GPS, and Turn off Bluetooth, and those radios will turn off automatically if they're not needed—for example, not connected to a Wi-Fi network, or using an app that requires GPS.

Location and Security

Plenty of apps, like turn-by-turn navigation and Foursquare, use the Galaxy Tab's ability to know your location. These settings control how the Tab handles knowing your location, as well as security options, like setting a screen lock.

The top section of this screen is labeled My Location, and it determines how the Tab handles location:

- **Use wireless networks.** Tap this, and the Tab determines your location by using Wi-Fi or mobile networks, via techniques such as triangulation.

Tip If you turn on multiple boxes in the My Location section, then the Tab uses the most precise available method for finding your location. So if you select "Use wireless networks" and "Use GPS satellites," for example, the Tab uses GPS satellites when possible, and wireless networks only if it can't connect to GPS satellites.

- **Use GPS satellites.** Tap this option, and the Tab determines your location via GPS satellites, which are a more precise means of locating you than wireless networks. GPS uses a good deal of battery power, so turn it on only when you need GPS services.

- **Use location for Google Search.** If you want Google Search and other Google services to use your location information to provide geographically relevant information in your searches, tap this.

The next section, Lock Screen, lets you lock your Tab so that only you can use it:

- **Configure lock screen.** When your screen is locked, all you normally need to do is swipe the lock to the left to unlock it—anyone can do it. If you lose your Tab, then whoever finds it can use it. Tap this if you want to make sure that you're the only person who can unlock the Tab.

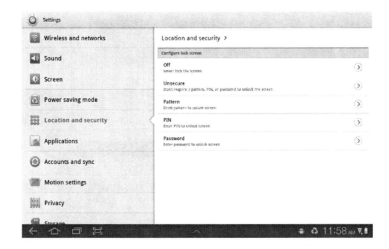

From the screen that appears, you can choose between a pattern lock, which is a special gesture you make on the Tab when you want to unlock it; a PIN, which is a series of numbers that need to be typed to unlock the Tab; and a password comprised of letters and numbers that needs to be typed to unlock the Tab. You can also choose to never lock your screen. And if you already have a screen lock, you can disable it here.

 Note Before creating a security lock, make sure to set up a Google or Gmail account, because if you want to reset your security lock, you need to use your login information from that account to reset it.

- **Owner information.** This lets you have your tablet display any text you want on the screen when it's locked—for example, "This Galaxy Tab belongs to Preston Gralla," along with contact information.

Next comes the Encryption section with only one entry:

- **Encryption.** This encrypts your Tab so that only someone with the right PIN or password can use it. Every time the Tab is turned on, the PIN or password has to be entered. This is separate from locking your screen.

The next section is titled Find My Mobile, with a single entry:

- **Remote controls.** If you're worried about losing your Tab and having someone get access to your personal data, check this box. You'll then be able to remotely track your Tab, lock it, and even wipe out its data. Just follow the instructions to do it.

Next is Passwords, another one-entry section:

- **Visible passwords.** With this option turned on, you can see passwords as you type them. This setup makes it easier to ensure that you're typing in passwords correctly, but it could theoretically be a security risk if someone looks over your shoulder at the passwords you type.

The Device Administration section also has only one entry:

- **Device administrators.** If your Galaxy Tab has been setup so that only certain people—device administrators—can make certain changes, here's where you manage them. Many Galaxy Tabs are not setup this way, so don't fret if when you tap this, you get the message: "No available device administrators."

The final section of this screen, Credential Storage, has four settings that are primarily used in concert with some corporate virtual private networks (VPNs). If they're required for VPN access, your company's IT staff can tell you how to set up and customize these settings. Otherwise, you probably don't need to touch them.

Applications

From here you can manage and uninstall apps, control services running in the background, and more:

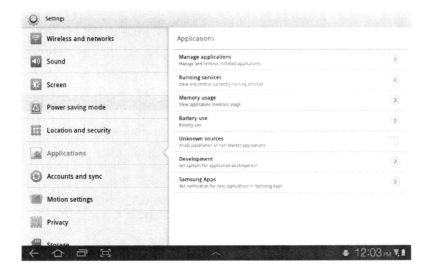

- **Manage applications.** This option lets you uninstall apps, manage them, force them to stop running, and more. Tap it, and a list appears of all the apps on your Galaxy Tab, in three categories: Downloaded (all apps you've downloaded), Running (those apps that are currently running), and All (apps preinstalled on your Tab as well as apps you've downloaded). Tap any category to see the list of apps, and then tap an app that you want to manage in some way.

Tip In the Downloaded category, you may see some apps that were preinstalled on the Tab, such as Maps. They show up in the Downloaded category because you've installed updates to them.

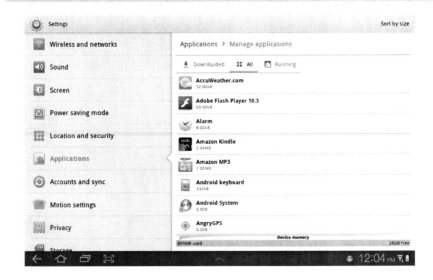

When you tap an app, you come to a screen full of information about it—its size, how much data it uses, the version number, and so on. Tap Uninstall to remove the app from your Tab. (You can't uninstall apps that were preinstalled on the Tab. However, if you downloaded any updates to the preinstalled apps, then you can uninstall the update and revert to the original version of the app.)

If the app uses your Tab's built-in memory to store temporary information—called the *cache*—you can free up that memory by tapping "Clear cache." There's also a "Clear data" option, but be wary of tapping it—that wipes out all of the app's settings, and you have to re-create them.

Some apps are set to run every time you start your Tab; if you want to change that so they don't start automatically, you can do so in the "Launch by default" area. If the app is running and you want to stop it, tap "Force stop."

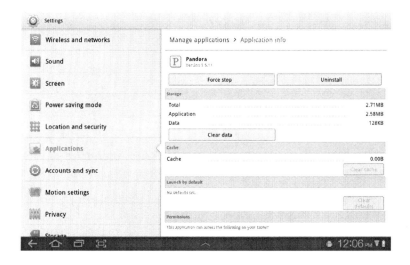

Tip At the bottom of the screen, you see information about the kinds of data that the app can access on your Tab or the services it can use—whether it can use the Internet, read system logs, and so on.

• **Running services.** Tap to see all the background services currently running on your Tab, like Maps, Music, Email, and so on. Tap any to come to a screen that lets you stop the service. Generally, unless you have the technical chops to know what you're doing, it's not a good idea to stop any running services, because doing so could stop various apps and the Tab itself from running properly.

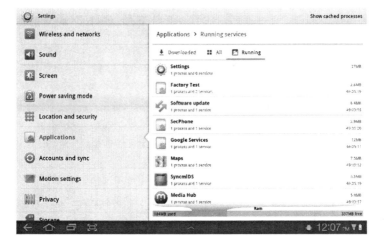

Tip If you're looking to close apps that don't need to be running, as a way to free up your Tab's RAM, your best bet is to use the nifty Task Manager built into the Galaxy Tab. Tap the down button at the bottom of the Tab's screen to reveal a half-a-dozen apps across the bottom of the screen. Then tap the Task Manager icon. From here, you can easily close down currently running apps, and tell the Tab to automatically get rid of any unnecessary background processes that aren't required..

- **Memory usage.** Tapping this doesn't really do anything more than tapping Manage Applications; it shows your apps and the storage they use—but so does the Manage Application screen.

- **Battery use.** Here's a useful screen that shows you what's been using your battery. It lists the biggest battery-users at the top, and then displays them in descending order, showing the percentage of battery each uses.

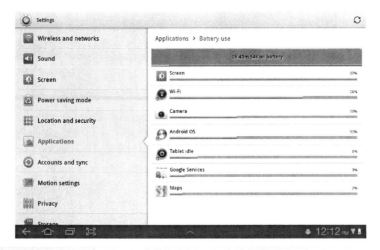

- **Unknown sources.** With the Galaxy Tab, you can find and install software not just through the Market, but in other ways as well—like by downloading it from the Web. Turn on this option if you want to install apps from anywhere, not just the Market. If you're very concerned about safety, turn off the box, since the Market checks apps for malware.

- **Development.** Are you an Android developer? If not, don't bother with this setting. If you are, it lets you set options for things such as USB debugging and whether the screen should stay awake when the Tab is charging.

- **Samsung Apps.** Samsung has developed specific apps for the Galaxy Tab. If you want to be notified when there's a new Samsung app available, tap here, and then make sure the box is turned on on the screen that appears.

Accounts and Sync

Here's where you manage the way your email accounts, including Gmail and other mail accounts, and social networking accounts synchronize and work. The first set of entries are for General Sync Settings:

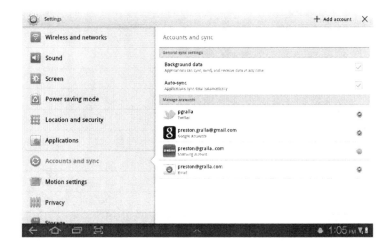

- **Background data.** Your Galaxy Tab regularly checks whether you've got email, looks for the latest weather updates, and sees whether there are updates to social networking sites you use on the Tab, like Facebook and Twitter. When it finds changes, it syncs them in the background. That's a good thing, but it uses up a bit of battery life. If you don't care about having the Tab check for new updates and want to save some battery life, turn this setting off.

If you uncheck the box next to "Background data," you can't use the Android Market. When you try to use the Market, you get a warning that you first need to turn on the "Background data" setting, and you're sent to this screen to do so.

- **Auto-Sync.** A checkbox next to this means your applications synchronize data automatically; no check means they don't sync automatically. No matter which you choose, you can still change sync on an application-by-application basis, as you'll see.

Next, you come to Manage Accounts, which lets you manage your mail and social networking accounts, including how they sync data, and their basic settings. You can also manage your overall Google account on the Tab. What shows up in this section varies according to what accounts you've installed on your Tab.

Email

Tap an icon for one of your email accounts (aside from Gmail), and you come to a basic setup screen where you can change your basic email settings. You can also delete an account from your Tab by tapping "Remove account."

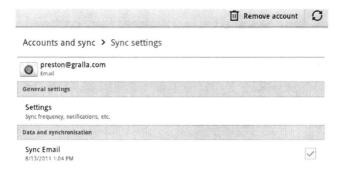

Tap Sync Email to sync your email. Tap "Account settings," and you come to a screen chock-full of settings:

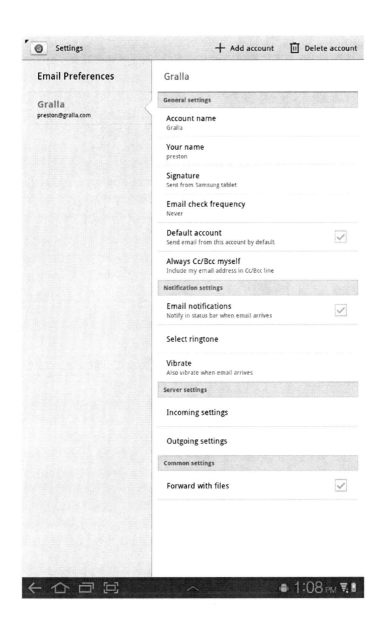

- **General settings.** Here's where you enter the most basic information about your account, such as its name (what the Tab displays for the account—think of it as a nickname that makes it easy to identify the account), and the account's "real name." So if you have an email account with an Internet service provider called MyBigISP, the real name of the account would be MyBigISP, but you might want to use the name "Home email." You can, of course, make the account name and the real name the same. There are other settings you can fiddle with in this section, including the name displayed on your messages ("Your name"), whether you want to append text to all outgoing email ("Signature"), how frequently to check for email, and whether this should be the default account for sending email.

- **Notification settings.** From here, choose whether you want to receive email notifications, which ringtone should be used for those notifications, and whether your Tab should vibrate when you get a new email.

> **Tip** To add a new account, tap "Add account" at the top of the screen.

- **Server Settings.** Time to get technical. These settings tell the Tab where and how to grab email that's sent to you and which server to use to send mail. In the "Incoming settings" section, you need information such as the type of mail server (for example, POP or IMAP), your user name and password, the port number, and so on. Get this information from your email provider, or from your computer's email program. "Outgoing settings" tell the Tab how to send outgoing mail. You need the same type of information as you need for "Incoming settings," so check with your mail provider or your computer's email software.

> **Tip** For more information about setting up your email account, the difference between POP accounts and IMAP accounts, and so on, see page 304.

- **Forward with Files.** This controls whether when you forward a message from your email account, you also forward the message's attachments.

> **Tip** To remove the email account, tap Delete account at the top of the screen.

Gmail and Google

The Galaxy Tab handles Gmail and your Google account differently than it does other email accounts, so they get their own settings. In part, that's because when you sign in with your Gmail account, you're signing into many different Google services, including your Calendar, Contacts, Google Books, and so on.

You don't enter information here about your incoming and outgoing server, because when you set up Gmail, the Tab handles all that automatically.

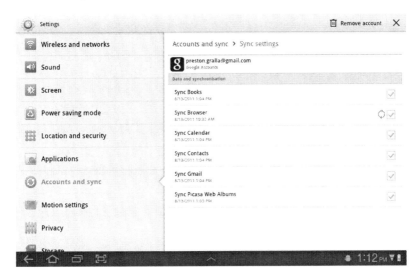

 Note You won't find options to customize Gmail settings, such as whether to get notifications, what ringtone to use, whether to use a signature, and more here. Instead, you have to do that from within Gmail. Open Gmail, tap the Menu button, and then choose Settings to do all that. For details, turn to page 299.

Instead, you choose whether to synchronize your calendar with Google Calendar, your contacts with your Google Contacts, your browser information (such as bookmarks) with Chrome on the PC, or your Google Books account, the mail on your Tab with Gmail servers, and Picasa Web albums, which are pictures and photographs on Google's Picasa site. If you uncheck the box of any service, then it doesn't synchronize. The screen also shows you the last time each was synced. To remove your Google and Gmail account from your Tab, tap "Remove account."

Add Account

If you want to set up a new email account, social networking account, or similar type of account, tap this button. You come to a page with a list of account types: email, Facebook, Twitter, and so on. Tap the account you want to set up, and follow the instructions (which vary for each type of account).

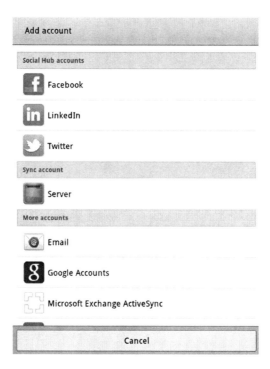

Motion Settings

Your Galaxy Tab can detect when you move the screen in a certain way, and translate that motion into action—for example, reducing or enlarging a photograph in the Gallery when you tilt the screen. Here's where you turn that on and off:

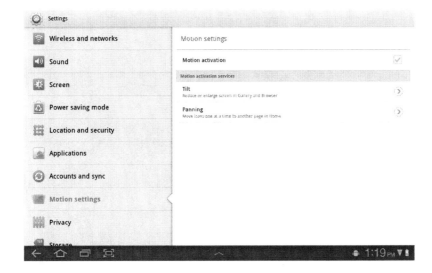

- **Motion activation.** This turns on (or off) motion recognition.
- **Tilt.** This turns on the tile feature that reduces or enlarges the screen in the Gallery and browser.
- **Panning.** This turns on the panning feature that lets you move icons one at a time to another panel from the Home screen.

Privacy

There are three settings in the Backup and Restore section:

- **Back up my data.** This setting backs up your Galaxy Tab settings and data to Google's servers so that if you have a problem with your Tab, you can restore the settings and data at some later time. Obviously, if you don't feel safe with your data riding an anonymous server some-where, turn this option off.
- **Backup account.** When data is backed up, it is backed up to the Google account you used when you set up the Tab. If you want to back up to a different account, tap this, tap "Add account," and then follow the di-rections for adding a new account and using it to back up your data.
- **Automatic restore.** If you uninstall an app, and later decide that you want to install it again, then if you have this turned on, the Tab automati-cally grabs the relevant data you've backed up using the "Back up my data" option and puts it back on your Tab when you reinstall the app.

In the Personal Data section, there's a single setting:

- **Factory Data Reset.** If you're getting rid of your tablet, you don't want anyone else to get all your data. Tap this button, and then follow the onscreen instructions for setting the Tab back to the way it was before you began using it. It deletes all your data, eliminates any changes you made to the Tab, deletes any apps you've installed, and makes the Tab look and work exactly the way it did when it was shipped from the factory. Tap it, and from the screen that appears, tap "Reset tablet."

Storage

Tap this, and you get the rundown about how much storage you're using, and what it's being used for. You also see the total amount of storage.

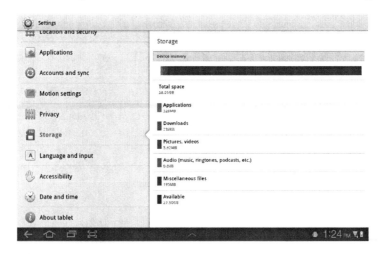

Language and Input

This section lets you change the language you use, as well as various input options.

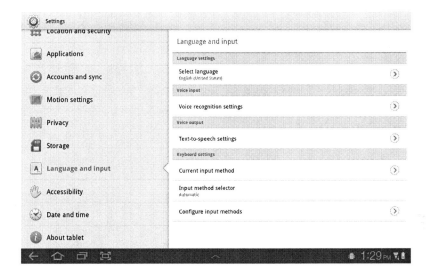

The Language settings section has one setting:

- **Select language.** Tap if you want to change your language. Choose the language from the list that appears. Depending on your Tab, you may only have a choice between English and Spanish.

A variety of apps, such Google Search, can recognize words you speak into the Tab. The Voice Input section controls how it works. It has only one setting, Voice Recognition settings. Tap it, though, and you've got these options:

- **Language.** Choose the language you'll be speaking into the Galaxy Tab.

- **SafeSearch.** Controls the kind of search results you get when you search Google using voice commands, by filtering explicit images and explicit text. The Moderate setting filters explicit images, and the Strict setting filters both explicit images and explicit text. Off turns off the filter.

- **Block offensive words.** Blocks the results of a voice search that contains offensive words. Turn it off if you don't want those results blocked.

Some apps, such as navigation, talk to you. The next section, Voice Output, lets you change settings related to the voice you hear. Once again there's only a single entry: Text-to-speech settings. But tap it, and you get inundated with settings:

- **Listen to an example.** Tap to hear a voice read text to you. Yes, it's robotic-sounding—that's the nature of text-to-speech.

- **Always use my settings.** Individual apps have a variety of settings for controlling how text-to-speech works. If you want to override those settings with settings of your own, tap this option. You can then set the two options just below it on the list, under Default settings—"Speech rate" and Language.

- **Default Engine.** You shouldn't have to worry about this setting—it just tells you what text-to-speech software the Tab uses, which out of the box is Pico TTS (TTS stands for *text to speech*). Tap here to choose between the Pico TTS and the Samsung TTS. If you've installed another engine, it will appear here as well.

- **Install voice data.** This item is likely grayed out, because the Pico TTS system is already in place. However, after you install another text-to-speech system, you may have to come back to this setting and tap it to complete the installation of the voice data required for that system.

- **Speech rate.** Tap to select how fast the text should be read to you. There are five choices, ranging from "Very slow" to "Very fast."

- **Language.** Tap, and then choose the language of text that you want read to you. In most cases, that's American English. But if someone sends you email in Italian, for example, and you want it read to you, select Italian. That way, the text reader knows the language it's looking at, and attempts to pronounce the words accordingly. For example, in Italian, the letter combination "ci" is pronounced the same way as "ch" in English.

- **Samsung TTS.** Settings here controls the voice affects in text-to-speech if you use the Samsung engine.

- **PICO TTS.** Settings here controls the voice affects in text-to-speech if you use the Pico engine.

The next section, Keyboard Settings, controls the keyboard, as you would expect:

- **Current input method.** Tap it, and you get a choice of the generic Android keyboard, voice input, the Samsung keyboard, the Swype keyboard, or the TalkBack keyboard. (See page 391 for details.) Hidden inside the guts of Android are some other useful keyboard settings. After you tap "Current input method," tap "Configure input methods," and then select Settings underneath the listing for the keyboard you want to configure. Here you can change settings specific to each of the input methods, like whether to auto-capitalize the first words of sentences, whether the Tab should make a sound when you press a key on the keyboard, settings related to how auto-correct should work, and others.

Accessibility

If you or someone who uses the Tab has vision problems or limitations, here's where you can choose options to make the Tab easier to use:

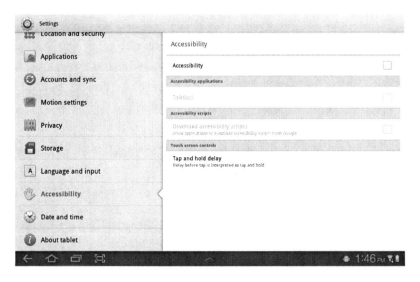

- **Accessibility.** To use either of the two accessibility services, you need to first turn on this box.

The next section, Accessibility Services, has one setting:

- **TalkBack.** This is an app developed by Google that can read what's on the Tab screen out loud. Developers can also use it to build voice reading directly into their apps. Tap it to turn it on.

The next section, Accessibility Scripts, has one setting:

- **Download accessibility scripts.** Google has developed scripts to help accessibility work better; turn this on to download them.

Finally, Touchscreen Gestures has one setting:

- **Tap and hold delay.** Controls how long it takes for the Tab to determine whether you're touching and holding something, or merely touching it. Tap this and you get to choose short, medium, or long.

Date & Time

Choose from these settings for the date and time:

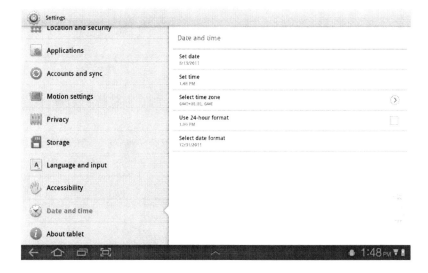

- **Set date.** Tap here to set the date.
- **Set time.** Tap to set the time.
- **Select time zone.** Tap here and choose your time zone.
- **Use 24-hour format.** Tap if you prefer the 24-hour format—14:00 instead of 2 p.m., for example.
- **Select date format.** You've got other options here if you don't like the U.S. standard (09/22/2011), including 22/09/2011, and 2011/09/22.

About Tablet

Go here for more information than you can ever imagine about your Galaxy Tab, including the version of the Android software you're running, your current signal strength, and much more. Much of what you find here is informational only. It's also where you go to see if there's an Android software update for you:

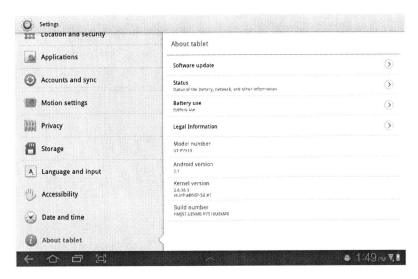

- **Software update.** Tap if you want to see whether there's a software update available. If there is, follow the instructions for installing it.

 Note Technically, you don't need to update your Tab's software manually by tapping "System updates." Updates are automatically delivered to you over the Verizon Network, via what's called over the air (OTA) update.

- **Status.** Tap for a mind-boggling amount of detail about your Tab's status, including its signal strength, the battery level, the Wi-Fi MAC address (a unique number that identifies your Tab), the IP address, and a barrage of techie details that only a full-time geek could love.

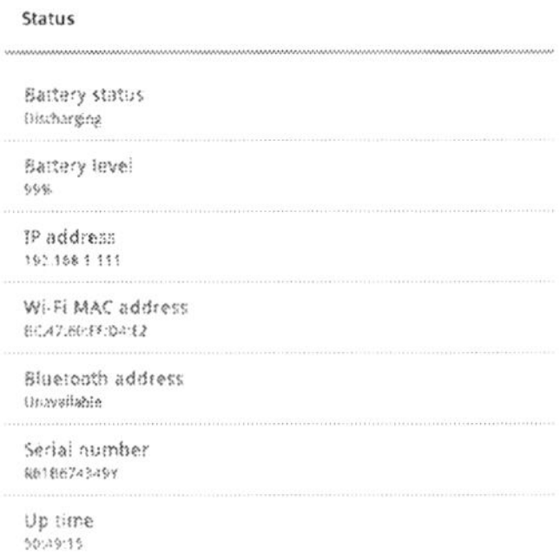

Status

Battery status
Discharging

Battery level
66%

IP address
192.168.1.111

Wi-Fi MAC address
EC:47:60:FF:0A:E2

Bluetooth address
Unavailable

Serial number
RB1B674345Y

Up time
50:49:15

- **Battery use.** This brings you to the battery use screen to show you what's using up your Tab's juice. You can also get to this same screen when you tap Battery Use on the Application settings screen.

- **Legal information.** Here's where you can while away the hours reading Google's terms of service and the contracts that govern the use of Android. If you're not a lawyer, you don't want to read this. In fact, even if you are a lawyer, you don't want to read this.

- **Model number.** Gives you the formal, techie name of the Galaxy Tab—GT-P7510.

- **Android version.** Lists the Android version number currently running on your Galaxy Tab.

- **Kernel version and Build number.** These are techie settings that you likely don't need to know about. However, if you need to call tech support, they may ask for these, so here's where to go when they ask.

Part 6
Appendixes

Appendix A
Setup, Signup, and Accessories

How you set up your Galaxy Tab varies according to whether you've got a Wi-Fi–only Galaxy Tab, or one that also includes a cellular connection. If you've bought your cellular Galaxy Tab at a Verizon or other service provider store, then the sales folks walked you through the process of activating your Tab and signing up for a plan. If you bought your Tab over the Web or at a retail store, you might not have gone through the setup process for getting your cellular connection. So contact Verizon or another provider for getting the Tab set up with a cellular connection.

If you've got a Wi-Fi–only Galaxy Tab, then setup is much easier. When you turn on your Tab and walk through its initial screens, it asks you for the email address and login information for your primary Gmail or Google account. (And if you don't have one yet, it prompts you to set one up.)

If you have a cellular-enabled Galaxy Tab, you want to get a data plan for giving the Tab everywhere-access to the Internet and email. Check with a provider for rates.

Accessories

You can buy plenty of accessories to get more out of your Galaxy Tab—there are Tab accessories designed to protect its case or screen, connect it to a car charger, and more. Here's some of what's available:

- **Cases.** Cases protect the Galaxy Tab against damage—when you drop it, for example. They also can hold your Tab at an angled position, facing you for when you want to watch a movie, for example, or video chat.

- **Keyboards.** The Galaxy Tab onscreen keyboard is nice, but for longer emails and word processing, it leaves something to be desired. Get a physical keyboard to do serious typing.

- **Screen protectors.** These thin sheets of plastic safeguard your Galaxy Tab's glass screen, greatly reducing the risk of scratches. They're so thin that you won't notice they're there.

- **Docking Station.** Charges your Galaxy Tab and holds it vertically so you can use it while it charges. It's also good for when you want to watch movies or video chat. You can also buy docking stations that include built-in stereo speakers.

- **Car chargers.** Plug one end into your Tab, and the other into your 12-volt power outlet, and you can charge your Tab while you're on the go.

- **Bluetooth headset.** With one of these, you can talk on your Galaxy Tab by speaking into the wireless headset.

- **Headphones.** You want these to listen to your music collection.

- **External speakers.** Want to share your music with others? Get external speakers to plug into the Galaxy Tab.

Places to Shop

There are plenty of places online where you can buy Galaxy Tab accessories, and so there's no room to list them all. Here are a few of the best:

- **Samsung.** You can buy accessories directly from Samsung, which makes the Galaxy Tab. Head to the main Samsung site at *www.samsung.com*, and search for *Galaxy Tab*.

- **Amazon.** This shopping site has a good selection of accessories. Search for *Galaxy Tab*.

- **Android Central.** This site sells accessories for the Galaxy Tab. (*http:// store.androidcentral.com*).

Appendix B

Troubleshooting and Maintenance

The Galaxy Tab runs on the Android operating system, so it's vulnerable to the same kinds of problems that can occur in any computer operating system. Like any electronic device, the Galaxy Tab can be temperamental at times. This appendix gives you the steps to follow when your Tab is having…issues.

Make Sure Your Software Is Up to Date

No computer or Galaxy Tab is ever perfect; neither is any operating system. So tech companies (including Google, which makes the Galaxy Tab's Android operating system, and Samsung, which manufactures the Galaxy Tab) constantly track down and fix bugs. In the case of your Galaxy Tab, those fixes come to you via software updates delivered wirelessly—called OTA (over the air) updates, via either Wi-Fi or a cellular connection.

So if you have a bug or other nagging problem with your Tab, there may already be a fix for it, via one of these updates. You get a notice that an update is available; you need to tap the notification to get the update started. Here's how to install updates when you receive an update notification:

1. If you receive a notification, tap it. Tap "Install now" to install it, or "Install later" to put off the update until a later time. Tap "More info" to get more details about the update.

2. Tap "Install now," and the update begins.

   You get a notice that your Galaxy Tab needs to reboot (shut down and restart) for the update to complete installing. Be patient, because it might take some time.

3. If you chose "More info" rather than "Install now" from the notification screen, then you see a page with information about the update. Tap "Restart & install" to install the update. Press the Back button if you don't want to install yet.

You can also check for updates manually:

1. From the App Menu, tap Settings.

2. Select About Tablet→Software update.

   You come to a series of screens in which you first select your country, and then accept the usual incomprehensible legal hoo-hah. If you haven't yet created a Samsung account, you have to create one now. If you have created one, sign into your account.

3. After you sign up or sign in, you'll be sent back to the Software update screen. Tap Update.

   The Galaxy Tab checks whether any updates are available. If none are available, then it tells you the Tab is up to date. If an update is available, the Tab tells you.

4. Tap the Download button to download the update, and then follow instructions for installing it.

Resetting Your Galaxy Tab

If you have a recurring problem that nothing seems to fix, including rebooting it, you may need to reset your Galaxy Tab—that is, delete all of its data, and return it to the state it was in before you bought it, with all the factory settings replacing your own. Your contacts, social networking accounts, email and email accounts, and so on all get deleted. Techies call this a factory data reset.

To perform a reset, from the Apps Menu, tap Settings, and then select Privacy→Factory data reset. Tap "Reset Tablet." That erases all the data on your Tab.

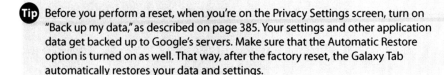

Tip Before you perform a reset, when you're on the Privacy Settings screen, turn on "Back up my data," as described on page 385. Your settings and other application data get backed up to Google's servers. Make sure that the Automatic Restore option is turned on as well. That way, after the factory reset, the Galaxy Tab automatically restores your data and settings.

Correcting Email Settings

The Galaxy Tab easily syncs with your Gmail account, but when you add other email accounts—like your work email or home ISP account—you have to enter all of the account and server information yourself. That's where errors can creep in, despite your best efforts. Even if you set the account up successfully at first, you may encounter problems later.

If Email Doesn't Work at All

If you're having trouble getting email to work for the first time, the most likely problem is that you've got a setting wrong, like your incoming or outgoing server. To check these settings, from the App Menu, tap Settings, and then choose Accounts & Sync. In the "Manage accounts" section, tap the email account that you're having trouble with, and then tap "Account settings." Tap each of the settings—Incoming Server, Outgoing Server, and so on—and make sure you've entered everything correctly. Even a single misplaced letter or number causes a problem. Check your ISP's website, or call your ISP to confirm the settings. You may have copied down the settings wrong, or maybe your ISP has different settings for accessing email on a mobile Galaxy Tab. If it's a work email account, call your company's IT department for assistance.

 Note Remember, if you have a Wi-Fi Galaxy Tab, you can send and receive email only if you're connected to a Wi-Fi network. So before trying any troubleshooting, make sure you're connected to a network.

If You Can't Send Email

Any computer—including your Galaxy Tab, which is, after all, a computer—uses *ports* to communicate with the Internet. They're not physical things; think of them as different channels. So one port is used for web traffic, another for sending email, another for receiving email, and so on. To cut down on spam-sending, some ISPs curtail the use of the standard port for sending mail—port 25. When you send mail using port 25 via these ISPs, they let your mail go to your ISP's mail servers, but not get sent anywhere from there. So your message never gets delivered to the recipient. To get around the problem, you have a couple of alternatives.

Try using a different port

From the App Menu, tap Settings and then choose Accounts and Sync. In the "Manage accounts" section, tap the email account that you're having trouble with, and then tap "Settings." Tap the Outgoing Server listing, and on the screen that appears, in the Port box, delete 25 and type *587*.

Use Gmail's outgoing mail server

You can use Gmail's server to send email from another account. On the Outgoing Server screen, use the following settings:

- For SMTP, enter *smtp.gmail.com*.
- For Port, enter *465*.
- For user name and password, use your Gmail user name (your full Gmail address) and password.
- Turn on the checkboxes next to "Use secure connection" and "Verify Certificate."

Encrypting Your Galaxy Tab

Worried about losing your Galaxy Tab, and that when someone else finds it, they can get access to all of your private information? There's a way around that—you can encrypt it so that anyone who wants to use it will have to type in a password or PIN to turn on the Tab.

 Tip You can also change the Galaxy Tab's screen lock, so that anyone needs a password or a PIN to unlock it. Turn to page 374 for details.

To encrypt your Tab, from the App Menu tap Settings, choose Location and Security→Encrypt tablet, and then follow the prompts.

Finding Help

If you're looking for more information or help, you have plenty of places to go:

- **Samsung's official Galaxy Tab support page.** This web page has plenty of helpful information, tutorials, tips and tricks, troubleshooting guides, and a searchable database of help. It's well worth the visit— *www.samsung.com/us/support*, and then search for *Galaxy Tab*.

- **Google's Mobile forum.** If you've got questions about Android, the Galaxy Tab's operating system, this forum might help. The forum covers many different types of mobile hardware, so you may need to search to find an answer—but given Google's great job at search, you shouldn't have to search long. Go to *www.google.com/support/ forum/p/Google+Mobile*.

- **Galaxytabforums.net.** This discussion forum is devoted to all things Galaxy Tab. You'll find plenty of other Tab users, offering help and advice. Get there by going to *www.galaxytabforums.net/*.

- **AndroidForums.com.** Here's another very useful forum where Android users congregate. The one for Galaxy Tab is *galaxytabforums.net*.

- **Android Guys.** If you're interested in news and rumors about Android in general, then this site is an excellent place to start. It's not specific to the Galaxy Tab, but if you're an Android fan, it's worth checking out— *www.androidguys.com*.

Index

Symbols & Numbers

A

G

Galaxy Tab
  about, **1–5**, **392**
  apps closed by, **88**
  company account setup, **337–339**
  default email address for, **302**
  disconnecting from computer, **228**
  encrypting, **402**
  folder structure display, **116**
  name of, changing, **364**
  playing music while using, **237**
  resetting, **105**, **400**
  restarting in troubleshooting process,
    105
  rotating, **58**, **252**
  Samsung support page, **402**
  screen size, **13**
  setup, **397**
  unlock restrictions, **374**
Galaxytabforums.net, **403**
Gallery, **229**, **245–257**
  album icons, **249**
  opening, **76**, **246**
  options, **256–257**
  photos
    uploads to Facebook, **167**
    uploads to Picasa, **258**
    viewing, **251–252**
    working with multiple, **254–255**
  saving email graphic to, **285**
  thumbnails, **246**
  toolbar, **252–254**
  videos in, **247**, **264–265**
  viewing email graphics in, **284**
games
  AirAttack HD, **109**
  Angry Birds, **107–109**
gas stations, in Google Maps, **182**
Gdocs, **344–346**
General settings, for email, **382**
General Sync Settings, **379**
genres, display music lists by, **234**
geolocation, and calendar, **327–328**
geotag information, **250**
global email settings, **299**, **300**

Gmail
  adding sender to Contacts, **286–287**
  adding signature, **295–296**
  attachments, **285–286**. *See
    also* attachments to email
  chat display, **290**
  graphics in, **283–285**
  horizontal vs. vertical view, **280–283**
  managing incoming mail, **290–293**
  organization, **289–290**
  outgoing mail server, **402**
  primary address, and Picasa account,
    257
  reading mail, **280–288**
  replying and forwarding, **288–289**
  search in, **297–299**
    advanced, **299**
    labels and, **296–297**
  settings, **299–300**
  setting up, **278–279**
  for sharing book, **204**
  Show/Hide details, **287–288**
  syncing Tab with Web, **278**
    settings, **293**, **300**
  widget for, **300–301**
  writing messages, **293–296**
Gmail accounts
  and security lock, **374**
  creating, **278–279**
  settings, **383**
  setting up multiple, **279**
Gmail icon, **53**, **282**
Gmail widget, vs. Email widget, **311**
Go off the record option in Google Talk,
    143
Google account, **98**
  and security lock, **374**
  settings, **383**
  setting up and managing, **52–53**
  syncing contacts with, **157**
Google Body, **126–128**
Google Books, **199**, **200–213**
  browsing, **205–207**
  managing books, **207–208**
  pushpins in, **206**
  reading books, **208–213**

Scan mode in, **210**
Setting button, **210**
Table of Contents button in, **210**
Text mode in, **210–211**
on the Web, **212–213**
Google Buzz, **290**
Google Calendar on the Web, **331–333**
for group calendar details, **323**
syncing
with iCal, **333**
with Tab calendar, **314**
working with multiple calendars,
328–329
adding event, **322**
Google Calendar Sync, **333**
Google Chat, **290**
Google Checkout
account, **97, 202–203**
email receipt from, **203**
Google Contact list, **279**
Google Docs, **341–346**
creating and editing documents, **342**
Google Goggles, **128–129**
Google Latitude, **182**
Google Maps, **49, 179–196**
as wallpaper, **25**
browsing, **180–181**
business location on map, **184**
directions, **185–187**
end point on, **186**
event location in, **327–328**
finding places, **182–185**
information from, **182**
Layers, **188–191**
locating address, **185**
location determination, **191**
pushpin for accessing contact address,
185
satellite view in, **189**
search, **191–193**
Starred Items list, **185**
Street View, **193–194**
terrain view in, **189**
traffic in, **190**
turn-by-turn navigation, **194–196**
Voice Actions to launch, **352**
zooming out, **32**

Google Mobile forum, **403**
Google Music Cloud Player, **121–124,
238**
Google Reader, for RSS feeds, **223–224**
Google Search, using location
information for, **374**
Google services, Android and, **278**
Google Talk
audio chat, **146**
chat process, **141–143**
contacts, **137**
photos, **136**
icons, **19, 142**
invitation to chat
responding to, **140–141**
sending, **139**
managing, **147–148**
More Options, **143**
options, **134–136**
search, **148–149**
starting, **133–138**
starting chat session, **138–140**
video chat, **144–146**
options, **146**
Google Tasks, **333**
Google, terms of service, **393**
Go to command (Voice Actions), **354**
Go To option, in Kindle, **215**
GPS chip, **191**
GPS icon, **19**
GPS locator, **2**
GPS satellites, for location determination,
374
graphics. *See* images; photos
group calendar, **323**
groups for contacts, **154–156**
gyroscope, **13**

H

Haptic feedback setting, **369**
HD videos, **271**
headphones, **398**
headset jack, **42, 45, 227**
height of text, in Google Books, **211**
help, **402–403**
for Google Talk, **148**
in Gmail, **292**

Windows 7, **229**
Windows Explorer, for file transfer, **228**
Windows Live Hotmail, **311**
Windows Media files, playing, **230**
Windows Media Player, **229**
  and .amr files, **359**
wireless headset, **398**
wireless networks
  for location determination, **373**
  settings, **361–366**
.wma (Windows Media Audio), **230**
.wmv (Windows Media Video), **230**
Word Choice window, **36**
Word files
  as email attachments, **285, 308**
  QuickOffice for displaying, **77**
words
  blocking offensive, **388**
  Hold finger gesture for selecting, **39**
  keyboard recognition, **42**
"Working" screen, for Voice Actions, **350**
world clock, **16**
wrench icon, **365**
writing messages in Gmail, **293–296**

Y

Yahoo, mail program, **311**
Yelp.com, **183**
YouTube, **270–274**
  Flash for, **270**
  playing video, **271**
  search for video, **272**

Z

Zagat.com, **183**
Zip code, Google Maps search for, **192**
zooming
  in Google Maps, **32, 181**
  photos, **251**
  web page, **59**
Zxing Team, Barcode scanner, **101**

Get even more for your money.

Join the O'Reilly Community, and register the O'Reilly books you own. It's free, and you'll get:

- $4.99 ebook upgrade offer
- 40% upgrade offer on O'Reilly print books
- Membership discounts on books and events
- Free lifetime updates to ebooks and videos
- Multiple ebook formats, DRM FREE
- Participation in the O'Reilly community
- Newsletters
- Account management
- 100% Satisfaction Guarantee

Signing up is easy:

1. **Go to: oreilly.com/go/register**
2. **Create an O'Reilly login.**
3. **Provide your address.**
4. **Register your books.**

Note: English-language books only

To order books online:

oreilly.com/store

For questions about products or an order:

orders@oreilly.com

To sign up to get topic-specific email announcements and/or news about upcoming books, conferences, special offers, and new technologies:

elists@oreilly.com

For technical questions about book content:

booktech@oreilly.com

To submit new book proposals to our editors:

proposals@oreilly.com

O'Reilly books are available in multiple DRM-free ebook formats. For more information:

oreilly.com/ebooks

O'REILLY®

Have it your way.

O'Reilly eBooks

- Lifetime access to the book when you buy through oreilly.com
- Provided in up to four DRM-free file formats, for use on the devices of your choice: PDF, .epub, Kindle-compatible .mobi, and Android .apk
- Fully searchable, with copy-and-paste and print functionality
- Alerts when files are updated with corrections and additions

oreilly.com/ebooks/

Safari Books Online

- Access the contents and quickly search over 7000 books on technology, business, and certification guides
- Learn from expert video tutorials, and explore thousands of hours of video on technology and design topics
- Download whole books or chapters in PDF format, at no extra cost, to print or read on the go
- Get early access to books as they're being written
- Interact directly with authors of upcoming books
- Save up to 35% on O'Reilly print books

See the complete Safari Library at safari.oreilly.com

Spreading the knowledge of innovators.   oreilly.com